VISIONS OF AFRICA

Series directed by Constantine Petridis

Curator of African Art
The Cleveland Museum of Art,
Cleveland, Ohio, USA

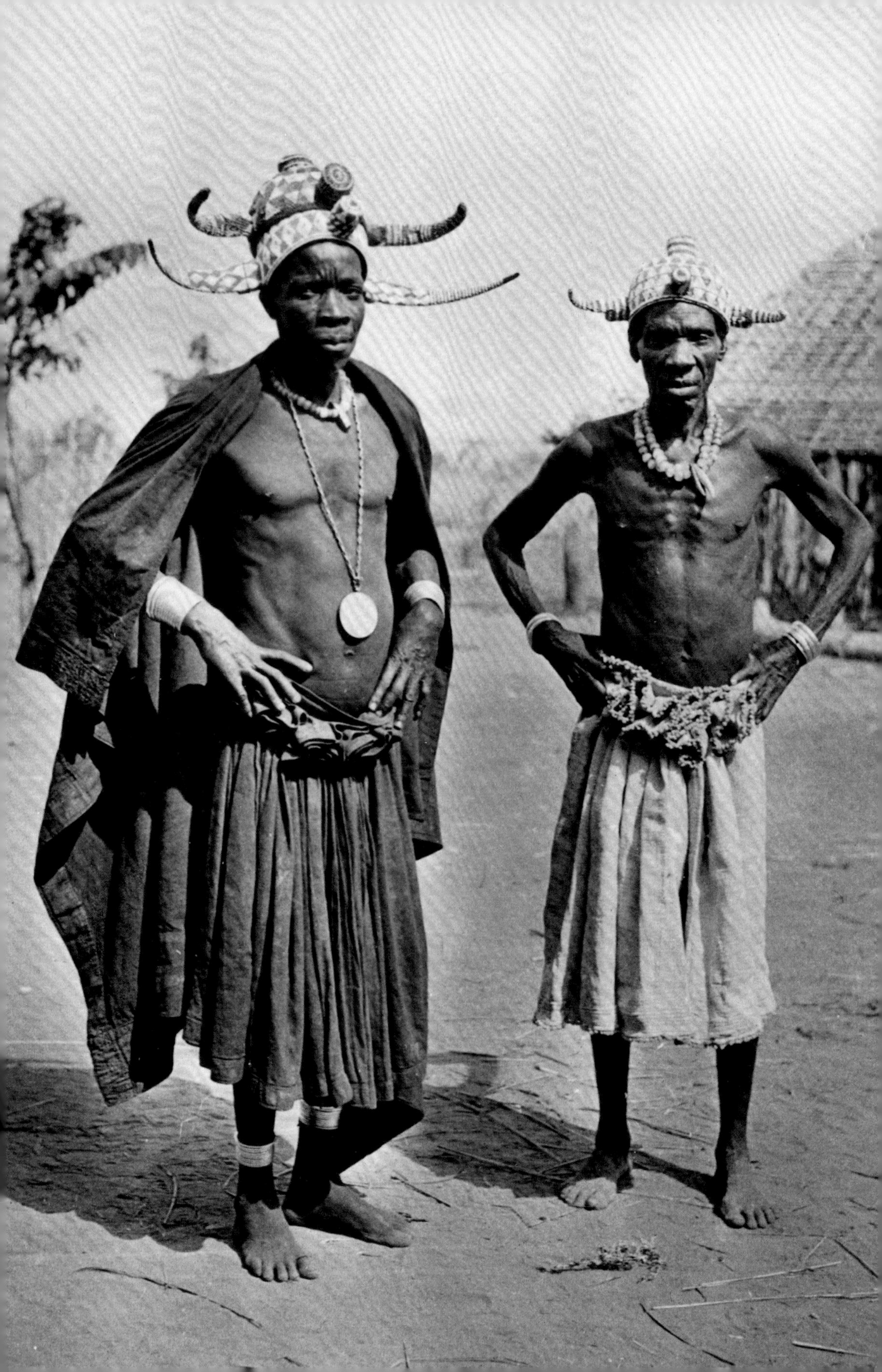

Arthur P. Bourgeois

YAKA

5 CONTINENTS

Editorial Coordination
Laura Maggioni

Editing
Emily Ligniti

Art Director
Fayçal Zaouali

Layout
Annarita De Sanctis

Acknowledgments
The publisher would especially like to thank
Marc Ghysels for his invaluable assistance.

ISBN 978-88-7439-515-6

First published in April 2014
by 5 Continents Editions
Piazza Caiazzo, 1
20124 Milan, Italy
www.fivecontinentseditions.com

Distributed in the United States and Canada
by Harry N. Abrams, Inc., New York.
Distributed outside the United States
and Canada, excluding France and Italy,
by Abrams & Chronicle Books Ltd UK, London

Cover
Central Yaka mask fragment (*n-kisyan-khanda*) (pl. 43).
Wood, pigment. H. 24 cm.
Jesuit Heverlee Collection, Royal Museum
for Central Africa, Tervuren, inv. 2334.

Back cover
Yaka masker in Muela Buanda. Photo: Eliot Elisofon,
1951. D. Gelbard Archives, no. 2098.

Page 2
Yaka regional chief and dignitary wearing beaded
hats (*misango mayako*). D. Gelbard Archive, no. 2110.

Table of Contents

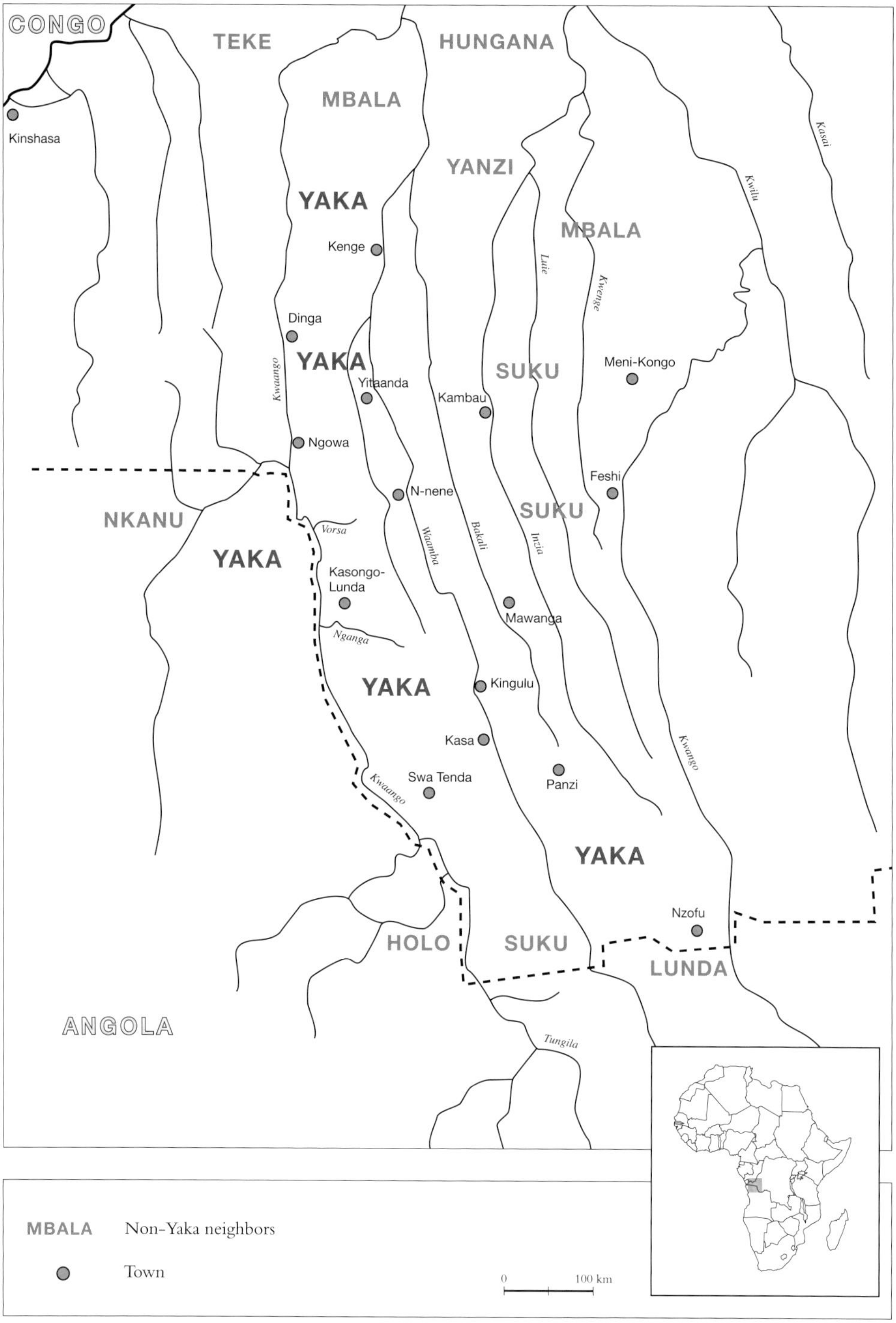

Yaka country in southwest Democratic Republic of the Congo (DRC) with neighboring ethnic groups with whom the Yaka have interacted.

Making Sense of Reality

Introduction

The study of the art of the Yaka, like that of any traditional society, is set in a continuum. Ethnic arts exist at the confluence of pictorial, oral, and functional traditions, none of which are apparent to the uninitiated eye scarcely able to recognize the subject, much less know how to respond to them. An understanding of the pictorial code utilized requires not only an elaborate commentary, but a survey of allied components as they echo throughout the original context. The oral component includes both historical narratives and popular folktales, while the functional aspects pertain to ritual actions and ceremony, while offering therapeutic effect and entertainment. It is essential, therefore, to understand the interplay of art objects with primary artifacts and overarching concepts within the society. Moreover, art objects are embedded in the history of a given people, with earlier and later examples and nuanced changes that occur in the social matrix. In the following pages, an attempt will be made to explore some of these dimensions in reference to the earliest of Yaka sculptural examples as preserved in European and American collections, along with the most striking examples in terms of form and expression

Curiosity about and preservation of Yaka art begins with the earliest explorers, merchants and traders, and missionaries in what was to become the Independent State, then Belgian Congo, then Zaire, and presently the Democratic Republic of the Congo. Numerous objects eventually found their way to the Royal Museum for Central Africa, Tervuren (Belgium); the British Museum; the National Museum of Ethnology in Leiden, Berlin, and Basel, and into both public and private collections around the globe.

Direct contact with the Western world began in 1879 with the Portuguese explorers Capelo and Ivens visiting one of the southernmost Yaka chiefdoms. By 1880 Von Mechow reached Kyambvu Nawsi's court and provides the earliest description. This was followed in 1885 by Schultze, Kund, and Tappenbeck, and then by Büttner and Wolff. Representatives of the Independent State were in the region by 1889 and included Lienart, Drag, Lehrmann, and Dhanis. Popokabaka became the chief place in the district and a garrison of soldiers was maintained at

Kasongo Lunda. However, effective colonial administration, missionary, educational, and medical institutions were not established until the 1920s.

The Yaka (or BaYaka) live along the Kwango River and its parallel affluents in the Democratic Republic of the Congo in the west of Bandundu province otherwise known as the Kwango region, and number between 300,000 and 400,000 people, with a population density of eight or nine inhabitants per kilometer. The land consists of high sandy plateaus and the wide, forested fluvial valleys of the Kwango, Wamba, and Bakali Rivers, which generally flow from south to north, where the vegetation is lushly dense and the climate humid, whereas the plateaus remain arid and lightly forested. Within this context the Yaka live by subsistence agriculture. In addition to hunting, fishing, and foraging for plants and small animals, standard crops include manioc, peanuts, and sweet potatoes, while more recently coffee and palms are grown, and herding of cattle has been introduced. The women perform the subsistence agriculture, and the men regard hunting as their most valued activity. Villages are relatively small, averaging from 50 to 200 inhabitants in separate hamlets. Dwellings are pitched-roof structures made of split bamboo; the traditional thatched two-room building was gradually replaced by larger dwellings featuring a porch. The twentieth century saw a rural exodus of younger males to urban centers such as Kenge and Kinshasa, an exodus that increased with the discovery of diamonds to the south in Angola. Thus for the past half century, villages are largely made up of the elderly, children, and women, with an absence of males for most of the year. To understand the uniqueness of the Yaka, some grasp of their history is important.

The Yaka regional chiefs, together with the paramount chief, the *kiambv* (pl. *biambv*), who resides at Kasongo Lunda near the Kwango River, each claim descent from Lunda conquerors in the seventeenth century. In oral tradition, it was Muni Putu Kasongo, one of the sons of the Lunda Mwant Yav at Koola, who with his twelve *bilolo* (sing. *yilolo*) or Luwa nobles—ancestors of the regional chiefs—subdued through warfare and by matrimonial alliances the ancient clans of the Yaka, Tsaamba, and Suku residing there at the time. In more recent history, forty-one *bilolo* govern a specific region with its cluster of villages; each in turn is governed by a chief or autochthonous Tulamba (Earth Chief), the possessor of the land, who continues as a ritual officer. In order to strengthen alliances, the *kiambv* often marries the daughter of his regional *bilolo*.

Although twenty-four successors are listed as succeeding Muni Putu Kasongo as *kiambv* that continue to the present day (Van Roy 1988 and Plancquaert 1971: 123–124), major secessions have divided the population; the first was that of Muni Kongo and the exodus of the Suku to the east under the sixth *kiambv*, Muteeba Yiinda—thought to have taken place around 1775–1780

(Van Roy 1988: 90). Under the seventh *kiambv*, Muteeba Tsiimba, the Ngudia Nkama, "sister" of the Suku Muni Kongo, fled with her people to the south to dwell among the Holo. Under the next three or more succeeding *biambv*, the Pelende Kobo, a *yilolo* or Luwa noble, refused payment of tribute and they became independent. A group of Tsaamba also retreated to the northeast, while other groups of each of these divisions submitted to Luwa control (Van Roy 1988: 80–90, 104). Throughout the region, daily life, beliefs, and healing institutions are relatively uniform, despite political affiliations. Yaka social identity derives from a reckoning of paternal descent combined with clan affiliation traced back to the maternal great-grandmother—the end product of historic contacts between the Kongo and Lunda spheres of influence.

Signs, Symbols, and Rites of Leadership

Like Yaka society itself and its kinship structure, the art of the Yaka is strictly hierarchical. Von Mechow (1880) describes the *kyambvu* Naweshi within his impressive fortified chiefly enclosure surrounded by forty warriors, as seated on a leopard skin and wearing a red bonnet and the multi-colored and beaded *kaphoonda* headdress of a Lunda lord, three brass rings on his ankle, with a wrap of imported cloth with folds in front, and the double-bladed *mbeele phoko* sword hanging at his side and his rifle behind him (Von Mechow 1882: 481). Although this was an official if not threatening occasion, it is a typical emphasis on symbols of power and status. On other occasions, an orchestra of musical performers with instruments such as *madiinad*, *matuumba*, *moondo*, *ngufu* drums, *masina* and *itaanda* xylophones, *tsaatsi* and *masakila* rattles, and *isaandzi* lamelophones supplied additional grandeur and occasions for dance (fig. 1). Aspects of these same symbols would be replicated by the *bilolo* or Yaka nobles at official appearances. At the other end of the social hierarchy, the *kalamba* earth chiefs would wear insignia such as the blackened *bweni* hat made of woven raffia, occasionally featuring a brim or visor (fig. 2), and also a *makeketi* necklace of pale blue beads and a leopard or lion's tooth or wildcat teeth and an iron bracelet called *mbulu*, *malunga*, or *nkunga*. Decoration of the head with feathers takes the form of a miniature openwork or woven construction rising in the shape of a cone that displays a burst of color-coded feathers. Varied chicken feathers are relegated to the lower-ranking individual, while that of the red-feathered *nduwa* bird is reserved to the *bilolo*, and the white heron *kanangi* and spotted guinea fowl, *khanga*, reserved to the *khambvu*. This was a shifting relationship, however, as insignia of higher ranks would be adopted but had to be removed in the presence of a higher ranked dignitary. We shall see a reflection of such ranking in the appearances of masks within *n-khanda* initiation.

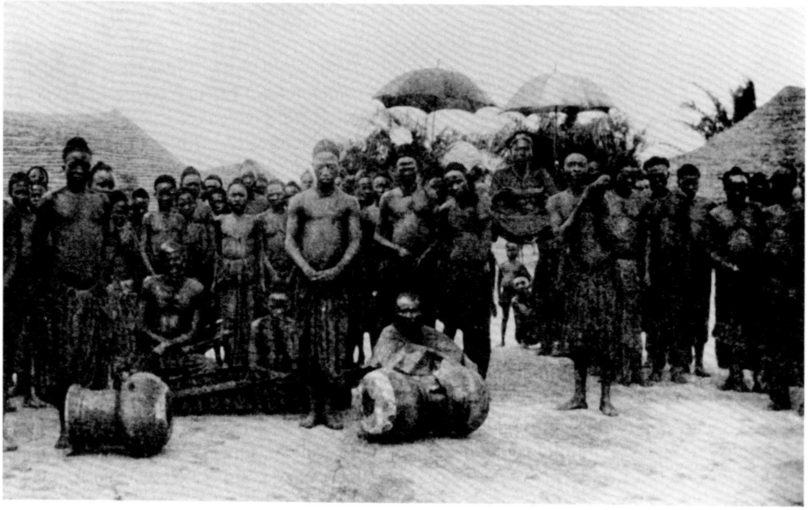

Fig. 1. Yaka paramount chief, Kiamfu Mulombo (1860–1865 to 1913), accompanied by his entourage. He is shown bearing the sword of rulership (*mbeedya phoko*), and a scepter dance wand (*n-nsesa*), wearing leopard tooth pendant, riding a litter (*tipoy m'seela*)—accompanied by an orchestra of two *mukupila* or double drums and a *n-taanda* xylophone. Near Franz-Josef Falls in 1903. Photo: F. Michel, 1903, Royal Museum for Central Africa, Tervuren, Photo Archive.

Elaborate headpieces such as the kalamba's woven *bweni* hat that was worn as a charm even while sleeping and thus necessitated an object of traditional furniture known as a headrest (*musaw* or *m-baambu*), although a headrest was also used by the head of a family. When lying on one's side, this small object supports the head just below the ear at the junction of head and neck. The lower portion includes either a finely carved column, an openwork "X" form, or freestanding imagery of the leopard, duiker, bird, or male or female human, or miniature pitched-roof dwelling. Most Yaka headrests had charm packets inserted into a prepared cavity or charms were otherwise attached. This served to protect the owner from malevolent influences while sleeping.

The double-bladed *mbeele phoko* sword of rulership is perhaps the most striking visual expression of authority (fig. 3). (Although the most essential symbol of paramount power is the copper-covered ring around his arm or ankle, containing fibers but also the tendon from a sacrificed victim—currently a ram but previously from a sacrificed maternal nephew.) The sword signifies the chief's protective role in maintaining social and moral order as well as the source of life. With it he embodies the founding ancestor and history of the chieftaincy. On another level it alludes to the chief's role in securing an abundance of food as well as its distribution. Sexuality is also implied in the expanded shape of the scabbard, as both phallic and vaginal with uterus,

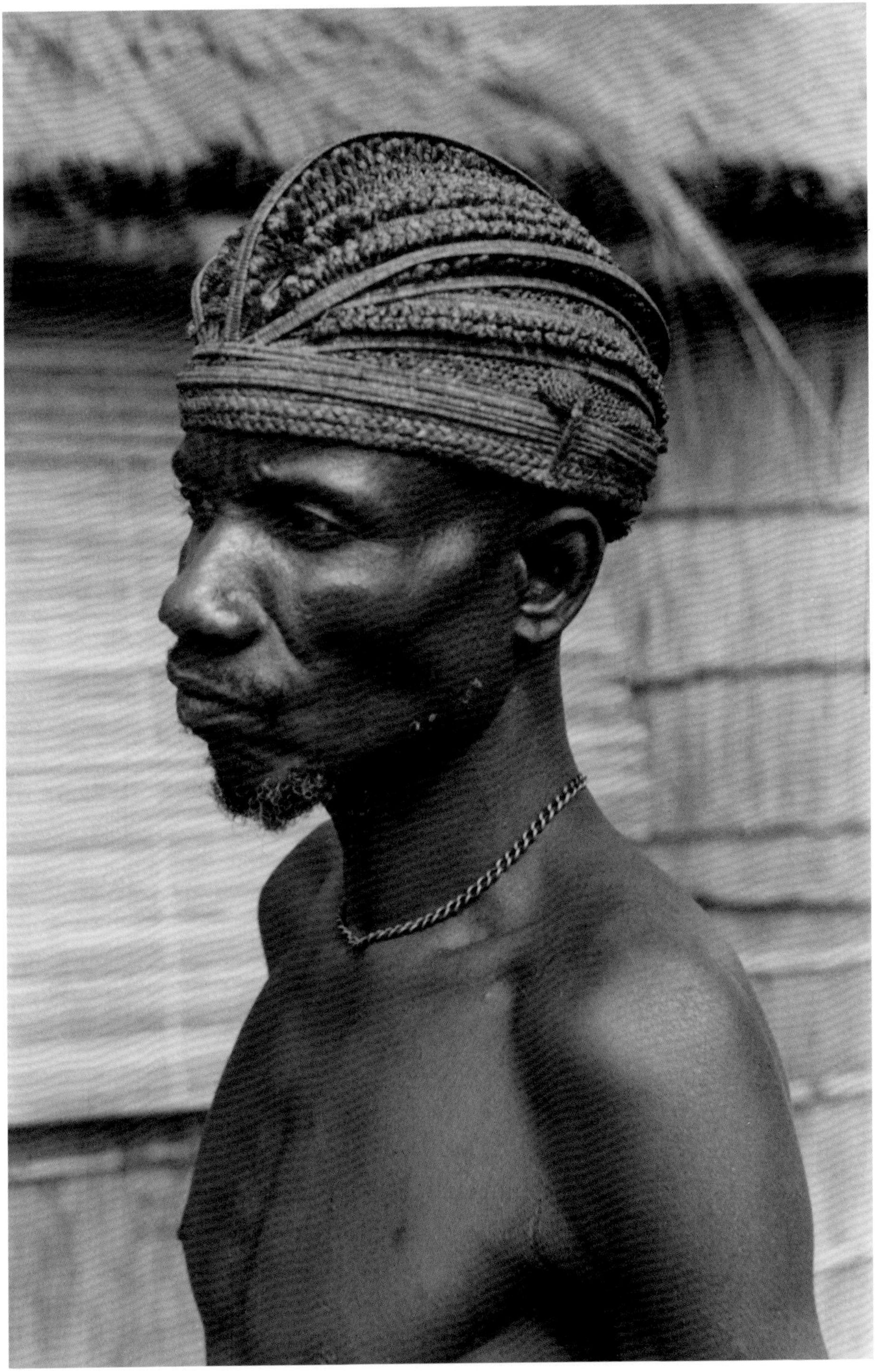

Fig. 2. Yaka earth chief wearing woven hat. Postcard: D. Gelbard Archive, inv. 2043.

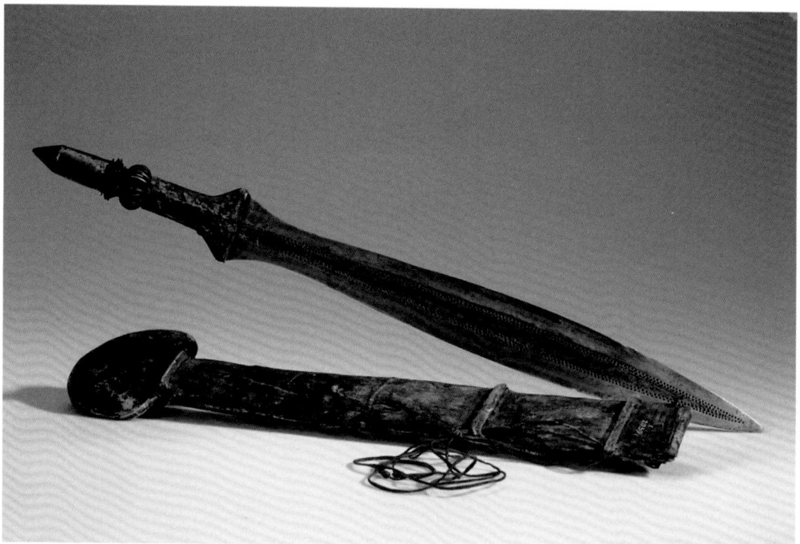

Fig. 3. *Mbele phoko* sword and scabbard serving both as a weapon and chiefly symbol of power and authority, 1869–1890. Collected on the Atlantic Coast. American Museum of Natural History, New York, inv. 1/2059 AB.

allusions to the rigid palm tree and its overflowing grog blossoms, and the parallel lines engraved along the length of the blade that evoke the virile rainbow-python *kyandzangoombi* (Devisch and Brodeur 1999: 180). Violence underpinning the office of paramount chief is implied by his use of the sword together with his intent to control witch power.

Yet this powerful and esoteric artifact, with all its forceful allusions, is best compared to its opposite, an everyday domestic artifact from the realm of Yaka women, namely, the humble *muswalu* or manioc sifter basket with its oblong form and constricted neck that bears similar sexual allusion (fig. 4). Woven by men, once presented it remains a distinctly female household object no male will touch. One might also select the *muyendi* burden basket (fig. 5) or the mortar and pestle used in making manioc flour with its resonating sound at daybreak in a Yaka village, or, again, the spherical *mondo* jug used for the transport and storage of water. Essentially, this is a woman's product with its decoration surrounding the long neck. Conceptually, they are life-sustaining artifacts: soft and pliable, even fragile, in the case of the *muswalu* or *muyendi* baskets and *mondo* jug, or rigid and resounding as in the mortar and pestle. The male/female allusions in each of these, including the *mbele phoko* sword, appear on Yaka masks and other carved artifacts.

The *ndzuundu* is also a significant item of leadership. It consists of two metal spikes approximately 10 centimeters in length, joined by a cord. Of indigenous

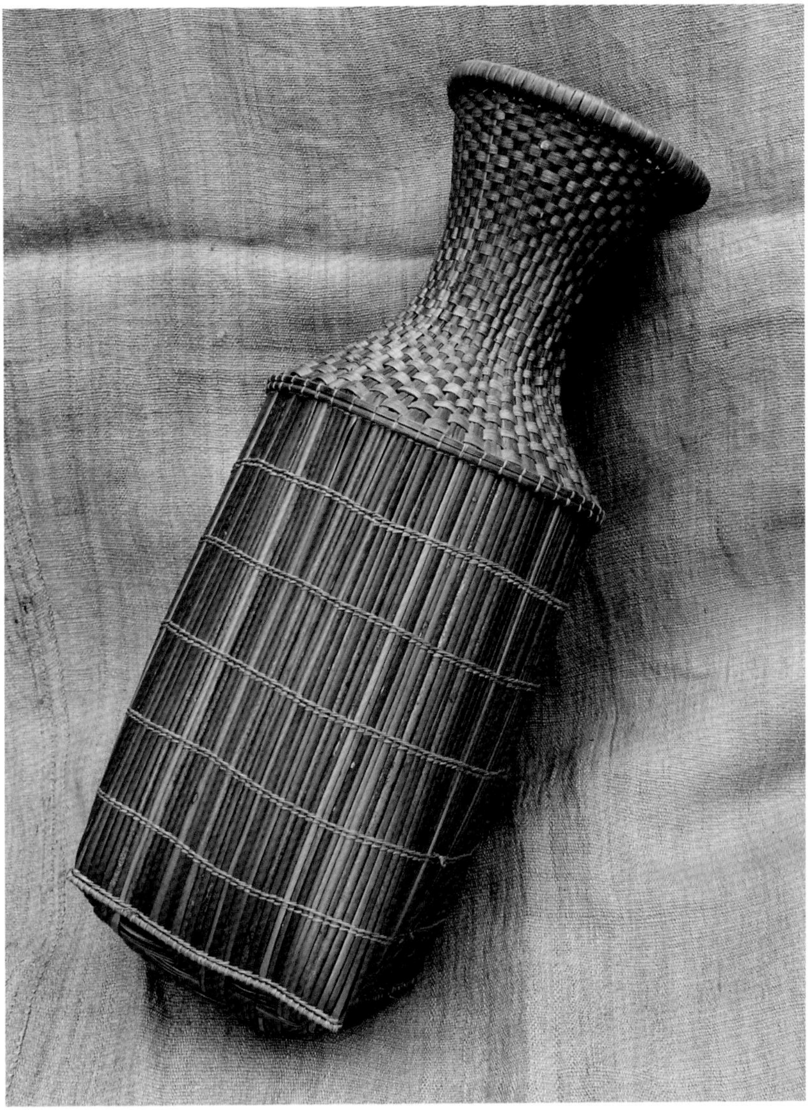

Fig. 4. *Muswalu* basket woven by men but used by women for sifting manioc flour. Its oblong form and constricted neck bear sexual allusion. H. 46 cm. Photo: Arthur P. Bourgeois, 1976.

rather than lunda derivation, this object is worn around the neck while eating or drinking, or the spikes are crossed or struck together following a meal. Another custom is to extend a hand toward the *ndzuundu* following a meal, and then to clap twice as a sign of respect (Van der Beken 1978: 21). Symbolically associated with the earth, the *ndzuundu* relates to the anvil of metal smiths. Pouring palm wine to the earth before drinking seems to be a related custom

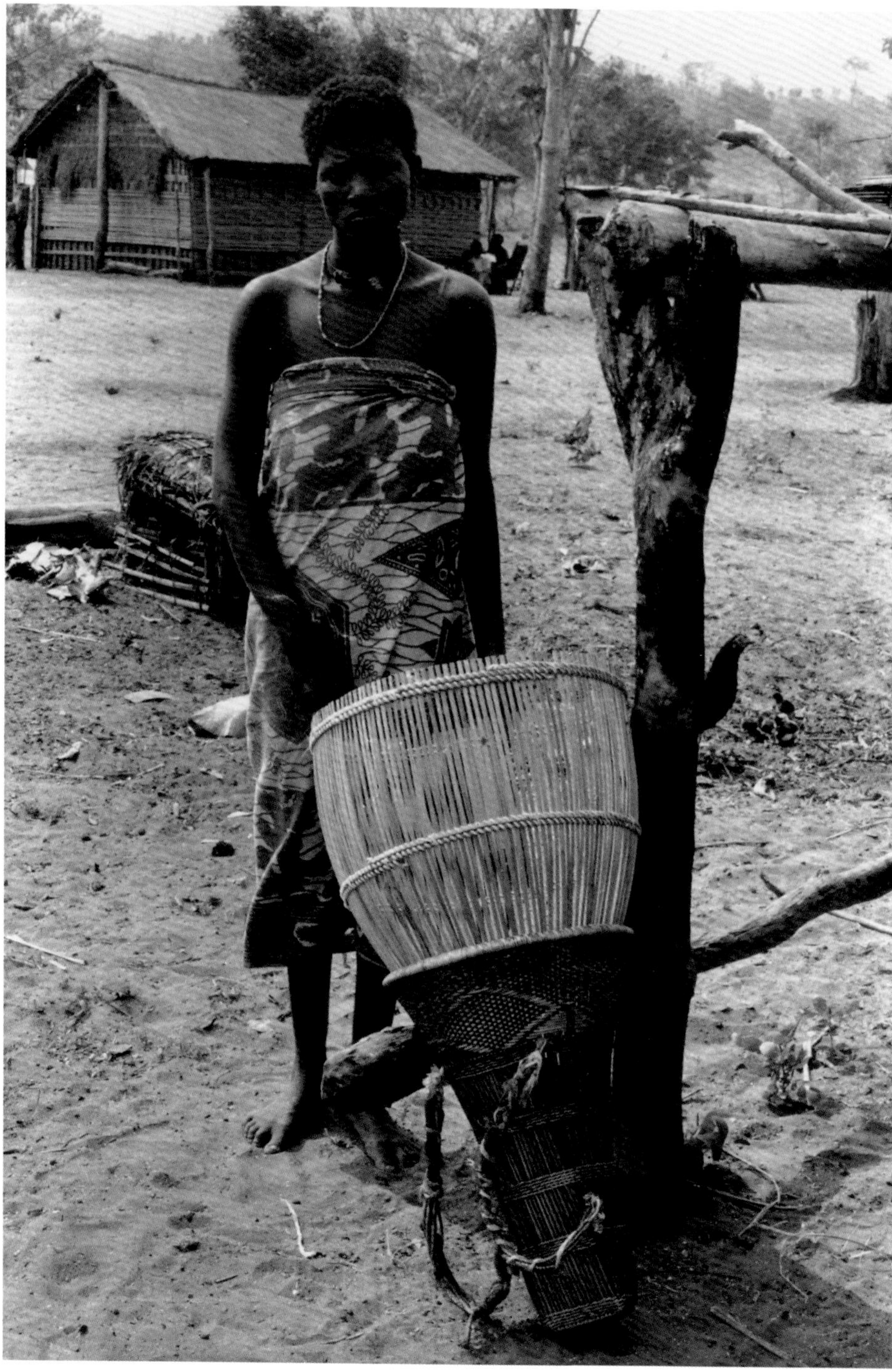

Fig. 5. Yaka woman with *muyendi* basket with *kizangala* extension. Village of Pasanganga, Popokabaka sector. Photo: Arthur P. Bourgeois, 1976.

as well as the use of a special vessel. Yaka enclaves neighboring the Suku similarly employ the *kopa* for this purpose (fig. 6). Northern Yaka chiefs from clans that proceeded the coming of the Lunda and land chiefs (*kalamba*, pl. *tulamba*), honor their ancestors either by planting *nsanda* trees (*Ficus dusenii*) or by constructing the *ndzo makhulu*, a miniature house that shields a row or two of forked stakes of the *n-kuati* tree (*Erythropheum africanum*) each signifying a named ancestor. One or more forked stakes are first placed on the grave site of an ancestor and later erected in the *makhulu* enclosure and consecrated in the name of the ancestor by applying a solution of reddened *khula* wood, and sprinkling the blood of a cock. The chief will go to the enclosure or *ndzo makhulu* on the evening before a grand communal hunt, daub them with kaolin, and on the following morning will distribute pieces of kaolin to those participating in the hunt. Thus, trees and by implication their parts and wood, are in themselves associated with ancestors and the *ndzo makhulu* structure, a parallel to curative cult structures such as the *mbwoolu luumbu* with statuettes and other *nkisi* shelters. Moreover, *n-yoombu* forked stakes are erected behind the "elephant" totemic shelter in *n-khanda* initiation to manhood. Chiefs of lunda lineages plant special trees called *m-yoombu* (*Lannea welwichii*), each commemorating particular ruling ancestors within a roofless rectangular enclosure, called a *bindzandza* (fig. 9). Balls of kaolin, *phemba bindzandaza*, are often kept within this enclosure. The vigor and tenaciousness of these trees is taken as a sign of the life-giving and life-promoting influence of ancestors upon their descendants. The tree in its upright and freestanding position models continuity of generations and descent. Older clusters of *miyoombo* trees, but without the enclosure, provide shade for communal activities within the village; hidden in the forest, and known as *yipheesolu*, they are places where masks associated with *n-khanda* initiation are sculpted or constructed.

Among the earliest artifacts of Yaka creativity to be collected by European explorers and early colonial officials in the Kwango region are the wooden
Pls. 7, 8 combs and hairpins (*yisanuna*) that bear miniature human or animal faces or full figures. Dating prior to 1930, the several hundred examples apparently were carved in the vicinity or to the south of Popokabaka, although they were traded extensively. A few examples appeared at the court of the *kyambvu* at Kasongo Lunda (collected by Büttner in 1886). Used by Yaka male dignitaries as hair ornaments, they display a broad variety of subjects and exquisite carving; otherwise little information is available about them. Clay tobacco pipes (*kinsu*) are a similar early Yaka item to be collected that feature ceramic pipe bowls shaped like human faces with turned up noses or mask-like features. Although they are not distinctly a sign of office, they bear the more

widespread function as a meditation piece; the dignitary while smoking is contemplating a solution to problems he is asked to resolve.

Yaka religious expressions concern the elders and ancestors, the *bambuta*, who in life and death command obedience and whose discontent is greatly feared. Respecting traditional ways and directives honor the *bambuta* and they are appeased by submitting offerings and gifts. Elders, ranging from lineage headmen to local, regional, and paramount chiefs, lead the public ancestor cult.

Leadership objects find their appropriate context in the *lukhaangu,* the installation of a regional or paramount chief, sub-regional and village chiefs. The following summary of *lukhaangu* derives from the research of R. Devisch (1981) and L. De Beir (1975a). Like most rites of passage among the Yaka, this takes place just before a new moon. Death and burial of a Yaka chief involves ritual absorption of his vital powers into a ball of kaolin, hiding the chiefly insignia, removal of his dwelling to the outskirts of the village, and nearly a year of official mourning. During this interregnum, the main political and ritual role is that of the *tsakala*, the chief's mother's brother, who as a ritual specialist mediates between subordinate populations and the ruling line of lunda descendants. Installation begins with an assembly of family heads together with a neighboring dynastic chief. Choice of a successor is formally announced and the sacred insignia of chieftainship is presented before the group by the *tsakala*. Spread out in a circle in the sand, a sacrifice is made and its blood sprinkled on the insignia in order to purify them from the blood of sorcery and restore them to their primal state (Devisch and Brodeur 1999: 175). This insignia, as presented above, includes the copper bound arm and ankle rings (*kazekedi*), double bladed sword (*mbeedyaphoko*), adze, basket, or receptacle containing among other items: a ball of kaolin (*pheemba*), a pair of spike-like anvils (*ndzuundzu*), and the incisor teeth of a leopard. That evening five individuals enter a dwelling backwards, curtained with palm fronds, for a period of silence and seclusion: the chiefly candidate, his main wife, the ritual officer of the installation (*tsakala*) together with the future chief's "brother"-assistant, and lastly his classificatory "sister." Those in seclusion wear a palm-frond fringe over their shoulders and across the chest. Care of the chiefly insignia is the task of the first wife. On this occasion, an augury is commonly performed by flipping the *kazekedi* bracelet onto the chiefly candidate's right arm. If it falls to the ground, this is a warning of rejection by the ancestors. Another form of prognostication is through a collective hunt for a clawed and spotted animal, the success of which indicates ancestral approval. At dawn, the *tsakala*'s representative with weapon in hand performs a war dance before the house of seclusion while others nearby fire off guns. The *tsakala* then leads each of the occupants out in a row; walking in a bowed manner, each with his or her

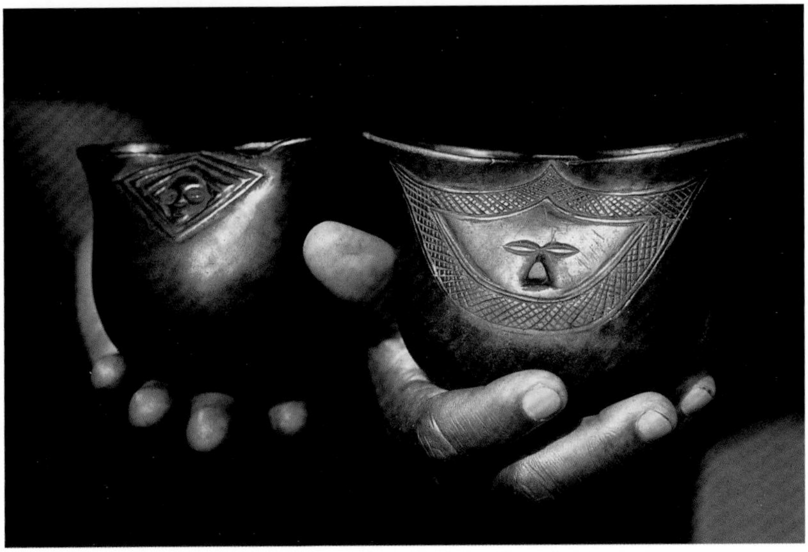

Fig. 6. Yaka-style *kopa* or ritual cups photographed among the Tsaamba-Suku, Kiamfu Kinzadi, Bandundu. Photo: Arthur P. Bourgeois, 1976.

hand on the back of the one proceeding, until they approach an enclosure draped with palm leaves. Their bodies are then rubbed with red clay taken from a termite mound and at sunrise and sunset they must stand on one leg with the other leg positioned against it.

Using the ancestral firestone, the new chief will light a fire for distribution within his village and finally, holding his buffalo tail fly-wisk, will begin the ruler's dance. This dance simulates an attack on a dignitary who sits at the opposite end of the council place. Here, mythical events of the lunda conquest are re-enacted in song and gesture. The new chief then wields his sword before the dignitary and finally plunges its blade into the soil beneath the person's feet. This representative of earlier populations then offers the chief a special cup of palm wine and his submission.

Subsequently, the chief together with his principal wife, *tsakala*, and his "brother" assistant will return to the ritual enclosure to be further inducted by a ritual specialist representing a neighboring regional overlord. White lines are painted from eyes to temples, a vine is wound around each participant, water is poured over them, they are sprinkled with mosses, and males dance nude before the group. The white kaolin clay lines refer to the new moon, revivify health, and sustain longevity, as well as assuring abundance of game, unity of lineage members, and purifying cult objects (Devisch 1993: 67–68). Within this ritual, the chief's power of supervision is conveyed. His wife presents the chiefly regalia to the new chief and all salute Kola, the land of lunda origin. A black ram is then caught by the excited crowd and sacrificed, and that evening a human ligament or its ram substitute is added to the ankle *kazekedi*. Dignitaries representing earlier populations pay their respects to the new chief, receive from him the pelt of a civet-cat, and in turn anoint the ruler with their own ancestral kaolin. The double bell and small anvils within the chief's insignia are then exhibited and the newly inducted chief organizes a regional tribute collecting tour. We shall see this replicated in the touring exhibition of masks following *n-khanda* initiation. After the investiture, an ancestral shrine (*bindzandza*) enclosure is erected in front of the chief's house in which a tree is planted representing each of his ruling ancestors that will be cared for by his first wife. To the rear of his dwelling a small ritual hut (*ndzo malala*) is also constructed that will contain drawn or modeled images of the chief's totemic animals: the leopard and crocodile. Equally, a vine is stretched from one wall to the other signifying *kyandzangoombi*, the rainbow python, and other objects make reference to sexuality, fire, hunting, and the forge. The chief acquires sovereign power through reconciling cosmic, social, and bodily opposites in mediating fertility and productivity of both subjects and land and control over aggression and sorcery. Henceforth, the chief is charged with placating his deceased predecessors through the preservation of bracelets and kaolin, performing sacrifices and libations in their honor, and offering prayers at ancestral tombs and the specially designated enclosures. The chief will serve as judge and peacemaker in the event of intervillage strife or predatory behavior toward strangers and dominate any negotiation with outside political or economic units. As a symbol of allegiance, sporadic collection of tribute remains his special prerogative, although certain symbolic items such as skins or parts of animals associated with sovereignty, e.g., leopard, buffalo, elephants, and white feathers of certain birds, must ascend the chain of delegated authority. Today, cooperative efforts between equally ranked chiefs are in response to external governmental pressures, other than at funerals and investiture rituals. Formerly, mutual cooperation between chiefs concerned resistance or aggression toward a common enemy.

Prior to the twentieth century, the Yaka adult male had a reputation as a fearsome warrior, and since the time of colonial rule, the prestige of hunting has been paramount to male identity. A hunter's conversation is filled with hunting episodes of surprise, reactions, successes, disappointment told and retold while engaged in more mundane pursuits. The hunter will often have a private hut in the forest where he can dwell several days or weeks at a time devoted to this pursuit. Successful hunting provides meat for a man's dependents, but its implications run much deeper. Not only is a man's social and self-image involved, but hunting is auspicious, signaling prosperity in other endeavors and truth in divination oracles. For example, good hunting is said to result in one's wife becoming pregnant and furthering the health and wellbeing of one's lineage. The wife presents a red ointment to her husband to wish him success and thereby retains "rights of the hunt" which include certain portions of the game reserved for her. The redwood paste, known as *khula*, made with palm oil is associated with the setting sun, fertility, pregnancy, and uterine blood (Devisch 1993: 66). Numerous restrictions apply to the hunter, particularly before a group hunt. They include sexual abstinence, avoidance of menstruating women, and the resolution of any hostilities or disputes. The hunter uses bow and arrow, antique rifle, lance, or a variety of snares and traps. Groups of hunters in a collective hunt, especially during the dry season in June and July, use long nets to encircle their quarry as well as dogs to drive the game. The larger and the more ferocious the animal he brings down, the greater the hunter's prestige. The skin, tusks, or teeth of animals capable of killing humans become tribute to the paramount chief.

Days before a collective hunt, men of a locality are alerted by means of a whistle sounded by the owner of a hunting dog. The hunting location is mutually agreed upon and gifts of palm wine and kola nuts are sent to the local land chief for his approval and as a request that he present the customary blood offerings to his ancestors. The types of animals commonly sought include duiker, antelope, wild boar, and buffalo. Before leaving for the hunt proper, all gather in front of the symbolic tree or ritual shelter of the land chief and present their bows and arrows, guns, or lances. Ancestors are invoked and traces of kaolin are drawn on the forearm, bow, or gun. Other than weaponry, the most elaborate artifact of the hunt is the whistle that is suspended from the neck of the leader of the hunt and is used to
Pl. 6 alert others as well as to call his dog. The whistle features a carved human head and a side extension bearing a single hole to modulate the tone. In the most elaborate variety, the shaft of the instrument is enveloped with the fore-shank skin of a duiker and a carved human head is prominent at the lower extremity. Others are more spherical in shape but with a similar although shorter side extension and modulating hole. Occasionally, a carved head is presented here as well. The simplest is adapted from the hollow horn of the duiker but without the modulating side hole. This form provides the generic name for all whistle types and it, together with use of antelope leg bones or certain hollow fruit pods or calabashes, provide prototypes. The associated image, worn as a pendant, has significance in protecting hunters from the influence of witches in ruining or bringing bad luck to the venture.

Charms that assure success in the hunt proliferate. While some are portable as packets, filled horns or shells that are specific to the different kinds of hunting, be it with bow and arrow, rifle, lance or traps of various kinds. Other charms are free-standing constructions or series of stakes kept in enclosures or open shelters that approach the creations of contemporary century artists. Elevated by forked supports, the *khoongo* component—found in several of the series charms—consists of a pile of logs of the *n-heeti* tree with one in the middle extended outward and carved in the form of a knife blade. This is flanked by a series of sculptured or wrapped stakes, termite concretions, banana plants, with one or more connected in the air by interlaced vines. Differing configurations are given different names. Each is prescribed by the diviner in response to particular situations and then constructed or installed by a specialist in that given type of charm. Hunting offers ready contact between the ancestors and their descendants and at the same time it is difficult to delineate where the ancestor cult ends and use of powerful charms begins.

SORCERY AND THE ROLE OF THE DIVINER

Sorcery involves unbridled desires, aggression, exploitation, abuse, revenge, darkness, deviance, horror, and death but also is a special or extraordinary knowledge, power and special kind of intelligence that a person possesses marked by success in social and economic activities. The predatory sorcerer or witch instinctively denies any social restraint and disrupts domestic life. A sorcerer is recruited by a relative who reveals to him or her a nefarious dimension. In popular imagination, the sorcerer as a hunter wanders the depths of the forest under the cover of night. While others sleep, he or she leaves their own body, traveling through the air or under the ground as an invisible bird or insect to meet in covens where they indulge their incestuous desires and feed on the raw human flesh of relatives. They make slaves of their victims, forcing their spirits to toil in fields or forests or perform errands. Witch powers permit its owner to be in several places at once, travel long distances in a few moments, or transform the human witch into an animal, for example, a wild boar, leopard, crocodile, or buffalo in order to stalk and kill one's enemies. Eventually, the witch self-destructs. In many ways it is the negative image of the ideal and what would happen ultimately if one strays from the ways of the ancestors. Whether real or imaginary, the sorcerer must be stopped or trapped. Charms, called *nkisi*, are essentially defense mechanisms and protection from predatory sorcerers and carried on one's person or that close off domestic or ritual areas where they are placed at entryways, on walls, ridgepoles, and beneath beds. Designed to trap or snare, discharge like a gun, assault and counter-attack the intruder, they are most often inserted in a shell, nut, horn, or small container. The packet of ingredients or *khawa* is thought to be explosive and potentially harmful to their owner and to the intended victim. The ingredients form a kind of pharmacology with elements that derive from plants, animals, or unusual objects whose characteristics signify the desired effect. Objects ordinarily and primarily associated with one sphere or occasion are applied to another or their names are used for that of another suggested by it. Opposites are brought together and combined or mediatory elements or categories are added or cooked for an effect that is more than the sum of its parts. Yet the combination of materials or associations does not exist in isolation but concerns a ritual vocabulary, formulae, and drama that involves the interaction of participants.

For the Yaka, human life and all hereditary influences descend though one's maternal bloodline which is the special concern of matrilineal elders and maternal uncles. In marriage, for example, the future life of offspring is legitimately transferred from the maternal ascent to the lineage segment of the husband following special gift compensations. But the maternal uncles continue to oversee all family life particularly in case of ritual prohibitions of illicit sexual relations where they demand compensations and impose fines in the name of the matrilineage. Blessings are conveyed by means of kaolin (*pheemba*) that is rubbed on the left arm from wrist to elbow. Disagreements with one's maternal uncle are avoided at all cost. Neglect of customary exchanges, infringement of rights, and theft result in discord and invite misfortune, illness, and death. In a similar way, curses might be called down by agnatic or patrilineal authorities. Upon infringement, the wronged elder may withdraw protection or reassert his status through sorcery or seek revenge by calling a curse upon the wrongdoer and his/her kinsmen. Curses are not random but are allied proper to one of some twenty specific kinds (the principal ones being: *khita, m-mbwoolu, ngoombu, haamba, n-luwa, khosi, mbaambi, n-hwaadi, leembi, yindongu, maawa, ndzaambi* and *yimbala*) that are thought of as entering the bloodline of the wrongdoer causing destruction until formally neutralized through specific rituals. Those individuals who have sought relief from the same curse or undergone the same curing process form a social group that cuts across lineage identity. Each involves possession-trances. For a victim, identification of the specific cause of a misfortune, strange event, sickness, or death is sought from a divinatory oracle.

This oracle, known as *ngaanga ngoombu* or *ngaanga weefwa* (fig. 8), is found in certain matrilineal kin groups but functions for all clients regardless of their origin upon ritual compensation for the service. Consultations are performed in the presence of the client's patrilineal and matrilineal witnesses.

A mediating object such as shell money (*nzimbu*), coin, or piece of cloth, having been in contact with the victim is presented to the diviner without comment and the diviner, without any previous information, must reveal the complete problem to the client at the initial stage as a demonstration of an ability for extended consciousness. Subsequent oracle utterances reveal the persons, events, sorcery, or curse that led up to the problem and an analogous past occurrence involving an ancestor of the victim that had been neutralized.

The calling of a diviner follows a given pattern: (1) seizure by a persistent illness; (2) trance occurrence with bizarre behavior; (3) testing for extrasensory knowledge; (4) formal training under *ngoombu* practitioners. Most extraordinary is the diagnostic *ngoombu* trance during which the victim leaps onto the roof of a village cabin and scratches apart the thatched roof amid high-pitched cries of "ko ko ko," all the while the head and body twitching and jerking like a chicken's. During this behavior the person reveals the name of the deceased diviner forebear responsible for the possession. The *ngoombu* candidate subsequently adopts a new name and a diviner's way of life, that include special ways of sitting, eating, washing, and speaking a diviner's argot known as *ki-ngoombu*.

Sacral objects associated with the divinatory process include the wooden slit drum (*mukoku ngoombu*) that bears a carved human head on its handle. The Pl. 11
diviner's chant gives clues to its essence, "Oh Mama, I beat my slit drum so that he will confide in my big vagina, *Yeebeetaka n-kooku maama, kangwaana phenya mbuta*"(Devisch and Brodeur 1999: 115)—a return to a primordial uterine space in order to initiate rebirth and healing. This instrument is the distinct symbol of the *ngoombu* diviner but is also used as the diviner's seat and as a container in which to prepare medicines. The drum has either been inherited from a diviner predecessor within the lineage or been placed upon his or her grave in symbolic contact with this individual who will serve as the oracle's voice. The *mukoku ngoombu* is, in a sense, a miniature and modified version of the message or "talking" drum, a heavy cylindrical slit-drum known as *mondo*. The latter, however, is struck with rubber-tipped mallets and is associated with the regional chief. It announces the chief's arrival, community gatherings, or a death; and formerly it was used as a call to arms. In northern Yaka examples of the *mondo* prototype, the narrow rectangular aperture stretches between two rectangular orifices, but the *mukoku* slit-drum normally does not include this feature. When struck, the diviner's idiophone presents shrill tones with intervals of ¼ to ½ tone. In the rhythms commonly played by diviners that I interviewed, duple simple meters predominate, offering an accompanying pattern to the diviner's chant. Three examples are as follows:

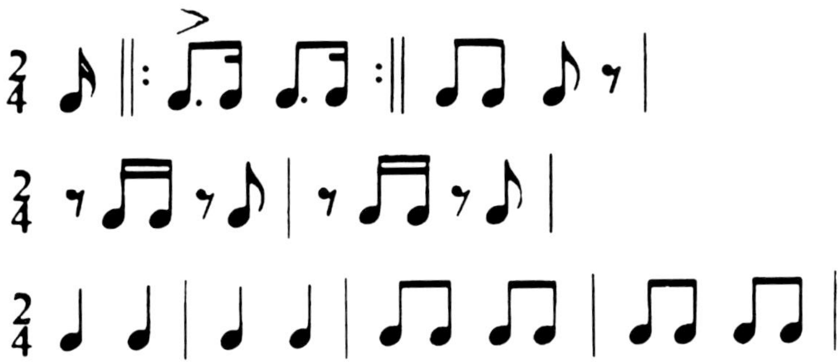

Diviner informants stated that the sculptured head on the slit-drum is "the head of *ngoombu*" or that "it is to decorate the *mukoko*." According to Devisch, who questioned Yaka diviners in 1972, the carved face together with the drum was described as "my very image," symbolically indicating the diviner's role as message bearer to all people regardless of their sex or origin.

The head surmounting the slit-drum, like Yaka freestanding statuettes in general, would appear to objectify the role of elders in mediating misfortune, sickness, and death. Implied is reference to the powers of extra-vision attributed to those in authority, enabling them to see past the appearances of ordinary life into the nefarious world of envy, witchcraft, and sorcery. This attribute is foremost with the *nganga ngoombu*, who crosses all divisions, limits, barriers, and who can see into the deepest darkness of the forest. Some Yaka slit-drums feature a duiker, bird, or tortoise image surmounting the carved head. Although diviners stated that these animal images had no significance other than as decoration provided by the sculptor, such representations are not meaningless. These animals are associated with various charms and charm ingredients. For example, the dried carcass of a *tseye* bird is included in the diviner's bundle to provide additional power to see misconduct; it was explained that this species has a reputation as an eavesdropper and informer. These same animals are a food source, having significance in hunting mystique, and also present analogies to human character types in folktales. For example, the duiker repeatedly and maliciously tricks other animals, especially the leopard, and animals otherwise symbolic of chiefly power and overwhelming force. The tortoise is associated with guilelessness, resourcefulness, and intelligence. The relationship between such imagery and divination is somewhat diffuse; it may be that the frailty of these animals and their ultimate triumph over incredible odds symbolically parallel the divination process. Surmounting animal imagery commonly appears on northern Yaka combs, statuettes, and in the form of puppet-like constructions on mask. Well-carved animal figures, like expressive faces on masks, also serve as personal signatures of prominent sculptors easily recognized throughout a given locale or region.

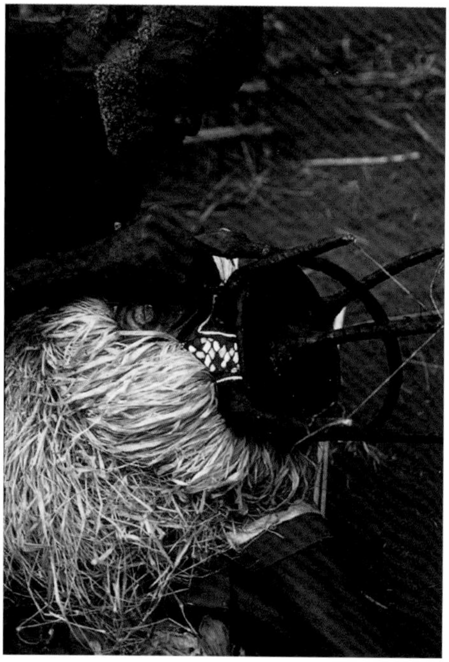

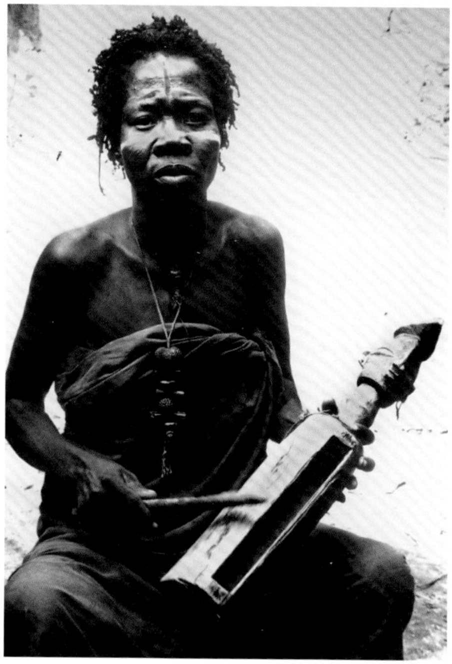

Fig. 7. Pakalupatu painting a Yaka mask, Pasa Ngaanga village, Popokabaka sector, Bandundu. Photo: Arthur P. Bourgeois, 1976.
Fig. 8. *Ngaanga ngoombu*, northern Yaka diviner, Mahunda Malaku, sounding a *n-knooku* slitdrum and wearing a neck pendant containing charm ingredients pertaining to diviners of the *wefwa muYaka* and *wefwa musuku* traditions. Masala-Yalama village, Bandundu. Photo: Arthur P. Bourgeois, 1976.

In the past, if a given individual is repeatedly accused of sorcery, the elders with the support of maternal uncles might force the person to undergo a poison oracle—a drink made from the toxic bark of the *phutu* tree of the forest. If the accused vomits the poison, this is a sign of innocence; if not, death would be instantaneous and his or her guilt confirmed. Presently, a chicken is poisoned and the person ostracized, however, the divinatory oracle identifies the curse and surrounding circumstances and concerned relatives establish reciprocity between kin and through ritual compensations in order to remove the cause. A search is then made for a ritual practitioner whose specialty is that particular variety of charm-curse and who will treat the victim directly or will initiate a member of the victim's lineage to control and neutralize its effect. During the period of treatment, a special dwelling is needed, specific prohibitions are imposed by lineage headman, appropriate formulae, songs, or dancers are taught, and the components of the particular charm are prepared. Ritual barriers are erected to protect the person under treatment often designated by a raffia curtain and secured with various charms such as the *mbindusi mitatu* charm. Made of intertwined branches of *n-kwati* (a savannah ironwood, *mbaamba,* a creeper used in traps and building houses, and *mboti* trees with the ends tied or capped, the *mbindusi mitatu* signifies the "twisting" effect of the disorder that must be reversed. If part of the paraphernalia includes a carved image, this is ordered from a carver, charm medicines are inserted into or rubbed onto the image, and the charm is activated with a blood sacrifice. Lineage members then share in eating the sacrificial animal and a lineage headman then makes offerings to the ancestors.

The cured victim or one being inducted is then ritually washed and returns to the village amid rejoicing. Once ritually incorporated, the charm-curse serves the lineage by protecting its rights over property and persons. For example, the statue or charm packet might be carried through a village as a warning against further depredations concerning thievery, or employed to force the culprit to make compensation or be used in judicial disputes to swear the truth. Thus social norms are reinforced under threat of being "seized" by the charm-curse. The variety of wood used in carving the statuette frequently has significance in itself, such as that of the small *yiseleti* tree of the savanna, as use of its concentrated sap can result in hemorrhages (Dechamps 1977; Devisch 1993: 305, note 7d).

Curative Statuettes

Of the twenty or so charm-curse institutions, among the northern Yaka, only five use carved imagery: *m-mbwoolu* and *ngoombu*—institutions that are transmitted in the maternal line—and *khosi, ndzasi,* and *mbaambi*—patrilineal transmitted institutions. However, only two of these contexts have distinct varieties of carved statuettes, namely, *m-mbwoolu-tsyo* and *khosi*. Such institutions are widespread in central African and known as "institutions of affliction"—Victor Turner's term for the classic sequence of a rite of passage (starting from Van Gennep's analysis, 1960) where the patient is detached from his/her kin group, put under the quasi-authority of the healer, changes identity, and is returned to the group but viewed as a metaphor of social drama whose re-enactment assures the continuity of the social structure while resolving immediate social conflicts expressed in sickness and misfortune (Turner 1967, 1968).

M-mbwoolu-tsyo statuettes appear in series that can number as many as twenty figures in a single ritual shelter (fig. 10). In general, they average from 7.5 to 35 centimeters in height and are characterized by the red *khula*-rubbed surface, the kaolin line across the forehead, and kola nut residue on the stomach. Individualized in carving, *m-mbwoolu* features statuettes with missing limbs, spiraled torso, expanding body sections, janus-form and doubles—one figure

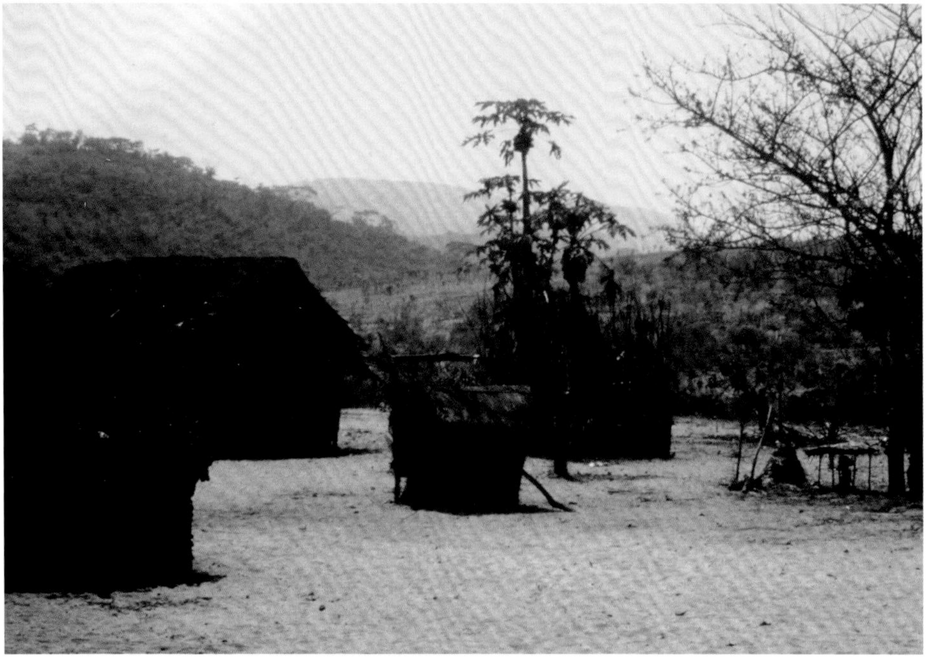

Fig. 9. Yaka village with enclosure with *m-yoombu* trees (right) and shelters with a variety of protective and hunting charms. Photo: Arthur P. Bourgeois, 1976.

above the other. As a series the Yaka conceptualize them as *bapfumu*, the chiefs, whose relation to one another is a miniature version of the political structure. Each shelter has its paramount chief and subordinate chiefs, often with wives, children, and retainers. The name of each begins with the honorific *nga*, "sir" or "madam," and refers to a forebear of the *m-mbwoolu-tsyo* institution that has appeared in a dream to either the victim or the *m-mbwoolu* specialist. A few have names that describe the form of the image; one example is Kabamba-Who-Has-One-Leg that is often the principal statuette in a *luumbu* shelter. Missing limbs, twisted body, or swelling torso appear to be representations of the situation in which the victim or his/her antecedents have been involved (fig. 11). Devisch notes the undulating shapes, twisted aspect, and slender limbless examples as depicting attributes of the electric catfish, particularly *ngaanzi*, one of the prohibited dietary animals with whom the person under treatment identifies (Devisch and Brodeur 1999: 143–145). The distinct sound is reproduced by the rasp used in *m-mbwoolu* songs and capable of sending the initiate into trance.

In Yaka terminology, *m-mbwoolu-tsyo* images are *biteki* (sing. *yikeki*), figures used to support or contain special concoctions. Without these applied preparations, which permeate the surface or, more rarely, are inserted into a small ventral cavity, they are without meaning to the Yaka and merely await employment by a ritual specialist. But when charged with these ingredients, they become *n'kisi,* "medicines-poisons" that "make-ill" (*kukwati*) through an invisible influence, or "make-well" (*kubuka*) by removing this influence. Owned by specific lineages rather than individuals, the *m-mbwoolu* pass from one generation to another through the "seizure" and subsequent cure of a man or woman who by this ordeal is entitled to become its ritual officer, the *ngaanga.* Originally, *m-mbwoolu* enters a lineage through the theft of some object placed under the *n'kisi*'s protection and becomes a hereditary "sickness" destined to reappear in future members. Its curative capacity can be induced only by the one who first invoked *m-mbwoolu* or by a special ritual practitioner qualified to activate it. Thus *m-mbwoolu* functions as both the calling and temporary abeyance of a curse. But once it has entered a lineage, *m-mbwoolu* offers some benefits. This "medicine-poison" serves the lineage by protecting property and assures the wellbeing of future generations. Moreover, lineage solidarity is furthered in *m-mbwoolu* ritual, and its *ngaanga*, or official practitioner, is assured a lucrative income.

Although complex to the outsider, *m-mbwoolu* unfolds in daily life as one of the most dramatic uses of figure sculpture in Central Africa even today. This assertion is best illustrated in the following example: a man in the village becomes very ill, and despite the help of herbs and European medicines, his condition worsens. His concerned relatives visit a noted diviner, a *ngaanga ngoombo*, who after consultation concludes that some member of the sick man's lineage has stolen an object protected by *m-mbwoolu.* As directed, the relatives seek out a *m-bwoolo* specialist and invite him to their village. Upon arrival, the *ngaanga m-mbwoolu* consults the lineage headman, and together they question the victim about his dreams. The young man has repeatedly dreamed of being capsized in a dugout canoe, thrashing helplessly, and is unable to reach land. Or he may have dreamed of serpents striking him or forcing him down an incline to a turbulent river. Assured that these are the dreams of *m-mbwoolu,* the *ngaanga* orders that an unoccupied hut be transformed into a ritual house, the *luumbu.* Numerous charms are suspended or erected within and a large pit is dug outside the entrance and enclosed within a high fence made of poles and brush. When finished, the *ngaanga m-bwoolo* begins his chanting: "Wait hundred rivers that eat the clans, I know you,/I see you as your victim has spoken. On the following day, the patient is rubbed with kaolin, and kola nut is chewed and spit upon his chest. The *ngaanga m-mbwoolu* then places a half-dozen statuettes within the prepared pit. The patient is lowered into this hole, and the family members are directed to fetch vessels of water and begin pouring them over his head. Around the squatting young man, the statuettes begin to float and bob in the rising water. Seated near the edge of the hole, the *ngaanga m-mbwoolu* continues his chanting, keeping rhythm by scraping a notched wooden rasp while the assembled villagers repeat his refrain: "Swim canoes swim/Swim Mat-sia swim/Swim Kabubu swim . . ." Possessed by a sudden force, the victim's body stiffens. Beating his flexed elbows against his thin flanks, he hysterically cries out:

"Aa mé, aa mé, amé,/Wretched am I, oho, oho, oho,/It is the river that takes people,/the river eats the Ngongo clan,/Ah, grandfather, eh, eh, eh, oho, oho, oho,/It is my grandfather who brought this upon me,/who set it loose./He stole goats, the goats of another,/When they left for work, when the owners left,/the owner said:/'Follow the one who stole my goats,/seize him, seize him, you my biteke mbwoolo,' You Matsia and great Kinkola,/seize the one who stole my goats. "Aa mé, aa mé, aa mé, Wretched am I, wretched am I, oho, oho, oho."

Then, drained of energy, the patient collapses. A line of kaolin is drawn across his forehead, daubs of red *khula* paste are placed on his temples, and he is carried into the hut.

The stereotyped "Aa mé, aa mé, aa mé" cry and accompanying gestures have thrust him into a new life as a *m-mbwoolu* child confirming the augury of the diviner and dreams. Awareness of the relative and situation that brought about the illness may have been revealed earlier by the diviner or may have already been common knowledge, but in the seizure of the immersion ritual the victim's anguished cry publicly tells all. In the days of rest that follow, numerous ritual procedures and dietary restrictions are explained to the *m-mbwoolu* child, and relatives are warned to avoid in his presence the names of snakes, the crocodile, or other river creatures capable of re-occasioning the seizure. His subsequent dreams are examined for clues to the particular *m-mbwoolu* personages that must be represented in sculpture to complete his cure. These are ordered from a local carver and then undergo an empowering process through contact with bones of dangerous river animals and wood of a tree struck by lightning, and by being immersed for days in a concoction made of particular tree barks and plants. After receiving a heavy coat of palm oil and red *khula* paste, chewed kola nut is spit upon the torso of each, and they are placed on a wooden elevation near the rear wall of the ritual house (*luumbu*). Following this, bands of raffia fiber are tied about the patient's neck and wrist, and the *ngaanga* returns to his village. For several months, the convalescent remains secluded. When his health is regained, the *ngaanga* returns for an all-night celebration with dancing and singing of *m-mbwoolu* songs to honor the young man. At dawn both descend to the river, the clothes and raffia bands of sickness are thrown into the current, and the initiate is ritually

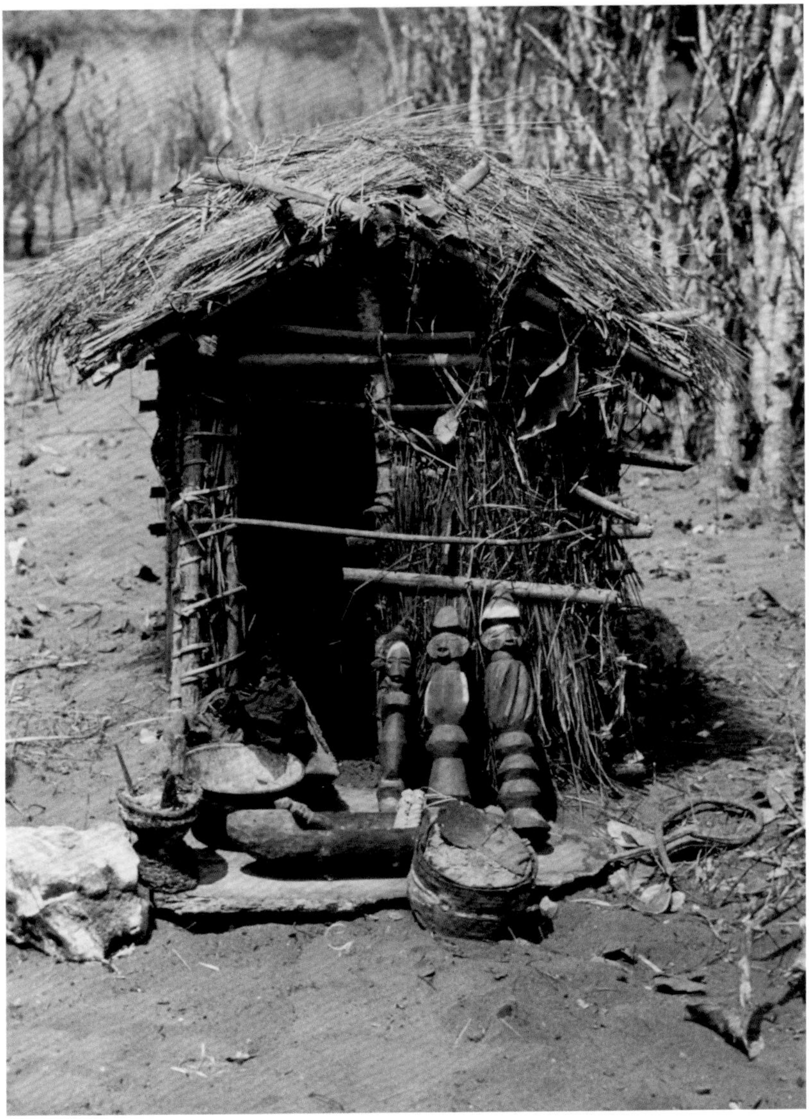

Fig. 10. Yaka shelter (*luumbu*) for *mbwoolu* and *tsyo* statuettes. Said to be one female and two male *mbwoolu* figures with boat containing two *n-ndedi*. The container with projections is for *tsyo*. Other *biteke* belonging to this series were on loan to lineage members. Kimbuku village, Popokabaka Zone, Bandundu. Photo: Arthur P. Bourgeois, 1976.

bathed. As the *m-mbwoolu* child returns to the village to complete participation in community life, he is met with a clamor of welcome.

Before departing, the *ngaanga* and his protégé erect a new structure in the form of a miniature hut as a special shelter for the new *m-mbwoolu biteke*. Kneeling

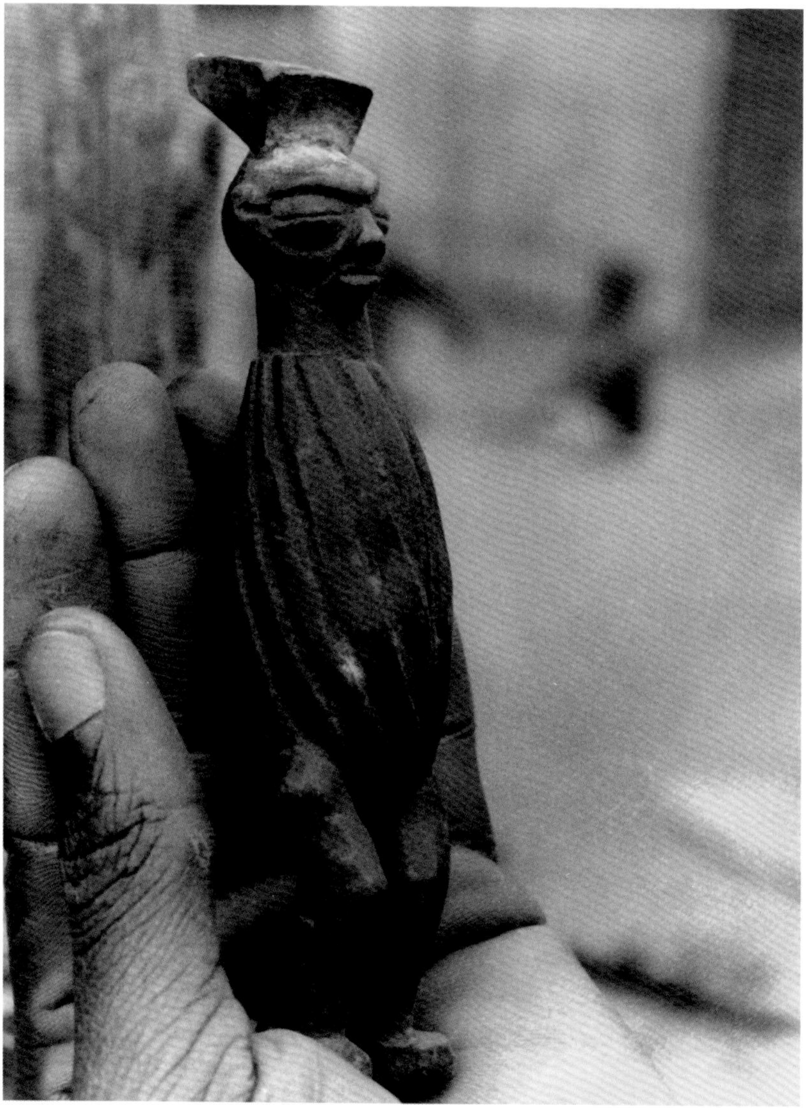

Fig. 11. *Mbwoolu yiteki* entitled "Sir Serpent" or "twisted". Pasanganga Village, Popokabaka Zone, Bandundu. Photo: Arthur P. Bourgeois, 1976.

before the row of carved figures, they salute them by clapping their hands, the right in the left, then the left in the right: they present their palms and press their knuckles to the earth. Then, taking a *yiteke* in each hand, they forcefully strike their shoulders, arms, and sides. Kola nut is spit on the stomach of each statuette, and finally they are carefully placed within the small structure together with special containers and offerings of food. The *m-mbwoolu* specialist will observe this ritual before dawn almost daily. Once each month, the *biteki* will be placed in the empowering rays of the new moon, a cock will be sacrificed, its blood sprinkled on the images and baskets, and the full repertoire of *m-mbwoolu* songs will again be sung. If the initial treatment of the patient is not successful or if there is a relapse, more images will be made and medicines will be taken, or another *ngaanga* may introduce the close "relatives" of *m-mbwoolu*, the *tsyo*, a series of associated rituals and images considered more powerful than *m-mbwoolu*. When *m-mbwoolu* sculpture is combined in the same shelter with those of *tsyo*, the auxiliary of *m-mbwoolu*, there is not much difference between the two types aside from their names and ritual use. Usually the *tsyo* are among the larger figures, but they also may lack appendages. Found only when *tsyo* and *m-mbwoolu* are together, however, is the *ndimba*, the boat carved in miniature, which is filled with river clays or is simply used as a receptacle for offerings and smaller sculpture such as the *ndedi* (see below). Occasionally, a mud- and kaolin-filled *ndimba* has at one end a carving of a passenger depicted with a trailing headdress. Although informants did not elaborate on the significance of the *ndimba* or its passenger, the reference here to river travel and submersion in *m-mbwoolu* chants, dreams, and ritual is evident. One informant claimed that the boat refers to the arrival of the *m-mbwoolu* institution by way of a dugout canoe.

Another dimension of the *m-mbwoolu biteki* is dramatized in popular narratives that emphasize their protective role, personalized attributes, and unyielding curse. This is best illustrated in the following story:

"There was a woman who planted a field of peanuts, and when they were ready to be dug a thief came to steal them. Each day when the owner came to the field she discovered still further depredations. Taking a *m-bwoolo yiteki*, she placed it in the center of her field to trap the thief and warned the children not to go there. The woman who stole peanuts arrived at the field and, not knowing that *m-mbwoolu* was there, began digging peanuts as usual. The *m-bwoolo yiteki* approached the thief and began to speak. When the woman saw this, she took her basket and fled, but the *m-mbwoolu* followed her and began to sing, 'That woman is a thief who carries peanuts in her basket, peanuts in her basket' (sung three times). When the thief heard the song she stopped, awaited the *m-mbwoolu*, seized it, and cut it to pieces. But the fragmented *yiteki* continued to follow her. The thief stopped again and burned the *yiteki*, but *m-mbwoolu* continued to follow and sing its song (refrain). When the owner of the field heard the song, she followed and the thief was caught. The owner demanded chickens and money in payment for the past thefts, but as the thief had no chickens or money, she caught the *m-mbwoolu* sickness. This is how *m-mbwoolu* came about, because of stealing." This narrative

was found in several versions among both the Yaka and Suku. A similar story relates to the *khosi* institution among the Yaka. Visually distinct are northern Pl. 12
Yaka *khosi* statuettes that are paired with a separate bag of charm ingredients or consist of paired statuettes that may be freestanding, joined back to back, or a single statuette with janus face, arms, and legs. Charm medicines are inserted either into the stomach portion or hang in pouches or antelope horn containers at the neck or waist. *Khosi* figures are the largest variety of freestanding sculpture throughout the region, averaging from 30 to 76 centimeters in height. The facial portion is painted or daubed with red or white clay or vertically divided with red on one side and white on the other while the body is decorated with red and white dots and loins are covered with woven raffia or cloth. This bi-coloration is said to recall the founding ancestors of the *khosi* institution, although this feature is equally found on *kakuungu* masks (see below). Moreover, it appears in the Yaka *n-ngoongi* "secret society" that is linked with *lukhaanga* (Devisch 1993: 300 n. 6; Plancquert 1930: 13–49).

Huber (1956: 265–290), Van Wing (1942–1943: 85–96), and Laman (1962: 91) provide descriptions of the use of *khosi* figures among the northeastern Yaka and Kongo. As an institution of affliction, the *khosi* institution was once common to ki-kongo speakers and thus included Eastern Kongo, Nkanu, Suku, Mbala, and other ethnic units and can be found as far away as Gabon (LaGamma 1996: 119–120). The name *khosi* means "lion" or "strong" in ki-kongo languages and the charm institution is mentioned in seventeenth-century missionary documents (Cavazzi 1687: 1, 184). Huber presents the typical narrative of how *khosi* came to a particular lineage through the theft of objects placed under protection of *khosi*, descendants suffering from severe headaches, a diagnosis by the *ngaanga ngoombu* diviner, treatment of the individual by a *khosi* ritual specialist, the selection of two young attendants/guardians that are trained to follow required rituals and seclusion for some months within a special cabin built outside the village. On the evening of their installation, special trees are planted before the house of seclusion and a cock is killed, its blood sprinkled over the newly planted trees. The ritual specialist, a *ngaanga khosi*, then invokes the charm to "drink the blood of the cock, not the blood of people," and *khosi* songs are sung. The attendants under special training in the interdictions learn an argot and songs as well as how to prepare and apply its medicines. The statuettes are commissioned or refurbished and placed in the *khosi* cabin. Resources are then gathered in preparation for the formal dedication attended by the *ngaanga khosi*, lineage chief and village.

On the designated day, the attendants climb the roof of the cabin with two fowls that they kill by biting through their throats before throwing them to the ground. Members of competing lineages then fight to possess them. A goat is sacrificed and its blood is applied to the statuettes and faces and arms of its attendants. The *ngaanga* then adds bits of other power items to the new medicine. The goat meat is then divided, and singing and dancing follow. Finally, the *ngaanga* followed by others carry *khosi* to the village where the statuette and charm bundles are placed in a special room of the chief's house, while different medicines are given to other members to be kept in their homes. Again, trees are planted in front of the lineage chief's dwelling and that of the new custodians of *khosi*. Sexual prohibitions are announced for that night. Subsequently, the lineage head and guardians will make food offerings, wash the *khosi* figure, rub it with palm oil, and renew its coloring on the first day of every new moon. The figure can then be used to protect property or persons and dramatically demonstrate invocation for this purpose.

Van Wing describes the *ngaanga* arriving carrying the *khosi* figure while his assistants accompany him playing small drums. The *khosi* figure is placed upon a mat and pinches of gunpowder are set before it. Kola-nut is spit on the belly of the male *khosi*. A hen is sacrificed and its blood sprinkled. The *ngaanga* then manages to give the spectators the impression that the *khosi* figure dances and moves spontaneously; then seizing it at the hips with both hands he address it. First he salutes the image, presents himself, describes the situation, and finally commands it to pursue, for example, a thief:

> Wring his neck
> May blood flow from his mouth,
> May blood flow from his nose,
> May blood flow from his anus.
> Break his spinal cord,
> In the name of the sovereign Mbumba,
> By the curse of Mbumba,
> What will you do then?
> Kill!

The assistants then sound their drums and sing. The *ngaanga* closes the session, is paid, and retires (Van Wing 1920–1921: 88).

Use of paired or janus-form figures, featuring a male on one side and a female on the other, fit, of course, with widespread traditional use of janus-faced masks and statuettes elsewhere in sub-Sahara Africa. In general, this feature references basic social duality where one side is female and the other male but also signifies an all-seeing capacity and general alertness of the power symbolized, be it that of ancestors or some specific entity. This janus motif, however, is not found in Yaka masking nor in that of their immediate neighbors.

According to Devisch's research on various charm institutions among the Yaka, the general male/female reference applies to the interaction of healer, patient, his or her kin group together with supporting neighbors who collectively expel the evil from the patient and turn it back to its source. Layers of the patient's reality are realigned or interwoven: the patient's afflicted body, his or her world of social relations, the spirit of the founding ancestor, and the life-bearing and life-threatening aspects of the larger life-world are treated. Through the healing drama, the patient is reconnected and fundamental relationships are renewed thus enabling the body to heal itself. In anointing both the patient and the statuette with red paste, the patient nurtures his/her self in a fetal condition and evokes the blood of animal sacrifice used in expelling affliction from the patient's body. White kaolin paste references the body's inner possibilities, broadly tapping the ancestral life source to mother's milk, semen, sap of the palm tree, and the lunar cycle. In brief, the combined male/female reference is a quest to optimized life (1993).

A variety of headgear is shown on *khosi* statuettes that vary from the *mpu* or *mpwa* raffia skullcap to a more elaborate headpiece known as *bweni*. The three-crested coiffure, known as *muhanda* with hair parted or shaped in such a manner as to create elevated ridges, was oiled, plaited, and arranged over an openwork support. All seem to be symbols of authority of land chiefs or previous political substrata but not that of current overlords. While the gesture of hands to chin or mouth commonly signifies reflection, sadness, and grief, the gesture of hands-together-at-the-upper chest pertains to a person confessing guilt or swearing secrecy but is also similar to the Yaka custom of a corpse prepared for burial. In its use, however, the image does not have narrative intent but serves as a support or container for various concoctions and as a personalized focal point of rituals that control, neutralize, and disperse malevolent influences.

Each figure is given a name; for example, the male aspect is entitled Ibanda, *masabu* or *ngudia-khosi*, and the female named *nkodia* or *magandu* and the patient is similarly given this name. The concoctions inserted into the figure or suspended from it might also include hair of a fearsome beast, a scrap of cloth from a deranged person, a morsel of goat meat or pork—forbidden food for a *khosi* patient. Raffia strings might also be tied to the legs of the figure by other ill relatives in order to please the elders/ancients and obtain a rapid cure. The customary offerings are a goat, bolt of cloth, and a chicken. Occasionally a hollow duiker horn whistle is attached to the figure and sounded by the patient when enduring pain. Still other horns are used as containers filled with copal or resin from trees struck by lightning. De Beir lists the ingredients of a *khosi* charm as deriving from

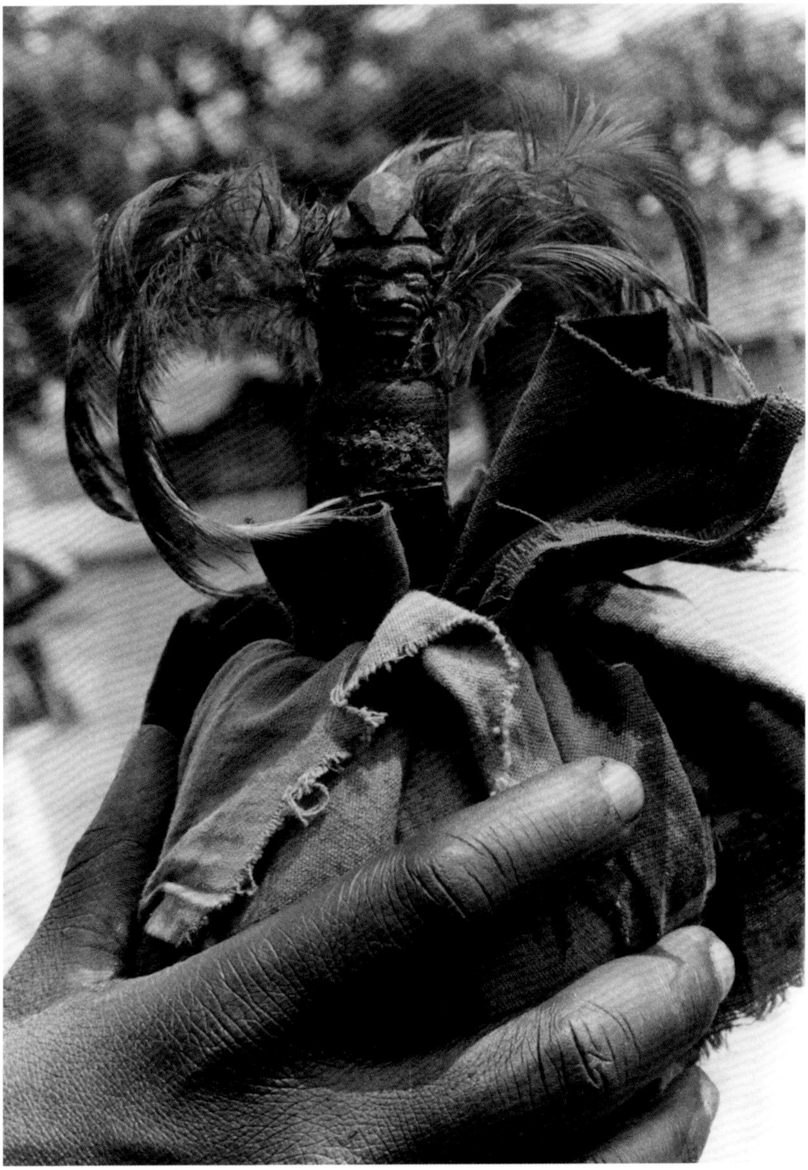

Fig. 12. *Phuungu* charm to protect one's kin group against witchcraft. Itunza village, Popokabaka region, Bandundu. Photo: Arthur P. Bourgeois, 1976.

the largest trees of the forest and includes the sacrifice of a goat rather than chickens (De Beir 1975b). Extensions of the *khosi* charm take the form of small stakes that are inserted in the fields to ward off thieves and as protective pendants worn about the neck in the form of two miniature duiker horns, either of horn material or schematized copies in wood (*binkoko-khosi*).

Statuettes used in the *n-luwa, mbaambi,* and *ndzasi* institutions, other than their intermediate size between *khosi* and *m-mbwoolu-tsyo* figures, are not distinguishable by sculptured form nor coloration but may have added coiffure of animal skin, burst of feathers, and profusion of attached animal-horn containers. *N-luwa,* also called *mwani phutu,* is linked specifically with Lunda-derived families that used the leopard and crocodile as totemic figures (Devisch 1993: 157) and carved imagery of chiefs that reflect courtly splendor. Some of the more refined statuettes of the past may derive from this context.

A multitude of charms enable the owner to do things that cannot be done by other means and to assure success. Generally, these take the form of packets and animal-horn containers with ingredients linked to a vast range of specific needs or desires. Those that include sculptured human images and categorized as *phuungu* bear enveloping materials about the torso or are flanked by packets protruding with sticks—of plants associated with savannah on one side and from the forest on the other, feathers, or bamboo cartridges (Fig 13). None of these involve a special initiation or communal ritual although blood offerings are made at their inception and food restrictions may be imposed. They are generally owned by the head of a patrilineal kin group and may pass from father to son. Need for a particular variety is designated by the *ngaanga ngoombu* diviner and the client then seeks a specialist for its manufacture. The primary function of the *phuungu* charm is to protect against witches and other enemies.

Miniature charms include a wide variety of undulating carved batons, tiny figures, or miniature slit-gongs and bellows strung on a cord together with decorative nuts or beads. These are worn around the neck or fastened to the forearm. They are generally extensions of charm/curse institutions but others such as the *baana maphasa* are worn by small children as part of a treatment for fainting or epilepsy with a second pair worn by the child's mother.

A charm category called *tsiinda* includes stakes or posts carved to represent a human head or face and surrounded by a collar of raffia fiber. Posts of this nature are extensions of specific concoctions placed within the earth beneath them. *Tsiinda* are found in several ritual contexts as a protector of boundaries and barricade against intruders as well as benefiting the hunt, and concern human fertility. *Tsiinda hata* are common landmarks within a village. Two prominent varieties within *n-khanda* initiation, placed along the main path, are termed Kambandzya and Kakuungu and refer to primordial ancestors that preceded lineage society (Devisch 1993: 312). Carved imagery of this type is usually rudimentary but may feature a janus face or head with an elaborate miter-like coiffure.

The formal interpretation of the human figure within this array of freestanding human imagery deserves an overview. Yaka imagery presents consistently schematized and expressively rendered creations of male and female figures in an upright posture. Stylized body positions include two-arms joined above the chest that rest and nearly meet on the stomach or that support the chin. Protruding pectoral muscles or breasts occasionally appear to the side on the torso rather than organically placed. The lower torso is treated either as a cylindrical shape or swells into a bulbous form that appears to fit into the spread of the upper thighs. Hips and legs are summarily treated with either a slight flex or are occasionally exaggerated to a near seated posture. Shoulders are either flat-surfaced or practically disappear in a direct attachment of arms behind the neck or upper torso. In either case, a dowel-like neck projects the head from lower body segments. The head is an oblong oval shape with a high domed forehead that can be dominated by a nose that is bulbous or upturned. The upturned nose is found on Yaka masks but is relatively rare in freestanding work particularly that carved since 1930. Ears expressively project outward from the head and are given a loop-like, almost circular shape. Eyes are given a closed or squinting aspect and appear in shallow cavities. The encircling hairline relief may enclose the face and touch the nares although this is more common among Yaka masks than in freestanding sculpture. Hair dress or head coverings present a multitude of variations.

There is, however, no absolute or easy distinction between Yaka carved statuettes and that of their Suku or Lula neighbors. Within the corpus of Yaka freestanding imagery there are subtle transitions between what can be termed core characteristics and the imagery considered distinctive of the Suku, Lula, Kongo, Teke, Holo, and Chokwe. Although the bulk of imagery can be rudely carved, those objects of artistic merit demonstrate a range of personal styles that are astounding in their creativity.

Initiation to Manhood

N-khanda (also known as *m-khanda, mukhanda,* or *longwa* among the Yaka) concerns initiation to manhood conferred upon uncircumcised youth. As an institution, it is known from the Kwango River valley to the Upper Zambezi River in East Africa where it is found among the eastern Kongo, Lula, Suku, Lunda, Chokwe, Lwena, Luimbi, Ngangela, Mbunda, Luba-Samba, and Luba-Hemba. In many cases it similarly follows the spread of lunda cultural influence since the eighteenth century. Its distinguishing elements are use of (1) similar titles used for both *mukhanda* officials and novices; (2) setting up a special pole or tree associated with feasting; (3) initial fireside celebration preliminary to circumcision rites; (4) prayers to the ancestors of the sponsoring village; (5) preparation of the site; (6) ritual washing; (7) extensive use of strengtheners and charms; (8) appearance of masks associated with ancestors;

(9) several coming-out events; (10) burning of the lodge; and (11) final purification and lifting of prohibitions. As found among the Yaka, its ritual and social activities may be subdivided into the preparations, circumcision, "bush school," and coming-out festivities but also includes abbreviated and simplified versions where certain masks or charms are not used due to missionary influence and school scheduling. The main purpose for initiation as stated by the Yaka is to have healthy and vigorous offspring (Plancquaert 1930: 62). *N-khanda* initiation has been documented by Plancquaert (1930: 55–118) based on observations made at Kimbao in 1927; Van Gool (1953: 853–888) at Kabila, near Popokabaka in 1941; Himmelheber (1939: 19–39) at Kabila and Kingulu; Devisch at Yitaanda and N-Tulumba (1972: 1–176), and my personal fieldwork at Pasanganga and Mvula Mwanga, near Popokabaka, in 1976.

Every three or four years, upon recommendation of village elders and those of surrounding villages, *n-khanda* is instigated by a village chief. Selection of initiation camp officials soon becomes the order of the day. Organizers and officials of *n-khanda* as well as the young candidates are given particular titles, each with its honors and assigned duties: *Kahyudi* to underwrite the expenses, organize the collection of gifts, and assume the role of headmaster. Two assistants to *kahyudi* are *n'lopo* and *bumbangi* who act as his substitute and help with the financial burden. *Bumbangi* is specifically charged with procurement and distribution of food and use of the feather-covered *mweelu* mask. His assistant is called *n-langala* who usually dances with the *kholuka* mask in the coming-out festivities. The charm specialist *yisidika*, also known as *makala*, often the village chief himself, provides the appropriate charm ingredients concerned with male fertility and may include the dreaded *kakuungu* or *mbawa* mask pertaining to his lineage. If further charm images and exhibition masks are desired, a sculptor (*nkalaweni*) is contracted who plays a secondary role as ritual officer. Two women are chosen for the roles of *yifika* and her assistant *ikumbi* who are charged with preparing foods and will be the only women admitted to the *n-khanda* site. Still other roles are assumed by previously initiated youth (*tolumbusi*), headed by *bumbangi*, who will act as guardians and assist other dignitaries—they must be responsible individuals and good dancers who will be featured at the conclusion. Families of the candidates will select *itapa*, one or more persons responsible for circumcising particular initiates. Candidates undergoing *n-khanda* initiation (*tundaanzi*) are divided into two groups likewise ranked according to age; the oldest (*mbala*) and second oldest (*kapita*) are given precedence as leaders to whom other youths are assigned.

Approximately one month before the opening of *n-khanda*, a collective hunt is organized in search of the duiker *tsetsi*; if successful, this is an omen of a prolific outcome of circumcision and *n-khanda*. Traditional gifts are then

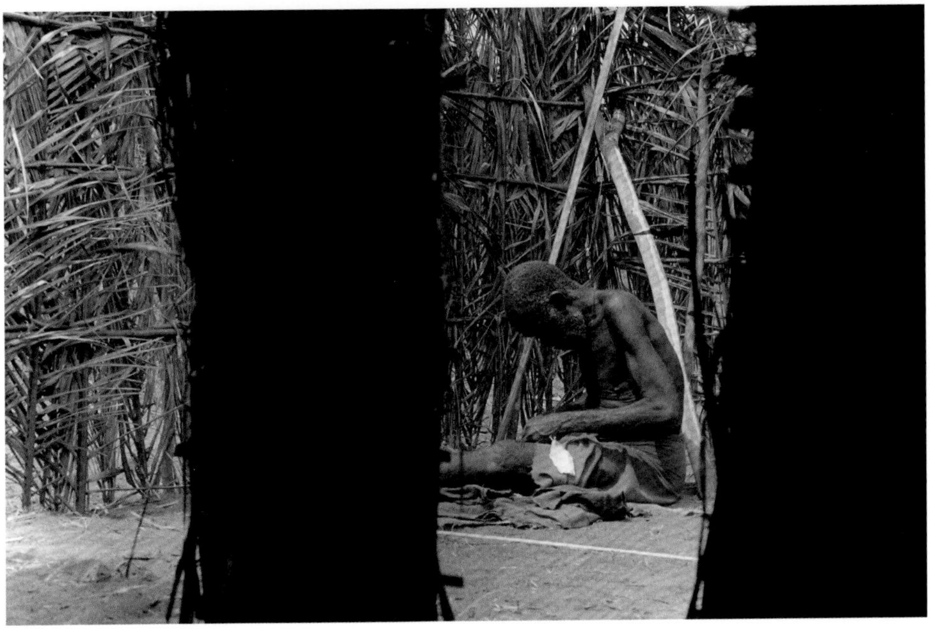

Fig. 13. Twin doors of initiation cabin (seen from within) with Yaka sculptor Pakalupatu constructing a mask coiffure. Pasanganga village, Popokabaka region, Bandundu. Photo: Arthur P. Bourgeois, 1976.

sought from relatives in the surrounding region by the young candidates. Meanwhile near the sponsoring village, an area is cleared and construction begun on a *nzofo* cabin with its adjacent double entrances that will be assigned to the initiates (fig. 13). This structure is further enclosed by a tall partition and all entrances screened by hanging raffia fronds. Next, charms are implanted by the ritual specialist *yisidika* throughout the site, the most esoteric of which are associated with the rainbow-python.

The opening of *n-khanda* commences with the young candidates, camp officials, male relatives, and visitors descending into the forest in quest of a *mukamba* tree (*Chlorophora excels*). When selected, it is shot with an arrow, felled, and transported to the sponsoring village. Songs on this occasion refer to the ancient origin of *n-khanda* at Kola, place of lunda origins, as well as mock women and invoke male solidarity. That evening, *kakuungu* or *m-bawa* masks with costumes of skin and palm fiber may appear in the village to terrorize women and children and seek out pregnant women. At dusk, *yisidika* assisted by other *n-khanda* officials insert charm ingredients into a hole and the *mukaamba* tree is replanted. A long chant is then intoned calling upon the protection of named ancestors; the young candidates are formally presented to the charm specialist and headmaster *kahyuudi*, then the evening concludes with an encircling dance around the fire and *mukaamba* tree.

Circumcision day begins just before dawn with family members carrying the novices upon their shoulders to the *n-khanda* camp. The operation takes place on route or within the initiation enclosure amid drumming and rifle shots and personal charms are placed in the initiates' hand. The initiate is required to endure fear and pain without a sound or cry at the risk of incurring insults from relatives and fellow villagers throughout his life. A charm offered by the charm specialist is tasted, and portions of manioc bread smeared with blood are eaten along with dried flesh of the duiker *tsetsi*—a clever animal conceptually identified with initiates. In a forbidden area behind the *nzofo* cabin, the foreskins are buried together with banana plants and the officials receive strengthening charms.

For the next several days, the newly circumcised remain in the open, are hazed by camp officials, and at sunset and sunrise forced to stand naked for long periods on one leg, putting one foot to the knee of the other with arms outstretched. This stance, termed *kataku*, imitates the crowing cock standing on one leg to announce the sunrise and is performed while singing songs of their role in the transmission of life. The straight leg represents virile erection (Devisch 1993: 64). Food restrictions are imposed and they are obliged to communicate in a *n-khanda* argot, an extensive series of word substitutions. Generally, on the third day following circumcision, the initiates are assembled and wear skirts of loose palm fibers; they are led singing to a cold rushing stream where the leaf and clay bandage loosen and the incision is cleaned. Three barricades blocking the path to the village are erected by the charm specialist *yisidika* in order to ward-off concealed envy or ill-will on the part of extended family members. The masks used throughout initiation partake of this same concern.

With the healing of circumcision wounds, a period of work and of instruction begins that traditionally lasted anywhere from one to three years improving existing skills ranging from constructing a dwelling and mat weaving to dancing. Use of appropriate proverbs and aphorism are taught in pleading one's case or in belittling subordinates. The main diversions during this period are group hunts and experience in trapping. Formerly, bearing arms as a warrior was an intrinsic part of instruction. The feather-covered *mweelu* mask is danced and might occasionally be worm by one of the initiates to steal animals or food from a nearby village.

MASKS IN COMING-OUT FESTIVITIES

Coming-out festivities begin with a great feast in the sponsoring village. One of the initiates or an official will first don the *mweelu* mask in seeking kaolin from the village chief and any charm specialist (*ngaanga*) and in encountering

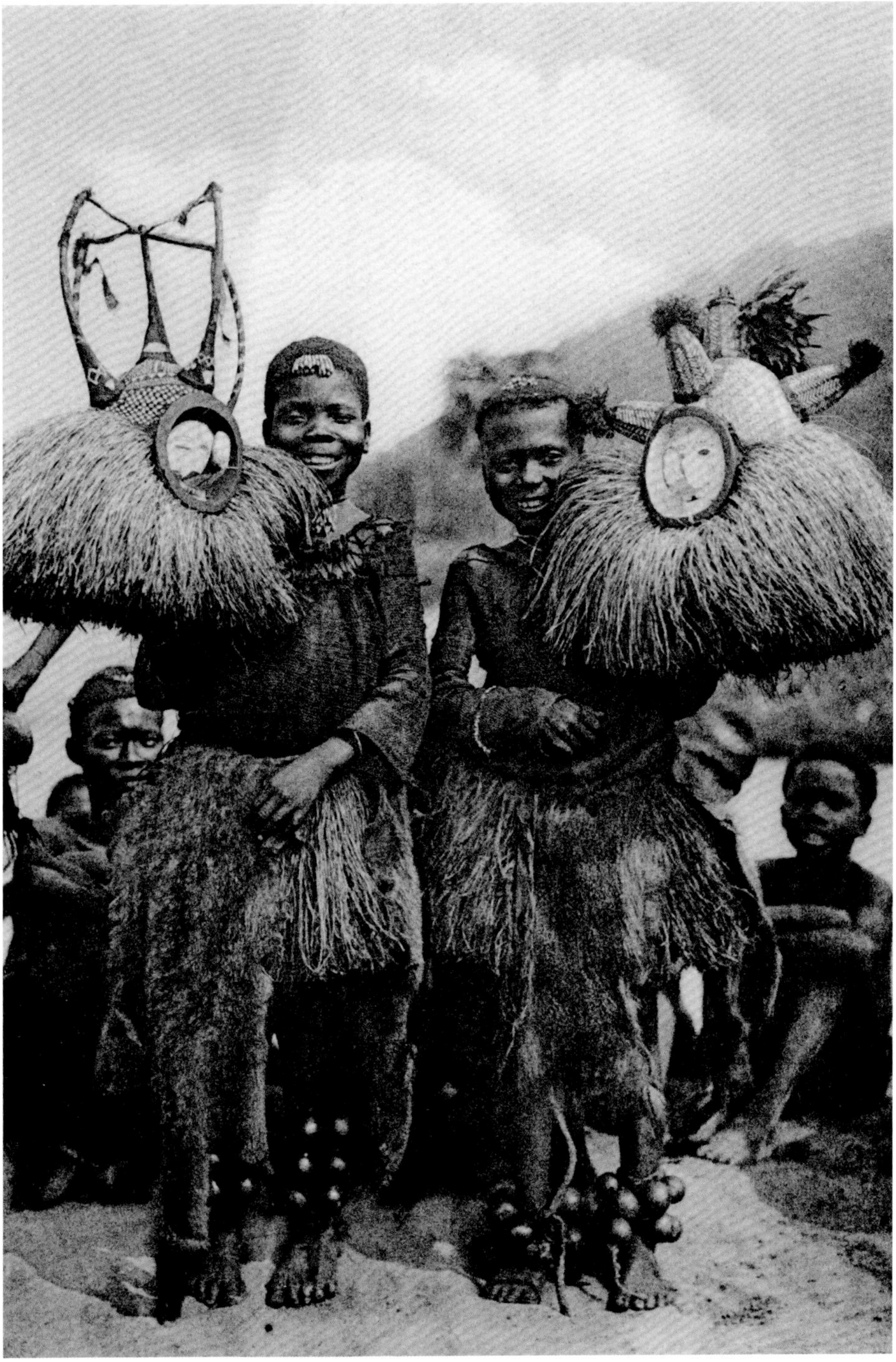

Fig. 14. Initiates in attire for their dance exhibitions. Photo: J. Van Doorslaer, S.J. Postcard: D. Gelbard Archive, inv. 2059.

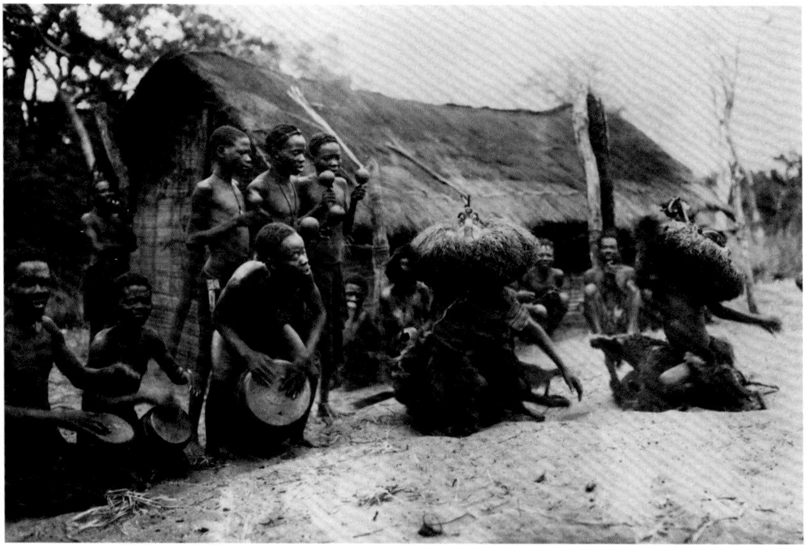

Fig. 15. Yaka masked dancers and orchestra. Postcard: D. Gelbard Archive, inv. 2127.

women. The newly initiated are then led into the village by the masked official who races them in a sinuous line, each holding his companion by means of an arm held between the legs—similar to the gesture found in chiefly initiation. *N-khanda* dignitaries and initiated, some of whom wear a series of paired masks with palm leaf ruffs while others wear only their fiber skirts. A large dance platform is erected within the village and serves as a stage for *n-khanda* officials and other dancers. Masked dancers do not mount this platform but emerge in pairs amid the pressing crowd. All await the dance of the *n-khanda* official, *n'langala*, who approaches carrying a partially covered mask, soon to be unveiled, upon his shoulder. This mask, known variously as *kholuka* or *mbaala*, features an elaborately decorated puppet-like scene in the coiffure that frequently incorporates some sexual humor. Amid his dance, the mask is displayed accompanied by sung verses. The overt sexuality of the verses and exaggerated pelvic thrusts might include showing a wood phallus or even shedding his clothing to display his own genitals. Not to be outdone, women approach with their *n-yende* conical baskets (Devisch 1972: 172–173). When the turmoil of the crowd has subsided, officials may again dance and the *kholuka* dancer may reappear but the crowd soon dissipates and the festivities end. Over the next several weeks, this is followed by a dance tour throughout the region in order to present the newly initiated and to collect gifts (fig. 15). Competition in dancing, singing, drumming, exhibiting the most surprising mask, and creating harmony between communities are also goals of such performances.

The dance of the young initiated with masks that I observed were performed in a flexed position with three movements of the lower torso to the right, then animated movements of the feet followed by three movements of the lower torso to the left while remaining on the same spot or making a simple jump forward without coordinating movements with other dancers.

Initiation songs that accompany mask dancers and dances of *n-khanda* officials fall into two categories: songs and refrains that nearly everyone in the audience knows (*nkunga*) and others composed and rehearsed in the initiation camp for the occasion (*bitoolu*). Those accompanying *n-khanda* officials stress the need for the young "to be visible," follow instructions of their elders, or brag of elder's efforts on their behalf. Other songs allude to the hardships of initiation, continuity of life from the ancestors, life overcoming death, or acquiring qualities and attributes of a true adult (Van Gool 1953: 882; Devisch 1972: 168; plus personal observation). One of the songs of the dignitary *kahyudi* and his assistant *n'lopo* speaks of their *n-khanda* experience: "We were unknown and now we are revealed a little." Other songs refer to the regional chief accusing him of killing many boys and suggest that he stop. Still others refer to the national government, the president, and MPR political party. Many are situational, often having little specifically to do with *n-khanda*.

A few examples are as follows:

Song of the *mvwala yamfu, yamfu* the singer:

(Solo) I am there,
where one displays the *N-khanda*
(Ensemble) He said: Arise to eat mushrooms (which are forbidden).
(Solo) I do not eat them, Eh! Eh! Eh!
(Solo) To the manioc field, mother, (where I cannot go) I don't feel well.
(Ensemble) To the peanut (field) where I could, I went there dragging.
(Solo) *Mweelu*! we le le! I brought out the *Mweelu* (mask)!
(Ensemble) Its name is *Mweelu* Eh! Eh! Eh! . . .

(Plancquaert 1930: 98).

Two varieties God (*Nzaambi*) create on earth;
Men with a penis,
women with a vagina.
You have not been introduced,
So do not build a house yet.

Leave us alone;
A child is already expected

You want a divorce?
You have no *zimbu* shells (to pay a new dowry).
So don't divorce
(Van Gool 1953: 882).

The dance exhibition begins with the *kanzenga mweelu* feather mask, obtaining the kaolin from a local dignitary. The older youths all painted red are clothed in loincloths of buffalo hide, wear white feathers in their hair, and carry double fly-whisks, as the color red in this context connotes existential completeness, a fulfilled and mature human condition (Devisch 1993: 66). The newly initiated wear fiber skirts (*ngombi*) with monkey hides hanging from their belts. Those wearing masks don a raffia knit costume (*kivuvu*), anklet bells or sounding nuts, metal bracelets, and amplify their gestures during the dance with fly whisks (*misesa*) topped with goat hair. Masks bearing a thick raffia ruff perform in a fixed sequence two at a time and the dance may last an hour or longer for each pair of dancers (fig. 14). Raphia palm and its fronds remain rich in cosmological and sexual symbolism, particularly in the tree's flowering and effusion of sap and as an icon of the life-bearing journey of the sun (Devisch 1993: 60–61). A solo performance of the *khuluka* (*mbala*) mask by a senior youth ends the performance. During intervals in the performance, a villager from time to time will press a coin to the mouth of the dancer or throw the gift on a hide or into a basket. Gifts collected during the tour are presented to *n-khanda* dignitaries upon return to the home village.

A final closing of *n-khanda* involves the most powerful mask-charm available. One by one the newly initiated are presented before the mask and bits of forbidden foods are placed in the mouth of each youth; thereby all restrictions are lifted. New adult names replace *n-khanda* names, and during the night the *n-khanda* masks and camp are set afire. Today the masks are either stored for reuse or sold. Under the supervision of *mbala*, initiates are carried on the shoulders of their guardians back to the village. This is followed by a village dance and feast.

Within *n-khanda* and *lukhaangu* chiefly initiation, a number of ritual parallelisms become apparent: appeal to a mythic lunda origin with its prestigious hierarchy as well as ancestral forebear; symbolic role of the females mwaadi, nambaandza and yifika with ikumbi in otherwise male dominated social contexts; planting of certain trees as living memorials; ritual use of palm fronds and fibers as screens, garb and in delimiting zones of seclusion signifying

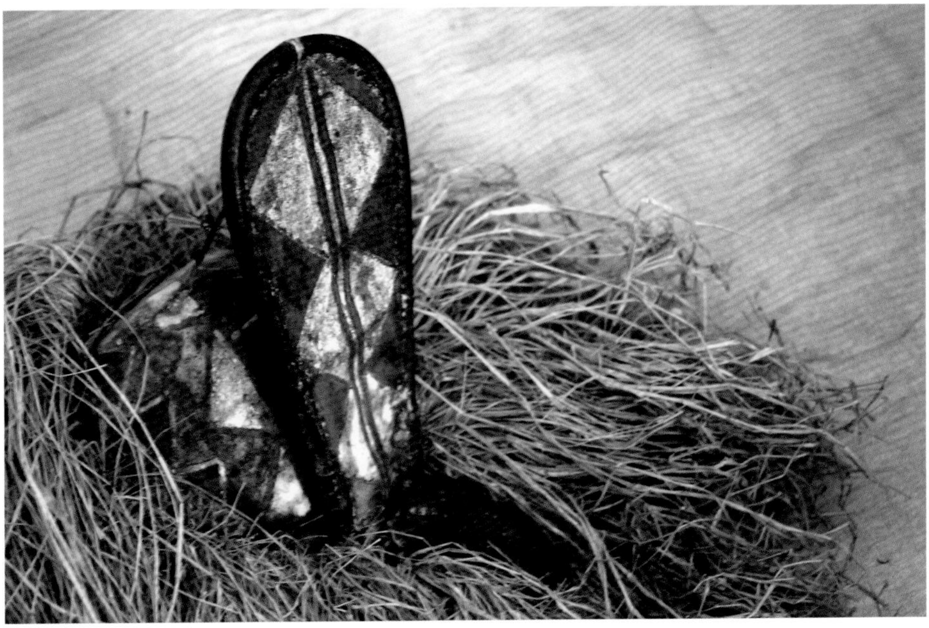

Fig. 16. *Kambaandzya* mask signifying both the duiker *tsetse* and the origin of *n-khanda* initiation. It is the patron of the sculptor. Photo: Arthur P. Bourgeois, 1976.

fertility; the successful hunt as a premonition to success in other endeavors; reference to the esoteric rainbow-python in ordering both society and nature; the chicken-like stance at dawn and dusk where initiates pose on one leg with the other foot positioned at the knee and arms outstretched; rebirth signified in the bowed emergence from seclusion; and lastly, a new identity by taking a new name.

Yaka masks used within *n-khanda* initiation belong to four structural types: (1) those that are constructed of various materials attached to a netted head cover; (2) those built on a splint frame attached to a paddle-like wooden face; (3) those masks carved from a single cylinder of wood into the form of a helmet; and (4) those carved in wood into an oversized facial form. The Yaka divide them according to function, those that terrorize rather than dance and masks that are used to entertain in the coming-out festivities.

The sculptor (*nkalweeni*) possesses his own fortifying charms and through the *kambaandzya* mask is associated with the master-sculptor who originally taught him (fig. 16). Although Yaka sculptors normally learn their craft from one's father, several indicated learning on their own, that is to say "stealing," through careful observation of a sculptor at work and later being forced to indemnify the individual. When a sculptor is remunerated for his services, a portion of this payment customarily is allotted to the master sculptor who taught him, or if deceased, an offering is placed upon his grave. A deceased sculptor is buried with this mask and subsequently other *kambaandzya* masks are placed upon his tomb. Regarded as "senior" and "oldest" of masks, it is the first worn in the evening before the appearance of other masks in coming-out ceremonies. It briefly dances and then receives gifts of bystanders who press them to the mouth of the wearer. In the dance tour, it is placed on the ground before the drummers as an honored emblem rather than being worn. Finally, at the end of initiation, it is returned to the sculptor who hides it in the forest and when decayed it is burnt and the ashes rubbed on his forehead, chest, and shoulders. *Kambaandzya* is constructed, rather than carved, in the form of a wooden armature like a cap with an oblong front brim mounting upwards and assuming a miter-like appearance (fig. 18: k and l). In front of the projecting brim is a small oval head nearly hidden in the surrounding fringe of raffia fiber. Over this surface is stretched raffia cloth covered with a black resin and brightly painted. The brim portion is frequently divided from top to bottom by a single pair of parallel painted lines that in conjunction with the head are the only visual clues to what is represented. Otherwise, the mask is covered with rows of painted triangles and cross-hatched areas set off in colors of white, red, blue, and yellow. The *kambaandzya* mask depicts or at least signifies the duiker *tsetse*. In some localities, *kambaandzya* is considered to be the patron and originator of the initiation institution and circumcision. *Kambaandzya* also takes the form of a cephalomorphic pole with a miter-like headpiece that is placed along the path leading to the *n-khanda* encampment and is similarly found as a charm in hunting shrines.

The *Mweelu* dancing mask is the most universally known Yaka mask where it emerges from the security of the initiation camp and from which other Pl. 28
dance masks seem only to be variations and extensions. *Mweelu* is a netted head-covering made of twined raffia fibers to which are attached painted calabash or bamboo sections that make up the facial features. The large beak of a hornbill bird—or less frequently the beak of raptorial birds—is added as a nose, but placed in an upturned rather than natural position as found on the bird. A profusion of feathers standing out in all directions is fastened to the netting that vary from speckled black or shiny metallic blue. The lower edge of the mask is fringed with a descending collar of loose fibers that are relatively short and do not attempt to hide the body of the wearer. Hidden within this fiber are one or more packets of charm ingredients. The remaining portion of the costume consists of a netted shirt with sleeves, a fiber skirt descending from the waist with dried monkey skins or those of wild cat attached to the belt, and two or more rows of seed-pod balls worn on the lower legs serving as rattles. In the dancer's hands are wands (*misesa*). The mask

first appears during a *n-khanda* worn by camp officials in charge of food supplies. In order to increase the normal rations provided by the village women, the *mweelu* mask descends upon the village to snatch edibles from their startled owners or may beg further foods by means of signs. The *mweelu* personage does not speak. Following an adequate preparation, the initiates themselves might don the mask for an occasional raid on the village. Within a given *n-khanda*, only a single *mweelu* mask is employed by the northern Yaka although multiple masks are reported from the Yaka of the right bank of the Kwango living in Angola as well as among the Suku. *Mweelu* is equally a charm of safe-conduct for the boys at their emergence from the *n-khanda* camp. Such use of this mask is widespread and found—and called by this name—among the southern-most Yaka. In some areas, it is considered to be the "chief mask" of *n-khanda* initiation. The term *mwelu* is often used to signify masks in general and as a prefix to other varieties. Mario Milheiros (1956: 97) describes the wild behavior of *mwelu* maskers beating people and hair or ear pulling, *matsala* being the father of the circumcision and *maiamba*, the mother.

Wooden helmet masks known as *hemba, yemba, gheemba,* or *mbala*, otherwise identified as Suku in African art literature, are found among the western and central Yaka from Mwanga and Ganaketi sectors eastward to the Tuana River and also to the southeast at Pandzi (fig. 17). On such masks the hairline curves inward toward the nostrils until it touches the nares. The raised area beneath is painted in colors differing from the whitened central area of the face and suggests a beard. The nose is emphasized either by its elongation, enormous proportions or presentation of an upturned feature. Beneath the front of the mask is a supporting stub-like projection or in later examples a full handle. The costume of the *hemba* dancer is identical to that worn by the *mweelu*-masked personage. The significance of the *hemba* mask as a charm extends to women with gynecoid illnesses who are presented charm strengtheners by the wearer of the mask. *Hemba* is also said to cure those suffering from hernia. If villagers have a prolonged period of bad luck in hunting, *hemba* masks are danced to obtain the blessings of the elders-ancestors in this regard. The *hemba* mask is said to serve as a collective image of all elders who have departed, particularly past matrilineage headmen (*leemba*), yet at the same time it remains a powerful charm with both dangerous and benevolent properties. Sculptured images above the mask include the duiker tsetse and bambi, tricksters of the forest and savannah; *kingundu*, a song-bird signifying good council; *nzangi*, a monkey with human-like intelligence; *yembi*, a pigeon; and *bata*, a duck. Each carved image refers to countless folk tales, proverbs, and hunting adventures, yet neither the behavior of these animals nor particular episodes are re-enacted in dance performances. From the region of Panzi on the upper Wamba River, helmet-shaped masks feature a reddened face and blackened coiffure, the hairline gracefully curving around face. Double-lidded eyes appear with the upper lid larger than the lower and separated by a narrow slit. The projecting chin and lips and degree of naturalism given to facial Pls. 45, 46 features and ears are characteristic. They are individually named *ngulu, mayamba, kangondi, tsumbu, mbala, lundemba, loku, lukalu, mbombo mnma*, and *kilesi*. In the performance of the southern varieties there is more individualization in behavior, accompanying songs, and audience response than in the north (Verwilghen, personal communication, 1976).

Among the northern Yaka, a complete set of masks may number eight dance masks that follow the appearance of the *mweelu*-masked dancer. *Kambaandzya* and *kholuka* are the most significant, the first and last of the series. Masks commonly presented between them appear in pairs and are called *tsekedi, myomdo*, and *ndeemba* and represent the two distinct groups within *n-khanda*, those under the leadership of the youths, *mbaala* and *kapita*. When financial means of camp officials are limited and the immaturity and limited dance abilities of initiates present obstacles, this intermediate group can be reduced to a pair of *ndeemba* masks. In each of these, the facial portion of the mask, together with supporting handle, is one piece of wood carved in the general shape of a paddle or scoop as seen from within and held before the dancer's face. The wood is taken from soft-wood forest trees, *dungoma ngoma* or *m-mungela* (*Alstonia congensis* or *Ricinodendron heudelotii*), that have dried for several days in the shade. The sculptor carves the facial portion with his adze (*khaandu*), a tool with a 15 cm long and 2 cm wide blade inserted into a wooden handle, and a small knife (*misendo*) for finer details. This generally takes a day to finish and is often done in advance within his home village. With a red-hot iron rod, holes are burned into the edges of the wooden face and wooden strips are then looped into the side and dowelled into the top to construct the headpiece. Facial features are boldly carved and flanked by projecting ears on the obverse side. Generally, a recessed circular or oval area surrounds the eyes, brows, and upper portion of the nose, and closes as it touches the nostrils. A projecting wooden decoration frames the perimeters of the face that minimally appears as a visor, more fully as a bonnet-like oval, or completely encloses the face in a circle or square frame. The nose occasionally presents a greatly elongated appendage that can rise upwards, bend back toward the face, and almost touch the area between the eyes. The Yaka regard the nose more than just an organ with a sense of smell but alludes to notions of body scent, seduction and sexual desire (Devisch 1993: 135). Although my informants insisted on its decorative effect on Yaka masks, Devisch maintains the upturned nose's relationship to cabin at the initiation site and the tree planted before it, together with Yaka

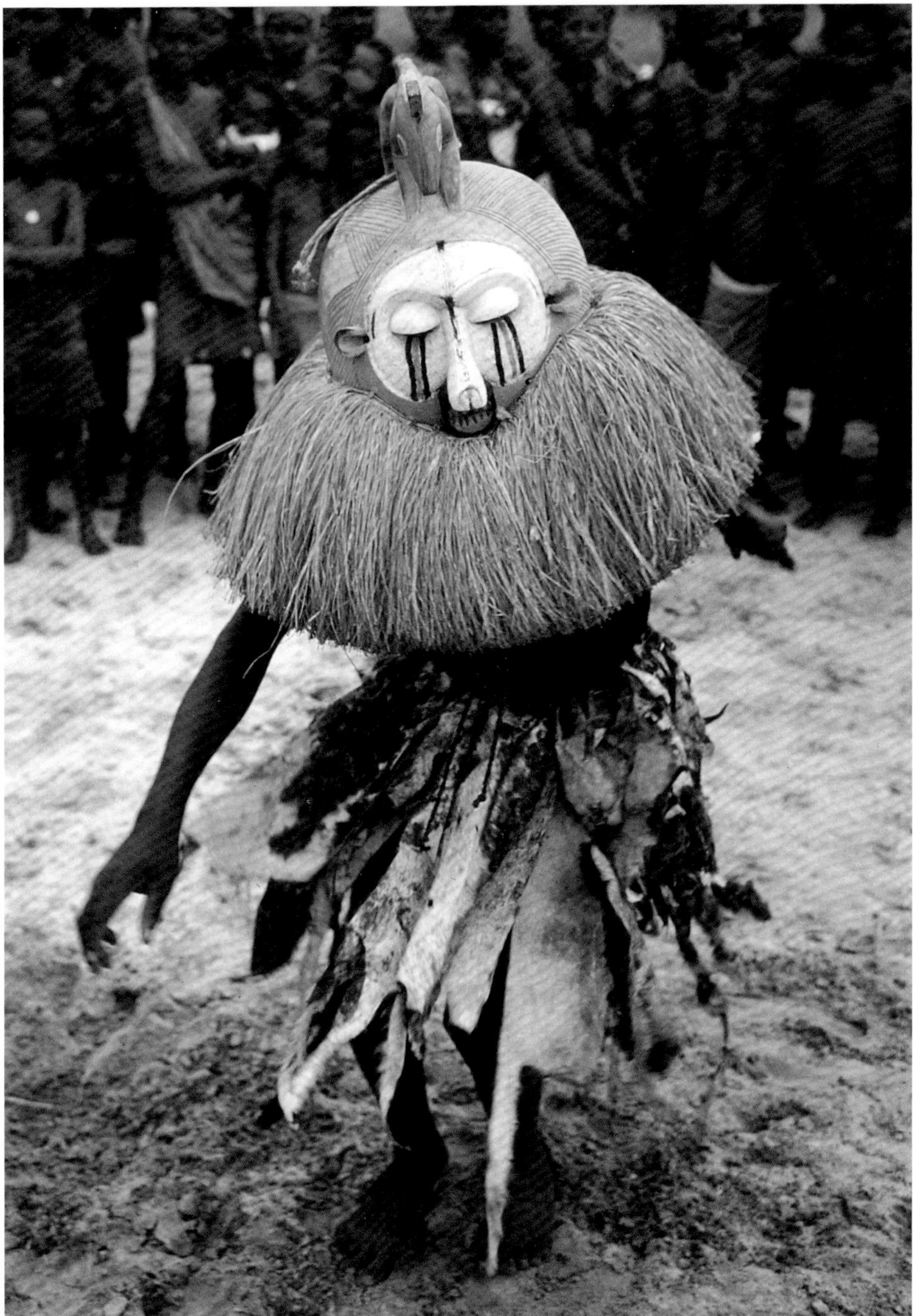

Fig. 17. Yaka initiation masked dancer in Muela Buanda. Photo: Eliot Elisofon, 1951.
Eliot Elisofon Photographic Archives, National Museum of African Art, Smithsonian Institution, no. EEPA EECL 4373.

phallic imagery regarding elephants (the elephant is regarded not so much for its size as its ability to explore hidden places with its truck [Devisch 1972: 155 and personal communication]). In this celebration of male force and potency, compared to the force of the elephant, men of the same age group may one day be forced to collectively repulse the violence of authoritarian rule (Devisch 1972: 175). Moreover, the nose of the mask together with the circular outline around the eyes can refer to the cosmic course of the sun and its fertilizing power that results in rain (Devisch 1995: 306–307). Following initiation, ashes from a detached nose of such a mask were added to the *n-khanda* initiation charm. Moreover, this flamboyant nose carving and the up-turned bird beak applied to the *mweelu* mask seem more than coincidental. Assertive ego-identity inherent in phallic parody and sexual pantomime in the context of male initiation reinforces male solidarity as distinct from women and children and is said to influence the regenerative potential of younger males. This change of status involves disdain for the asexual world of childhood and identifying with assertive male characteristics.

A fabricated portion completes the head shape of the mask that consists of a dome or cone-shaped construction made of wooden strips with woven raffia or cotton cloth tightly stretched and sewn over this armature and painted with a resin (*n-hondasala*) that takes on a tar-like appearance when dry.

A variety of traditional forms appear on the constructed coiffure ranging from simple cone shapes to a central spire rising from the crown of the head supporting from one to four horizontal disks and flanked by antennae-like projections. The tip of each projection is connected by means of a raffia fiber string and decorative strips of colored cloth. The central spire commonly features a pompon of feathers. Multiple squared or rounded projections attached to a dome-shaped headpiece also appear. Still others will feature one to three crests running from front to back. Such mask coiffures appear to derive from traditional head pieces and hair styles formerly worn by Yaka notables. Panels of painted designs placed below, between, and above projection present triangles, diamond, crosshatch, herringbone, zigzag, camber-shaped, and checker designs. Star-like configurations of triangles appear on the elevated disks. All such designs are merely termed "*n-khanda* designs," and according to my sources, do not have individualized names or esoteric meaning. Although Annemieke Van Damme-Linseele in her work on *Nkanu* initiation designs reports that the triangular geometric shape represents the three pillars of social life (the base represents the matrilineal clan; the right side, the patrilineal family, and the left side, the maternal grandfather) when the top points up, the geometric motif also symbolizes the first human being or the male sex organ; if reversed it stands for the female sex. Diamond-like patterns delineate ritual space and a call for help from sorcerers; linked together they recall the patterns on the back of the Gapon viper (2001: 32–33). Preferred colors among the Yaka are white, red, black, blue, and orange mixed with a binder made of palm oil and *n-hondala* resin. Painting of the facial portion of the mask follows the basic carved divisions. White is applied to the inner face area "to make the mask more visible" and surrounded in red or blue or gray-black. Projecting ears are painted blue, red or white. The projecting eye cylinders or double-lidded eyes are boldly treated in a juxtaposition of bright orange with a deep blue or a dull red and blue. The placement of color complements, or opposites on the color spectrum, presents a jarring visual effect. Eyebrows, descending nose line, and tear streaks are marked in blue although the latter may be paralleled with orange. Tear lines descending from the eyes are said to represent the sufferings of initiation.

Within the dance series of masks, the naming of masks is a decision left ultimately to the sculptor and *n-khanda* officials. Masks are generally ranked according to size with the largest or most expressive faces used for those of higher rank. Animal faces rank lowest in the series but this can occasionally be reversed for dramatic effect or if the image is regarded exceptionally well made. Higher ranking masks similarly feature coiffures with the highest projections and multiple disks. Creativity of individual artists is highly acclaimed and extraordinary examples are sought and often commissioned from more than one sculptor. Outstanding sculptors are recognized by regional chiefs by granting the title *Kimvumbu* (Himmelheber 1939: 39).

Kholuka masks, which appear last in the series, are noted for the puppet-like figure or group of figures attached to the coiffure although *ndeemba* masks occasionally present an image added to the central spire or one that replaces the

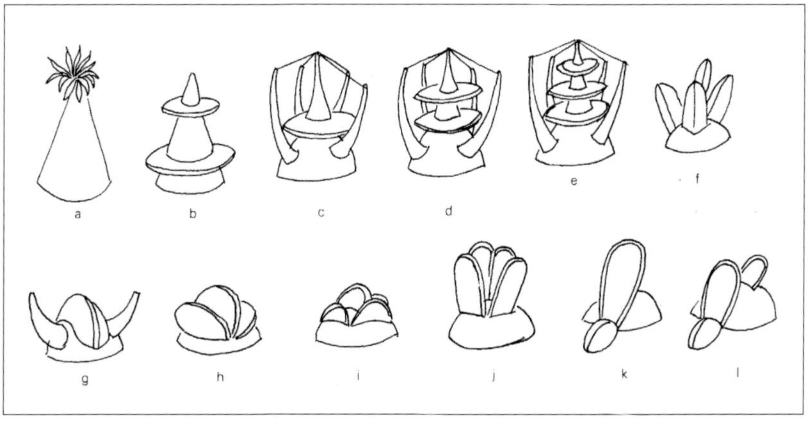

Fig. 18. Northern Yaka mask coiffure variations.

facial portion of the mask. The image is made of basketry or splints of wood covered with cloth with only the extremities such as head, hands, feet, and genitalia carefully carved of wood. The most popular of Yaka masks, *kholuka*, is associated with an unusually extroverted performer that completes the dance exhibition festivities both in the sponsoring home village and at dance tour performances. Puppet-like images feature sexuality and procreation scenes presented in both human and animal models; mammals, birds, fish, and reptiles descend or peer toward the wooden facial portion of the mask; and genre scenes of domestic dwellings, teapots, cups, or Europeans or Africans in various roles and uniforms. These images partake of motifs sung by the *kholuka* performer and song leaders in the coming-out festivities. Yet aside from its entertainment aspect, it remains a significant mask-charm containing ingredients derived from powerful charms. To the ingredients are added the ashes of the nose of a destroyed mask, thereby retaining ritual continuity with a previous *n-khanda*. Pls. 41, 42

In a minimal sense, *ndeemba, miondo,* and *tsekedi* masks are also mask charms. Women and children are forbidden to view their construction or see them before the dance debut, and an uninitiated individual would suffer harm in casually touching such masks. Otherwise, the masks do not receive blood sacrifice or special offerings, and they are not directly used to heal or injure. As in the coming-out festivities or in the dance tour, they can be regarded as charms of good luck.

Among the southernmost Yaka—from the Kasongo Lunda southeast to the Kingulu sector and Kasa chiefdom and to the southwest toward Suka-Mbundu (Guillaume Falls) on the Kwango River—other named masks appear at the end of initiation in addition to the *kambandzya* mask, namely, the masks *kawesi, mbaala, mfumu-n-khanda, lundeemba, tsakala, kiala, mangolo-mbolo, kosi, luhalu,* and *kakoku* (Verwilghen, personal communication, 1976). Here some varieties do not have wooden faces but are completely made of raffia cloth and surmounting puppet-like scenes are absent.

Rather, horn-like slats of wood encircle the mask, a comb-like element protrudes from forehead crests, and onion-shaped seed pods are affixed to the coiffure. Perceived from the interior, the wood facial portion of a mask is carved

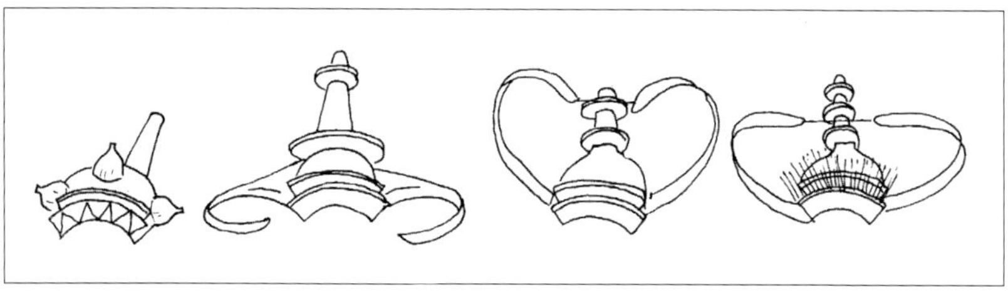

Fig. 19. Southern Yaka mask coiffure variations.

in an oval shape but without a supporting handle. On the obverse side, heavy camber-shaped eyes protrude slightly but are sharply undercut, or an eye-hole is pierced just beneath them. Overall facial colors vary but may show a band of red or blue crossing the eyes or area immediately below the eyes. At the
Pls. 47, 48 crown of the head rises a pole-like extension encircled by one to three small disks. Occasionally the disk or one of the forehead visor-like elements is left as an openwork construction revealing a pattern of triangles, rather than covered with material and resin. Less attention is given to detailed painted patterns on the coiffure than in the north.

Masks of Power

Kakuungu as well as *Mbawa* masks are reputed to be the most powerful as well as among the oldest of all *n-khanda* initiation masks. But, first, *kakuungu* deserves separate description and commentary. Characterized by inflated
Pl. 52 cheeks, massive features, and a prominent chin, *kakuungu* masks average some 84 centimeters high. The basic painted colors are red and white with the chin area generally white or the face vertically divided with red on one side and white on the other. The mask is worn surrounded by a full-length fringe of loose raffia strips and partially covered with skins of larger animals. Seed pod rattles are suspended amid the fiber fringe. Its massive human imagery is specifically designed to instill fear. Some *kakuungu* masks show a band or coiffure carved in relief on or above the forehead. Owned and sometimes worn by the charm specialist, *isidika*, it was only one of a series of charms employed to assure the wellbeing of boys. Customarily, it appeared on the day of circumcision, the day of departure from the *n-khanda* camp, and occasionally for the subsequent breaking of food restrictions. A *kakuungu* mask might also appear in the event of a crisis; for example, to cure an initiate who had begun to hemorrhage following circumcision. The general function for *kakuungu*, however, was to prevent witches, the *baloki,* from entering the camp and causing harm to the initiates, and for this purpose the mask was often kept in a special shelter within or near the initiation site. The emergence of *kakuungu* in the village was considered particularly harmful to pregnant women. Moreover, the mask wearer possessed the ability to detect a pregnancy even before the community or family was aware of it. He would seize the woman, holding her by the foot, and order the child to go out. To avert harm, shell money was paid by relatives, and the victim was treated with kaolin. If this was not done, it was said that the child might be born malformed or might even resemble *kakuungu*.

Among the southern Yaka, *kakuungu* would come out at a new moon in order to cure. With token gifts of eggs or money, the sick approached the cabin where the mask was kept. The *kakuungu* wearer emerged, accepted the gifts with one hand while hiding the eyes of the mask from the donor with the other, and then turned the mask away. The patient would then be treated with another charm held by the mask wearer (Verwilghen, personal communication, 1977). A common manifestation of the sickness associated with and attributed to *kakuungu* among the northern Yaka is sterility. That is, if a man or woman was thought to be sterile, members of the person's lineage approached a diviner, a *ngaanga ngoombo*, and if the principal cause of the condition was attributed to *kakuungu,* a *kakuungu* owner was sought to give the appropriate remedies. As noted by Himmelheber (1939: 33), the treatment involved confrontation with the mask in a small hut for a period of several days. The presence of the mask to normally fertile women, however, would cause sterility. Although it is the heaviest wooden mask carved by the Yaka and their Suku neighbors, *kakuungu* had a reputation for tremendous jumping feats. Accounts that I collected tell of *kakuungu*'s ability to jump from the village into the middle of the forest, and to jump over cabins or even the tallest palm trees—an attribute of sorcerers. Its ability to travel great distances in only seconds was also recalled. Another of its reputed aspects was that of controlling the weather. The mask was used to bring rain as well as drive away an approaching storm. Himmelheber (1939: 33) reports the use of a *kakuungu* to threaten a tornado as it approached, but this function was also performed by other charms. Its ability to control weather as well as to perform jumping feats is cited in sung verses associated with this mask.

In the preparation of a *kakuungu* mask, the charm specialist was obliged to immolate a goat to protect present and future members of the lineage against the *kakuungu* sickness. The meat was divided among lineage members, and a cock or hen was sacrificed and given to the man who would serve as the designated guardian for the new mask.

A *kakuungu* mask is considered well made when it can instill fear at first glance. It is equally well made when all the features that characterize the mask are distinctly carved and painted in red or white, and the mask is dressed with skins of large animals. In discussions pertaining to *kakuungu*'s two colors (red symbolizes blood, vengeance and evil; white refers to blessings and health) the white chin was invariably described as a beard. An explanation for this is found in the popular notion that old people with white hair or beard often have anti-social powers and occasionally prey upon their kinsmen as witches—a notion derived from their having outlived their competitors, and the belief that nothing happens by accident. *Kakuungu* was not considered to be a personification of an ancestor, although Devisch (Devisch and Brodeur 1999: 101) refers to *kakuungu* along with k*amwaadi* as primordial culture heroes, nor do they embody spirits. Solar symbolism associated with *nkanu kakuungu* imagery is sited by Annemieke Van Damme-Linseele (2001b: 252–253), particularly in concentric circles on the forehead and cheeks, emphasized by lines and quartered sun wheels painted on the mask's superstructure and its bloated form linked to the earth-related termite queen insect. Symbolic attention to celestial phenomena among the Yaka, the sun (*taangwa*), the moon (*ngoonda*), and stars (*themuthemu*) are culturally encoded references to the land of origin and subsequent migrations. The menacing full moon assumes an aspect of the Kyaambvu and the morning/evening star, Venus, known as *kathumumbwa*, as principal wife and mother of the people (Van Roy 1988: 193, note 37–38). Other stars of night can represent their courtly warrior-retainers, the first to appear is notably their palm-wine tapper—while shooting stars, on the other hand, denote the path of witches.

The northeastern Yaka formerly used a companion mask to *kakuungu* known as *kaseba* that was slightly smaller and regarded as female. In addition to being worn, it was placed upon a pole in the initiation camp as a charm to drive away rain.

Use of *kakuungu* masks ended with the widespread destruction of traditional charms in the mid-1950s and their replacement with what was considered to be more powerful foreign variety. Since nineteenth-century European intervention, several such movements have occurred (see below). But when the illness associated with particular charms again broke out in various lineages, and newer charms were unable to counter it, the traditional ones were reinstated.

Although details concerning the origin, use, and preparation of *kakuungu* charms conflict—Himmelheber attributes the origin to the Nkanu (1939: 33) while Devisch (1972: 158) mentions a Suku origin—a general pattern becomes clear. *Kakuungu* masks and charm posts, either used within or outside initiation context, principally protected and effected fertility. Negatively, the sickness could include a gamut of misfortune ranging from sterility to insanity, although each necessitated the augury of a *ngaanga* practitioner. The power of the charm, like that of other lineage charms, seems to derive from the specialist's recitation of verbal formulae while preparing particular ingredients, thereby activating the influence or curse of past practitioners. As embodied in a wooden object, *kakuungu* could act as either a mobile instrument that dramatically demonstrated its powers or as a stationary charm that guaranteed protection.

Mbawa is similarly a powerful charm to *kakuungu* but draws upon imagery of the *Syncerus caffer*, the massive black African buffalo known as *pakasa*. In nature, the bovine stands up to 1.5 meters at the shoulders and may weigh a ton (900 kg). The animal's heavy horns span over a meter, curve downward, then up and inward and form large bosses at their bases. Formerly found over most of central, east, and southern Africa amid open or scrub covered plains, open forests and reed beds bordering rivers and swamps, their herds number from a dozen to hundreds and commonly graze and browse early in the morning and again at dusk but are also known to be nocturnal rovers. When wounded it can be the most dangerous and is often noted to circle around and stalk the hunter, lethally using its snout and curved horns. Unprovoked attacks are attributed to the animal's revenge for previous injuries. The Yaka proverb, *pakasa yitangulalal m-vuuka*, sums it up: "The buffalo disappears like a witch preying upon its foe" (Van der Beken 1979: 124). The white heron *Bubulcus ibis* is often found in a symbiotic relationship with the buffalo, feeding upon its parasites. *Mbawa* masks equally appeal to the powers of chieftainship. Yaka chiefs are commonly thought to control aggression and sorcery by necessarily indulging in witchcraft, preying upon kinsmen or subjects as victims in order to hold in check witch powers on the part of competitors. Reference to the buffalo is apparent in the chiefly regalia not only in the form of a black buffalo tail flywhisk (*misesa*) held on judicial occasions and the *kabondo*, a wide belt of buffalo hide worn by the chiefly candidate at his installation but also in Lunda derived headgear with encircling horns and the leader's towering plumed bustle of white feathers, the *tsala zi pheembele kanaagi*, of the white herron (*pheembele*), the bird associated with the pakasa buffalo. Thus the paramount chief with community sustaining powers reigns over his subjects as the pakasa bull rules the herd and daily concerns of subjects are whisked away like so many annoying flies.

The earliest example of a horned mask collected by Verhaevert before Pl. 49
1910, from a Yaka village designated as Sisacidi, is documented as "reserved to war dances and worn by a chief who conducts the combat." Made of cane splints into an immense spherical form, its surface is covered with raffia cloth. Horizontally crossing the forehead is a raised fiber pad ornamented with a series of small calabash fragments painted red and white. Oval ears painted white project from the sides. Eyes are mere holes pierced in the cloth but highlighted with eyebrow-like tuffs of wart hog hair. The long padded nose of fibers is painted with red and white lines; the nares and open mouth are indicated by buffalo hair although nearly hidden in the surrounding ruff of flowing raffia fibers. The two conical horns wrapped with polychrome painted cloth terminate in two wooden points. Yet between the horns and above the head was originally a raffia pompon decoration similar in effect to that of chiefly *tsala* headpiece. This variety of *mbawa* mask, made of wood splints covered with woven raffia, is not too dissimilar from the eastern Yaka

Pl. 50 mask collected in the Kimbao locale on the Inzia River, by Père O. Butaye with exception of the vertical nose structure separately carved of wood like the mouth with pointed whitened teeth. In the Kasa locale of the southern Yaka a fiber *mbawa* equivalent is called *kambwamba* and from Panzi locale to Kapita-Tsuka near the falls of the Kwango River they are carved completely of wood in a naturalistic depiction of the buffalo which allow the wearer to peer out from its mouth when positioned horizontally on the head. The use of horned Mbawa and Pakasa masks in the concluding rituals of *n-khanda* initiation, its association with weather control, curing of the sick, and reference to leadership is widespread. Yet the image is not a mirrored copy but frequently a simplification and distortion of the animal's most expressive qualities, its massive preponderance, threatening bearing, and keen perception. The creature in nature is reinterpreted, re-presented for social purposes. Previous habits of thought, feeling, and action are disrupted and reflective speculation liberated as suggested by Victor Turner (1967: 205). Wildly lurching, whirling, and careening in its performance, the unpredictable, vindictive, and terrifying aspects not only of the *pakasa* animal in the hunt but the human interactions of community life are manifest.

Broader View of Meaning and Style

Meaning in Yaka masking can be abstracted from individual varieties and viewed as educational instruments. The use of wood as a medium alludes to masculine properties; ideal males are presumed to be strong and firm like bone in contrast to women, who are soft and tender. Another level of signification concerns life force. According to Devisch (1972: 158) the vital force or life principle (*m-mooyo*) of the Yaka—which affects bodily transitions, invigorates, and animates—is thought to be concentrated in both male semen and hard, bony structures of the human body such as the skull. Although Devisch does not relate this to facial features of masks, visual characterization of the human head and exaggerations of sense organs of the face in masking can be viewed as explicating vital force by dramatizing the functions of listening, smelling, speaking, and seeing. As presented by Devisch, listening implies reflection and understanding and accepting via the ear for the Yaka. Speaking authoritatively implies the assertive power of ancestral words and wisdom. A keen sense of smell denotes comprehension of signs that pass unnoticed to others as well as an anticipation of the smell of sexual intimacy. Finally, sharp vision implies superior perception and memory of distant persons and situations, including the ancestors and the deceased. Super-vision, an attribute of chiefly investiture, detects a path toward unity and permanence in plurality and transience, and order in disorder.

Masks equally partake of powers deriving from the elders and their predecessors and are used as corrective devices in establishing a social equilibrium. They are larger than life as they dominate a moving form of skins, netting, and raffia fiber. Like the elders, they are concerned with present and future procreation for posterity and collective survival. Certain masks exhibit harsh and aggressive behavior, others defer to more powerful varieties. Still others demonstrate a proficiency in dancing or trickery in obtaining provisions. Additional charm packets are frequently attached to the mask. Most bear in their coiffure elevations or projections associated with authority or power, and their bi-colored or multi-colored surface accentuates the overpowering presence. The massive face and cheeks of *kakuungu*, the enormity of the bovine *m-bawa,* and the wild unkempt appearance of *mweelu* are each highly visible and accentuate their arcane reputation. The sexual feature of the upturned *mweelu* beak, trumpeting wooden noses, bawdy imagery, and gyrating pelvic thrusts of dancers announces assertive masculinity. Organs such as bulging eyes, prominent mouth and teeth, protruding ears, and enlarged fleshy nose draw attention through colors and carvings. In addition, dance masks present downcast eyes, and tear streaks descending from the eyes giving them an aspect of mourning.

Moreover, the varieties of construction, leadership paraphernalia, statuettes, masks, and other objects surveyed in the preceding pages can collectively be viewed as extensions of the Yaka ethos that seeks to integrate and extend the social fabric, neutralize antisocial acts, and ensure the transmission of future life. This is illustrated on many levels: (1) the honoring of ancestors that affirms identity and kin relationships; (2) leadership paraphernalia which asserts authority and emphasizes the mediatory role of elders for social well-being and fertility; (3) divination equipment functioning as part of a system for restoring social interdependence; (4) statuettes as personalized supports for ingredients concerned with prohibitions and transgressions; and (5) masks and sculptured posts as personalized extensions of charm specialists that shield and protect potential fertility against harmful influences. In short, each is concerned with human life, its protection and continuity, which for the Yaka is the core of both their religion and creative aesthetic.

Although I have proposed a "*mukanda* masking complex" that Baumann (1932: 15, 1–54) and Crowley (1982: 206–221) and others have detailed stretching from the Chokwe across Central Africa (from the Kwango region through Angola and Katanga into Zambia and Zimbabwe), others such as Luc de Heusch (1982: 416–478; 1988: 31–44) and Annemieke van Damme-Linseele (2001b: 207) have proposed that mask forms may derive from circumcision and puberty rituals that pre-date the spread of the *n-khaanda* institution or that melded into the institution with Lunda-Chokwe political influence.

Although the convergence of similar ways of decorating certain masks are particularly noticeable (disks, bulging cheeks, horn-like extensions), the diversity of material used together with the variety of forms of carving (from helmet shapes to large and small face masks, to masks of feathers over netted coverings) would appear to support the idea of still more ancient local traditions. Use of masks by proto-Bantu speakers within this region would appear to be self-evident. Representations of birds, varieties of duiker, antelope, and buffalo were likely inspired by the natural environment while their adaptation of differing structures of authority depended upon historical circumstance. Similarly, Annemieke Van Damme-Linseele (2001: 194) views statuettes featuring "knees flexed, hands folded on the torso, and the breasts in the angles thus formed" as a primal proto-Bantu commonality manifesting itself in more recent times in sculpture from the Teke, Yaka, and Suku, through Chokwe to the Mbala, Hungaan, and Pende. She views this essentially fetal position more in line with earlier burial practices. Lema Gwete (1978: 289–290) and de Mahieu (1967: 128–131) argue this flexed posture as an allusion to dance. On the other hand, this posture can be viewed as a stylistic rendering developed from the carving process and working from a cylinder of wood more than having a specific iconographic meaning. Throughout the Kwango region, if not the whole of Central Africa, use of the human image featured in statuettes broadly refers to elders and living/dead elders in a meditative posture rather than as a cadaver or a prenatal condition or dynamically postured in a dance.

Outside Influences

Influences on Yaka art from outside sources must equally be considered. Our tendency is to consider given African styles of sculpture as isolated traditional forms with an indefinite ancestry. It is possible that the whimsical imagery not only of Yaka smoking pipes but the assortment of puppetry atop *kholuka* masks and carved on combs may have been stimulated or at least augmented by imagery on nineteenth-century clay imported pipes (see Bourgeois 1995: 17–26). Of particular note are the figurative Gambier and French Jacob pipe. The bearded Jacob pipe with its reinforcement by a metal ring of iron or copper and carrying its maker's mark to the side of the short stem finds a direct counterpart in Kwango ceramic pipes. Late nineteenth-century clay pipes from Europe with figurative bowls featuring the heads of international celebrities or comical characters or whimsical animals all serve as potential outside influences. One in particular deserves attention, the one depicting Alley Sloper with an extended and turned-up nose. Whimsical treatment of Kwango ceramic smoking pipes with their human or bird or animal imagery is unique to the Central African corpus. Although elaborated bowls and an occasional female image appear on Bas-Congo ceramic pipes, nowhere else does the whimsical play such a dominant decorative role. Also no archeological pipes from the Kwango are thus far known. Most Yaka pipes were likely made in the Popokabaka locale if the diagnostic Yaka turned-up nose is taken as an indicator. If so, elements of this imagery such as the turned-up nose may illustrate at least an interesting syncretization in the nineteenth century whose influence lasted among the Yaka until at least the 1930s. Manufacture of Yaka ceramic pipes appears to have ceased following Himmelheber's visit and description in 1939.

In subtle ways, a combination of colonial management and missionary influences has left a mark on Yaka art, not the least of which is a restraint on sexual imagery. Roman Catholic influence in the Kwango Region began in the east with the Jesuits and Sisters of Notre Dame de Namur at Kisantu in 1901 and at Ngowa (near Popokabaka) in 1915 led by Jean-Baptiste Hanquet. This, as well as another mission established at Kingunda (near Kasongo Lunda), were school-chapels with students residing not at the school but continuing to live in their respective villages. Although Hanquet led a violent campaign against "fetishism" and certain dances—Hanquet is described as forcibly seizing fetishes, cutting them in pieces with his knife before throwing them in the fire at Kubu-Longo (in the present territory of Pelende) —he succeeded in suppressing initiation to charm institutions that required weeks of cohabitation of its young male and female guardians (Ruttenberrg 1967: 49). Himmelheber reported mission efforts in fighting traditional *n-khanda* as late as his visit in 1938/1939 (personal communication, November 1975). However, Hanquet's Jesuit successors gradually adapted to local custom including approval of *n-khanda* initiation. Particular accommodation was made to polygamous family life and modification of indigenous ways urged only when abuses were apparent. Himmelheber (1939: 27) reports *kholuka* masks featuring a particular colonial official on his motorbike and medical staff with microscope in puppetry-like images. Several examples present bearded Europeans in pith helmet that I suspect represent prominent missionaries.

In 1940 the Bamvungi religious movement spread into the northern part of the Kwango Region that was prophetic, anti-European, and anti-fetish and promised that the Belgians would disappear and the "Balama" (the Germans) arrive and inaugurate a period of abundance without forced labor or work. In this episode, which affected the regions around Lusanga, Kabama, Ikomba, and between the Kwango and Lubishi Rivers, all ritual sculpture was thrown out and burned and the Bamvungi lasted until the economic resurgence between 1943 and 1945. In 1955, the Holy Water movement reached the Yaka from the east by way of Kimbau. Feeling that their traditional "fetishes" had become the tool of witches, they were destroyed and a massive quest was to substitute the "fetish" power of the missionaries. At first mission stations among the Yaka ignored this but with time, crowds of villagers demanded cooperation until missionaries preferred to take this in hand in order to direct it less to incur anti-European sentiments. Efforts were made to explain that holy water without prayer was useless because prayer alone was capable of banishing hatred and vengeance from the heart and combating sorcery. Each village was then assigned its weekend to obtain all the blessed water that it desired provided that they participate in a religious program of instruction. After six months the crowds ceased to participate in these meetings and traditional charms were gradually reinstated in the villages. Researchers such as Igor Kopytoff (1960), working among the neighboring Suku, suggests that such movements and their repetitiveness indicate that the process of occasional and even violent reformulations, whether internal or acculturative, may be an inherent part of the very workings of the same system of ideas.

Let us conclude with a Yaka proverb: *N-kisi wakinina dithimb dya ngoma*. Literally, "the mask dances to the rhythm of the drum" (Van der Beken 1993: 248) that is, the masked dance is inspired by aspects other than itself, namely, a surging rhythm. In this sense the pictorial, oral, practical, and historic aspects together manifest the richness of Yaka art and its context. But the proverb can also mean: "When I see the possibility of obtaining what I desire, I will make the effort but not before." Yaka arts are a means to an end, namely, they are vital to continuity, identity, and survival. Not only do they continue to the present day but reveal to us the Yaka reality.

Plates

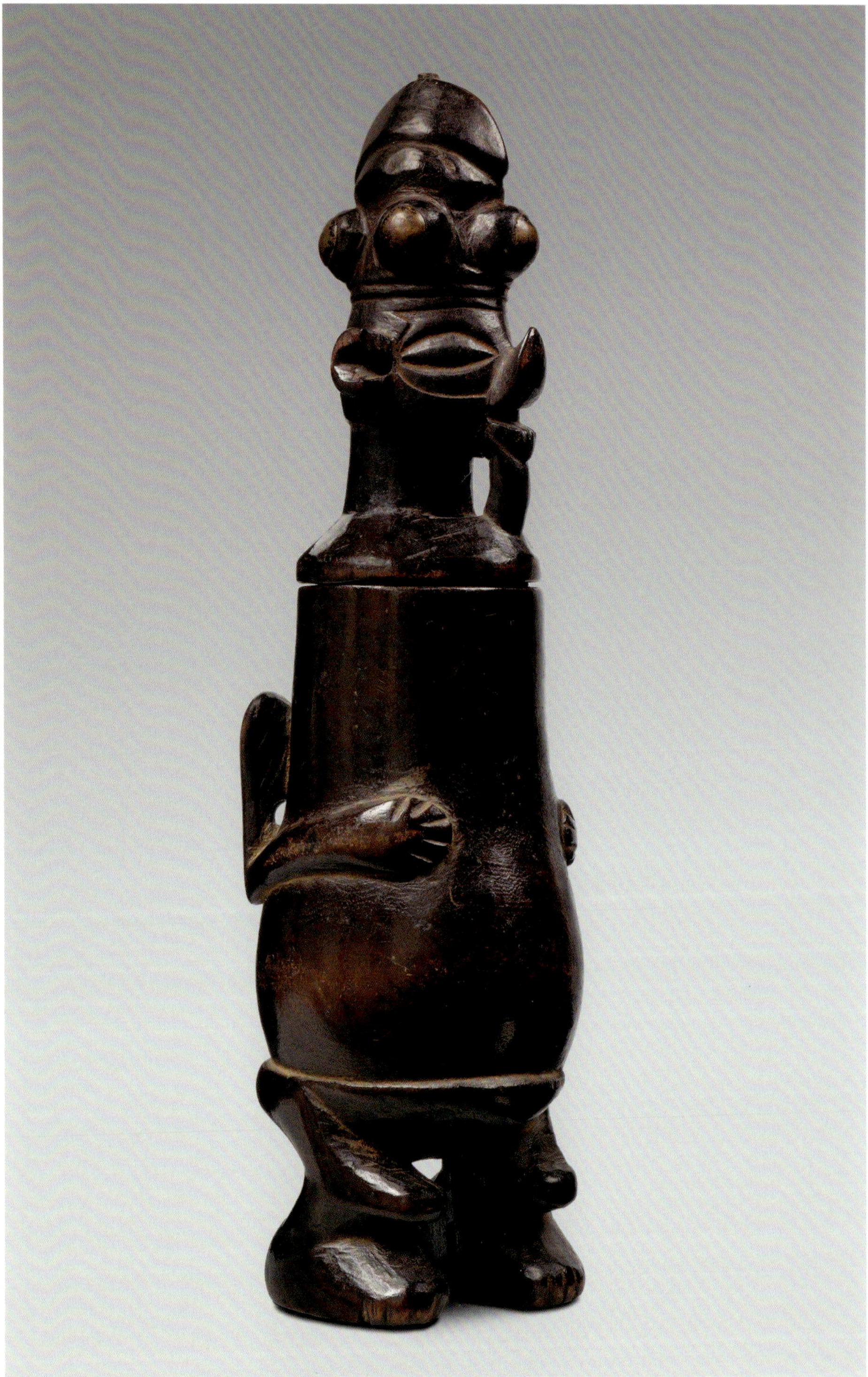

1-2

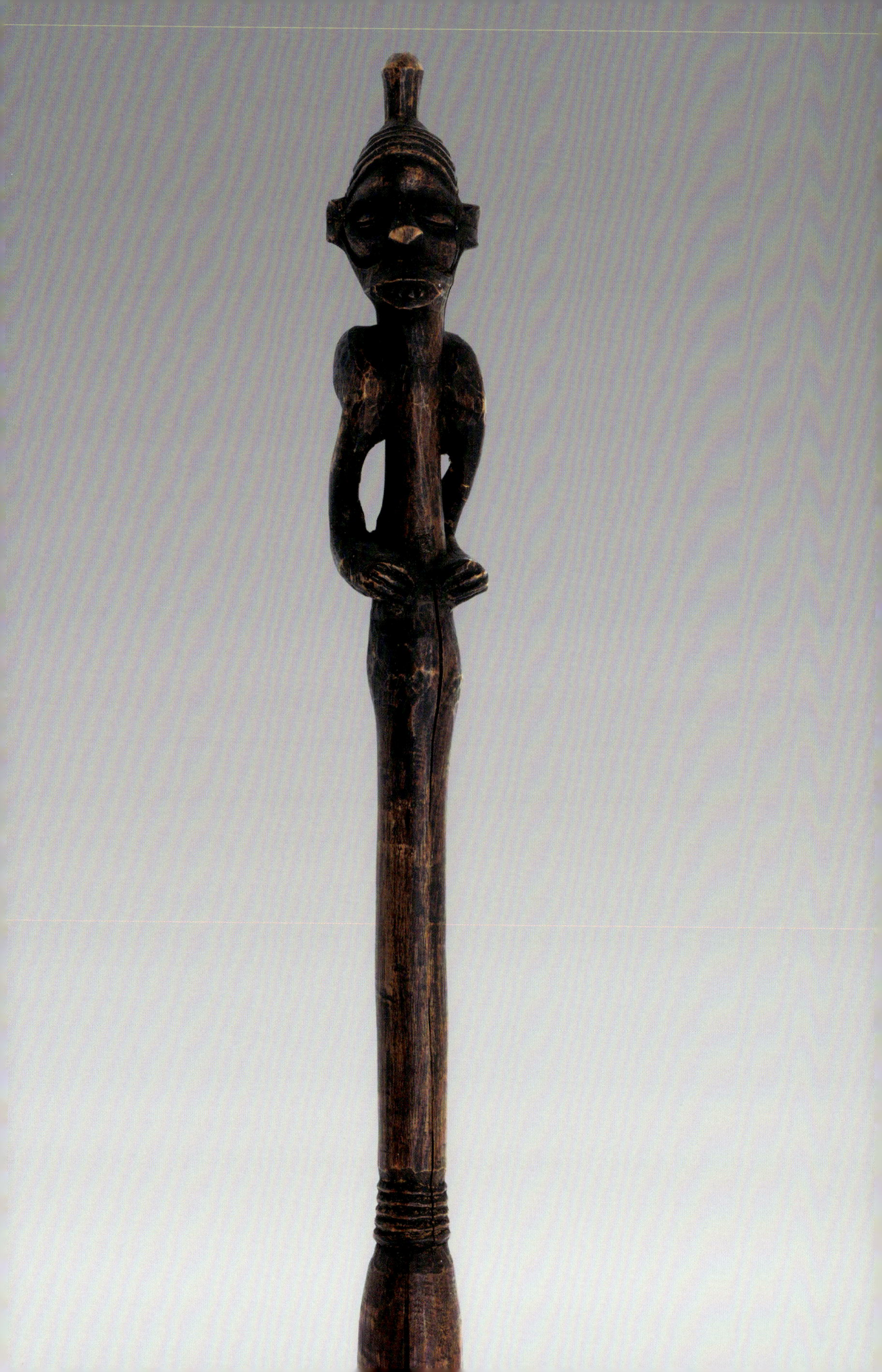

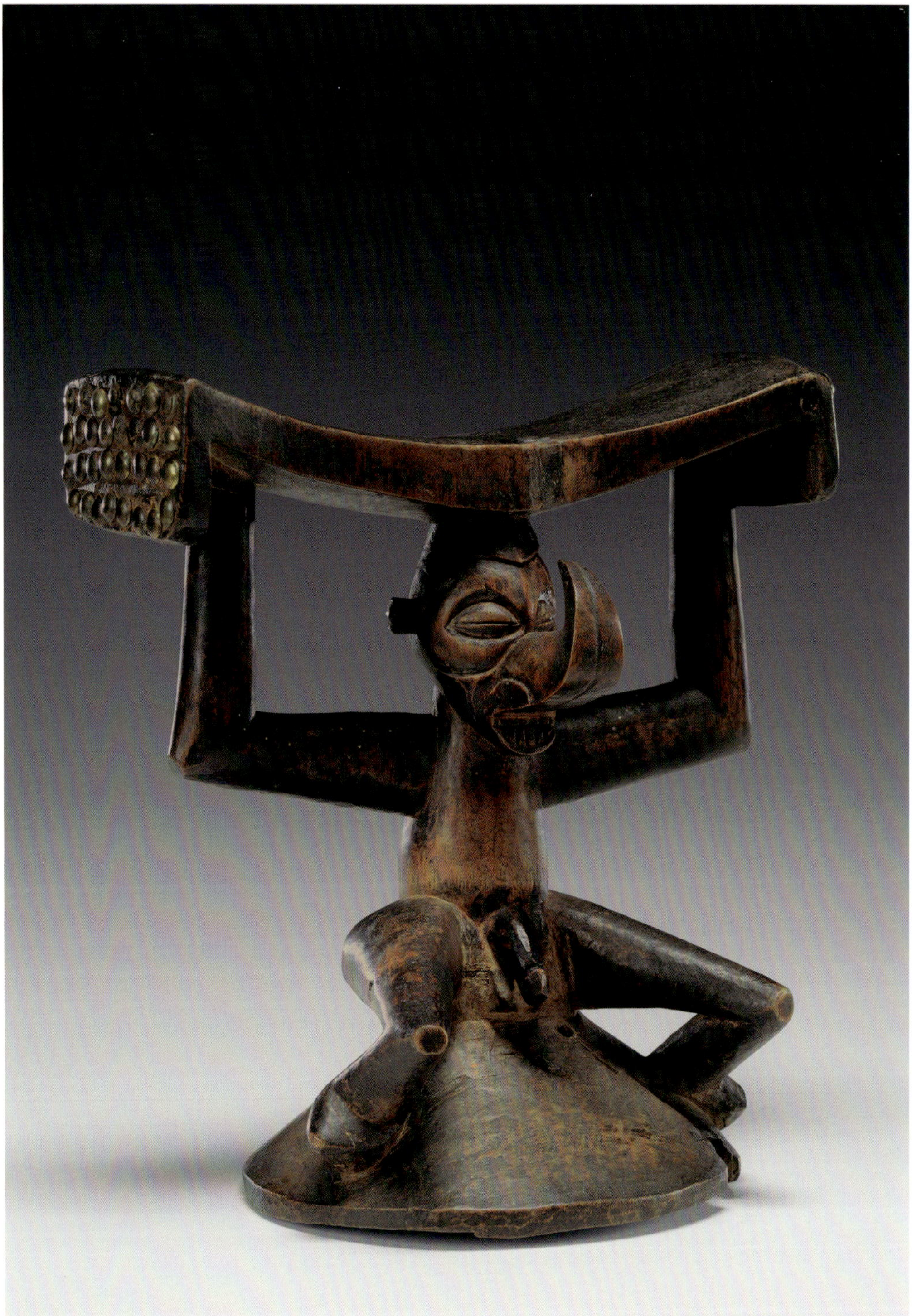

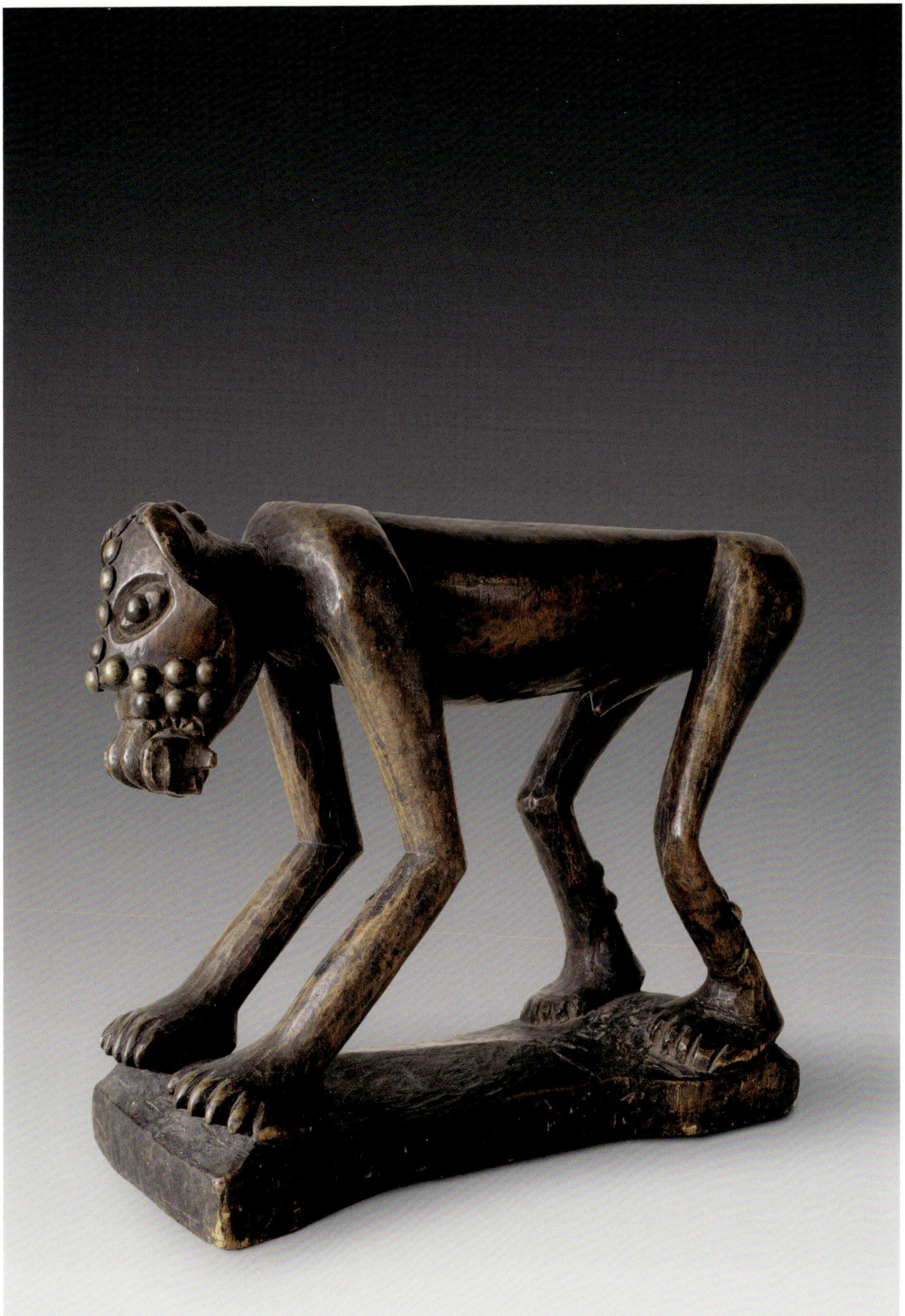

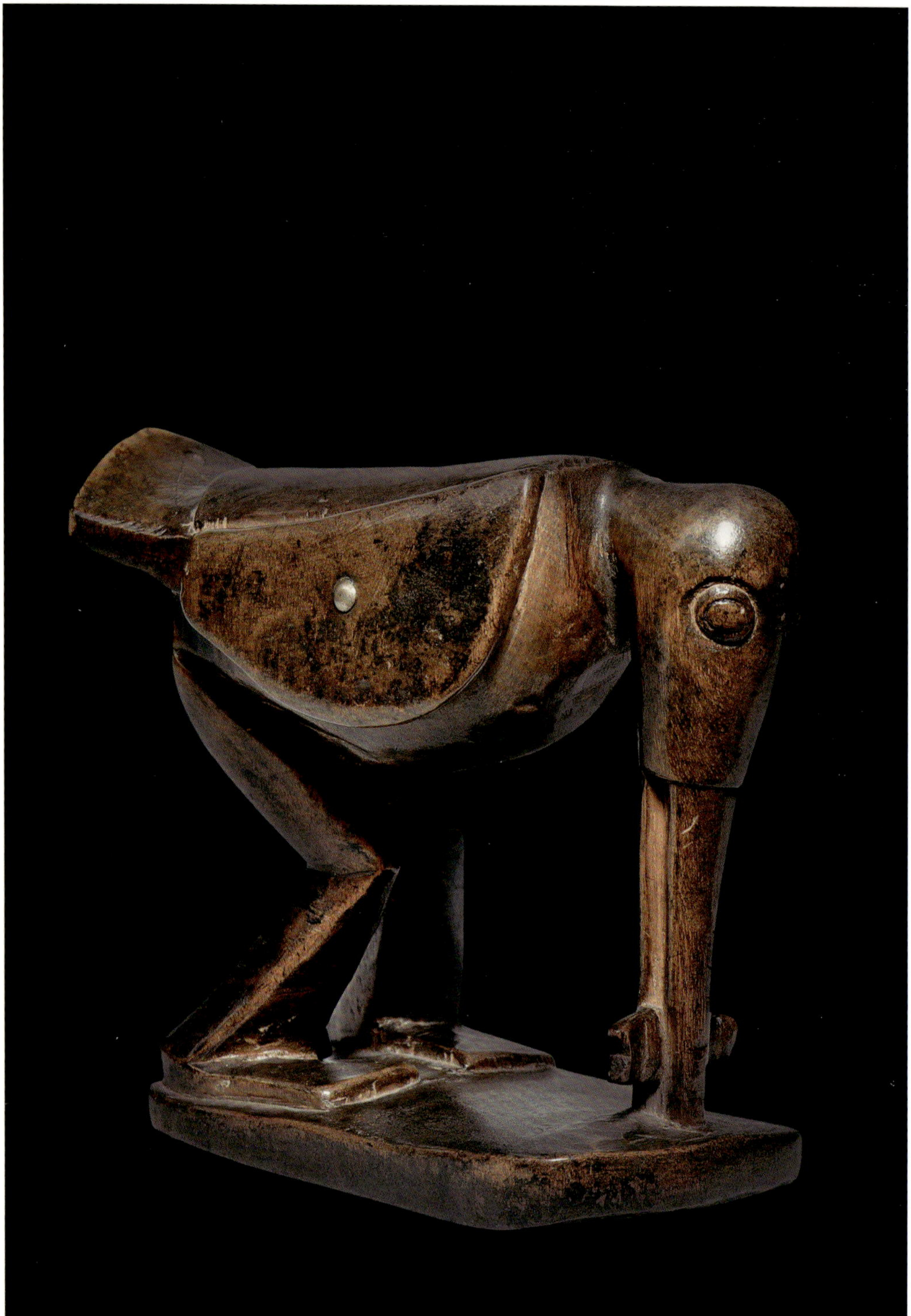

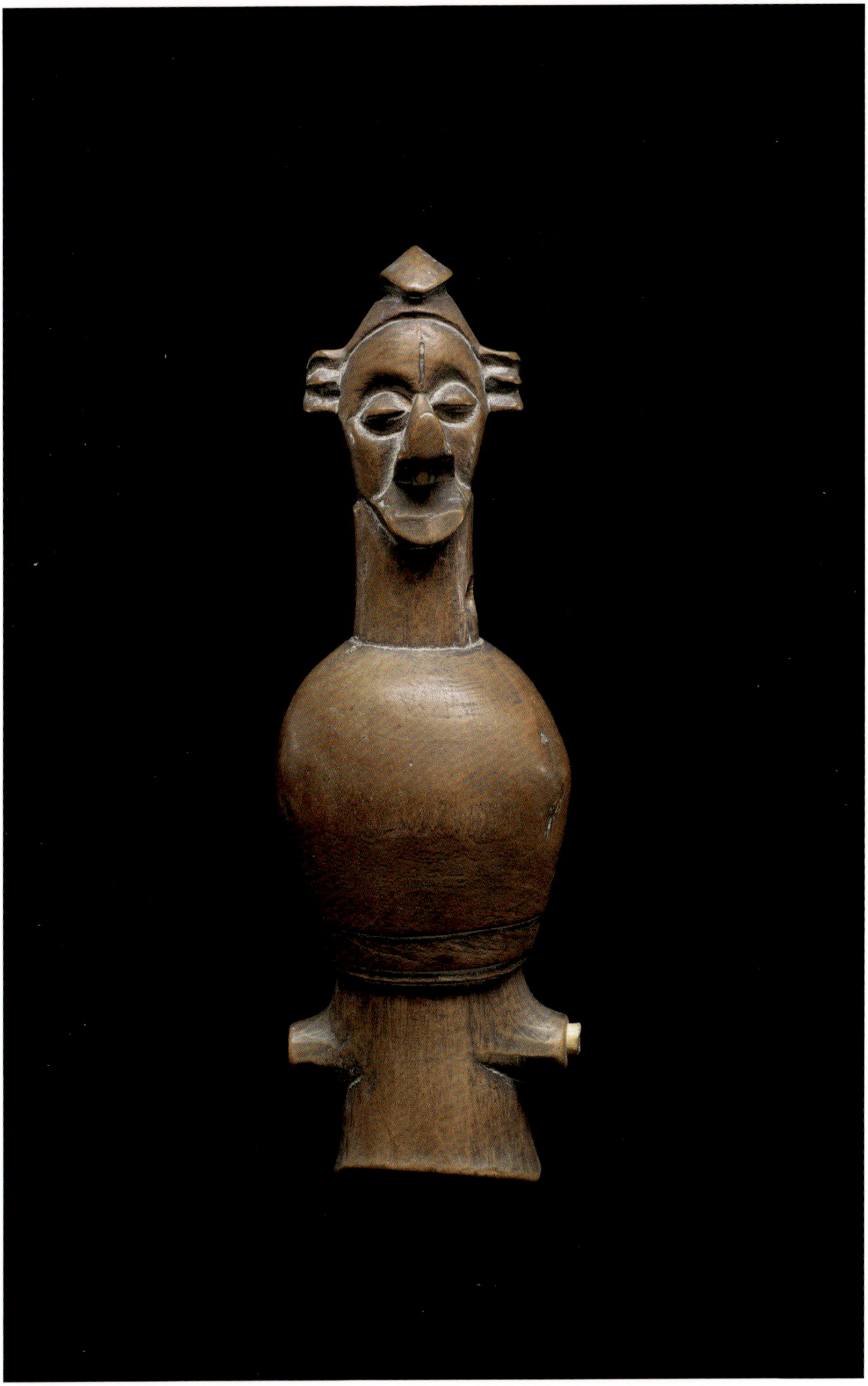

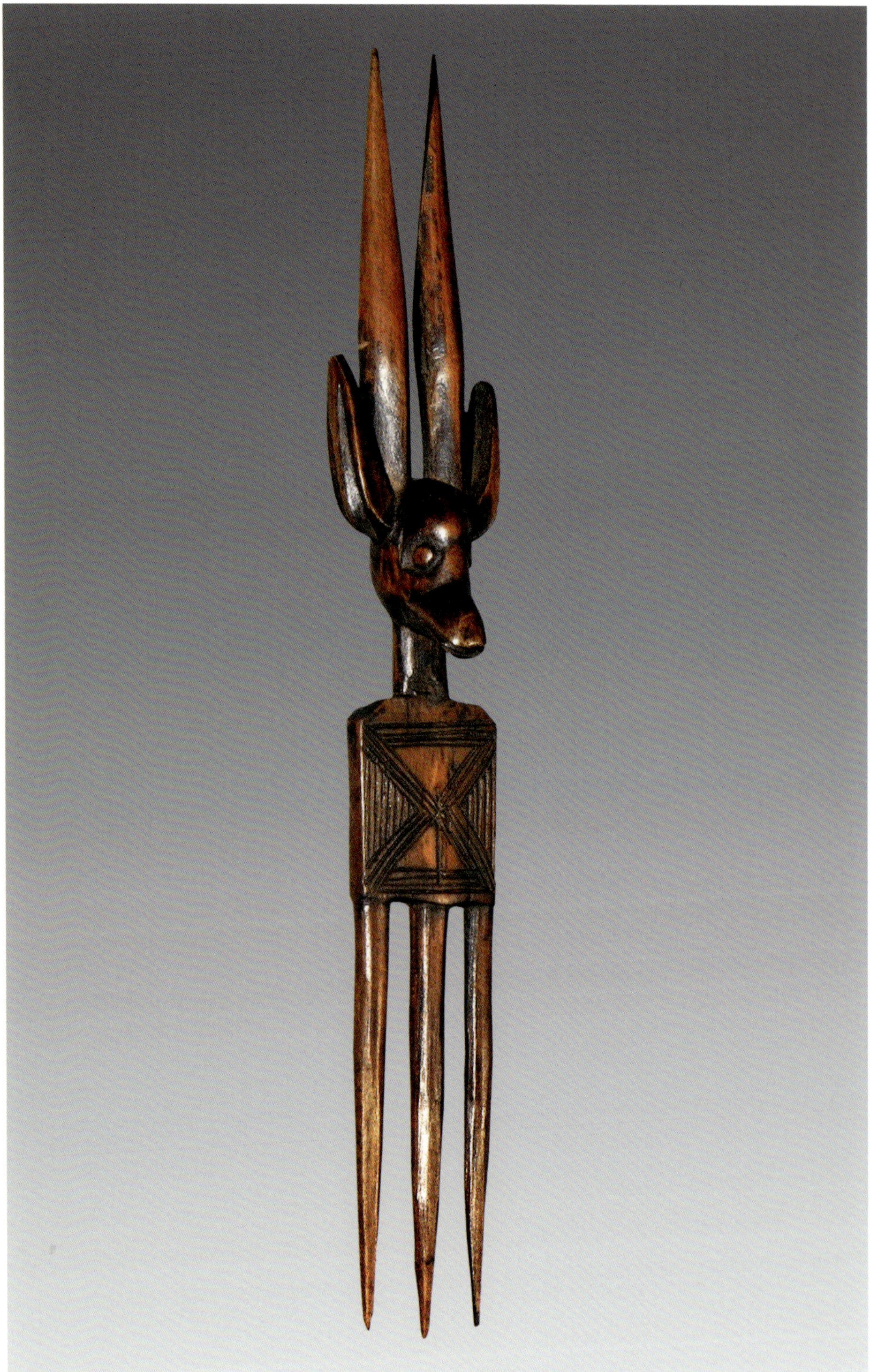

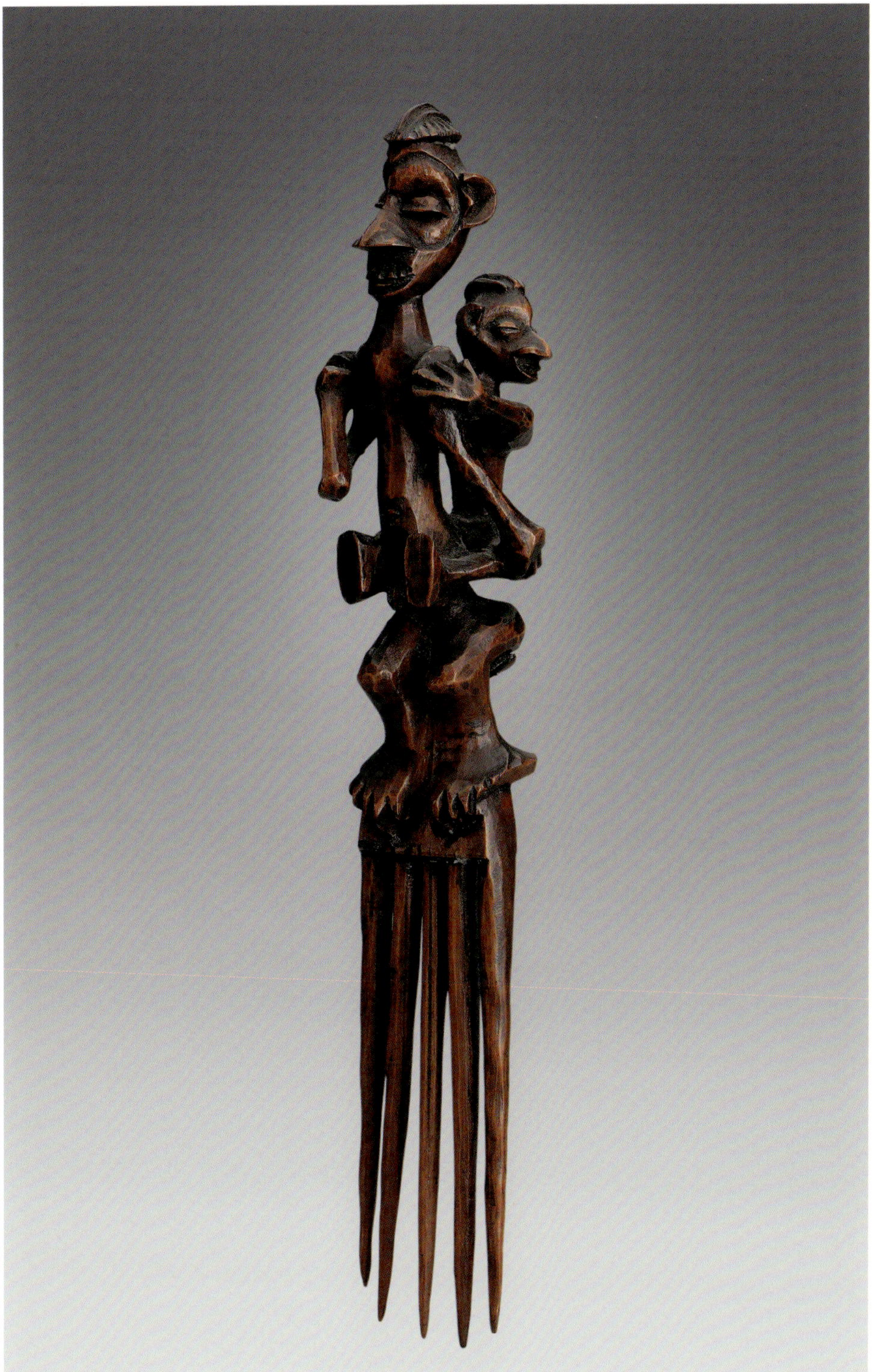

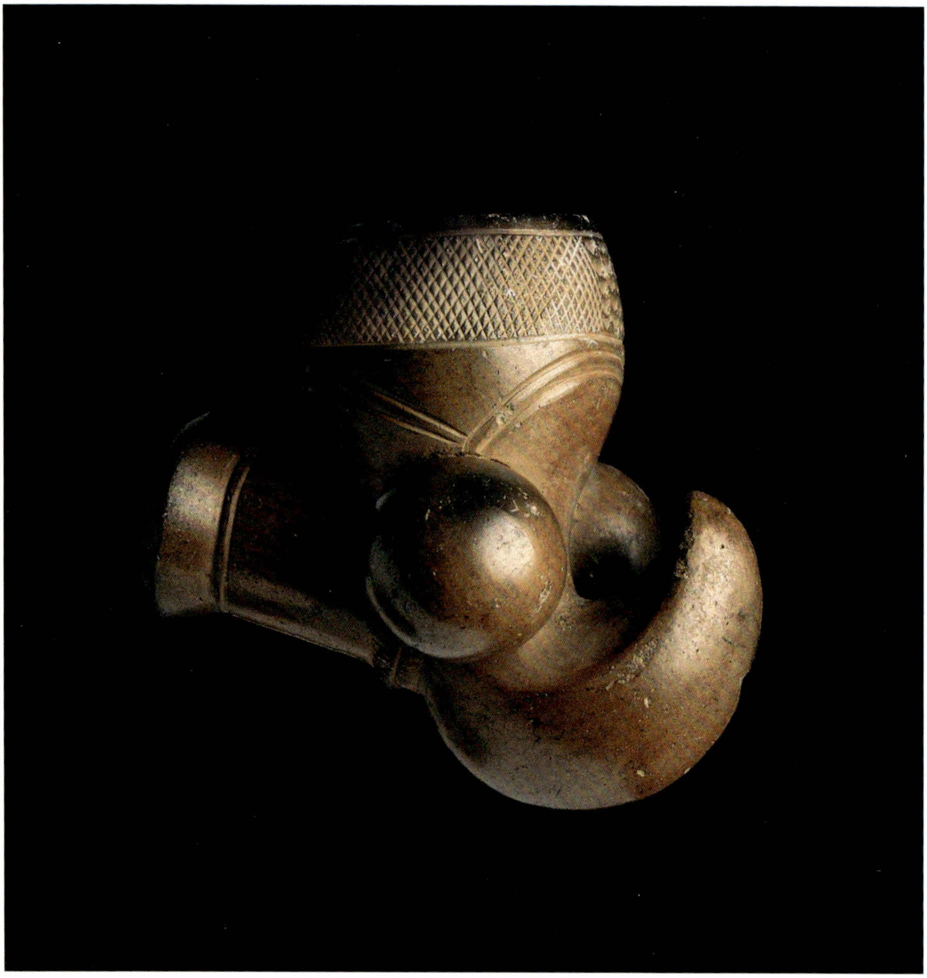

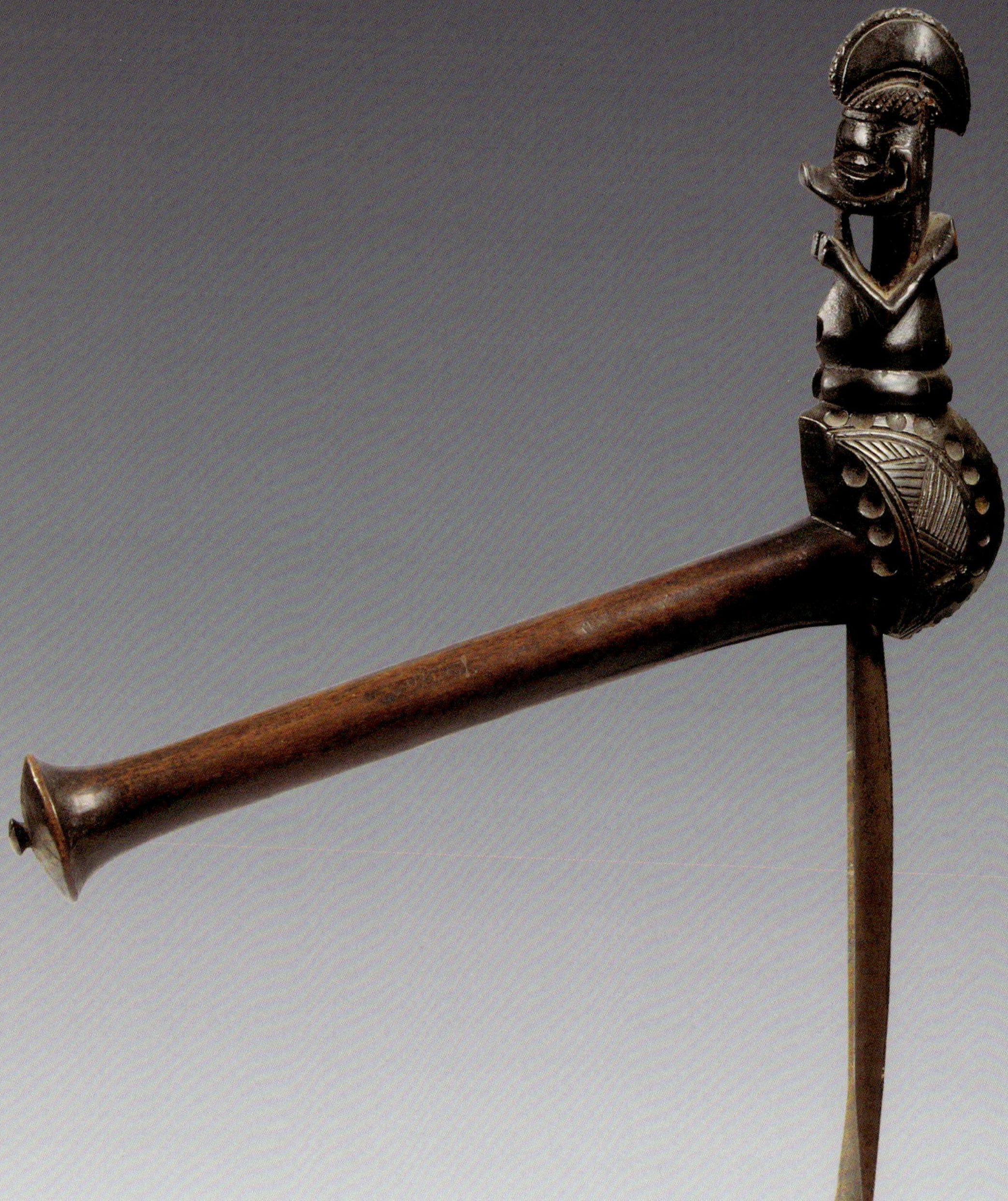

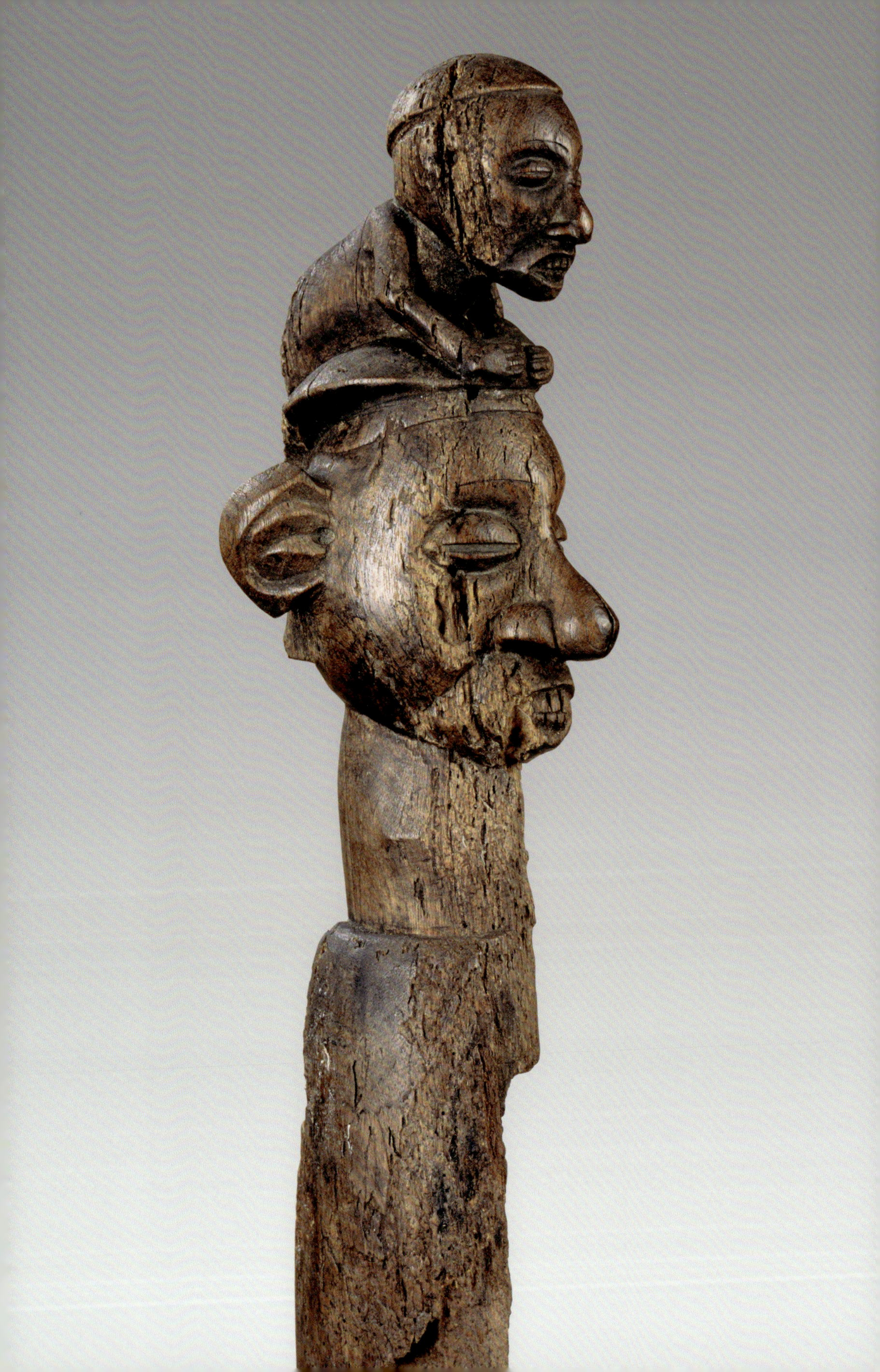

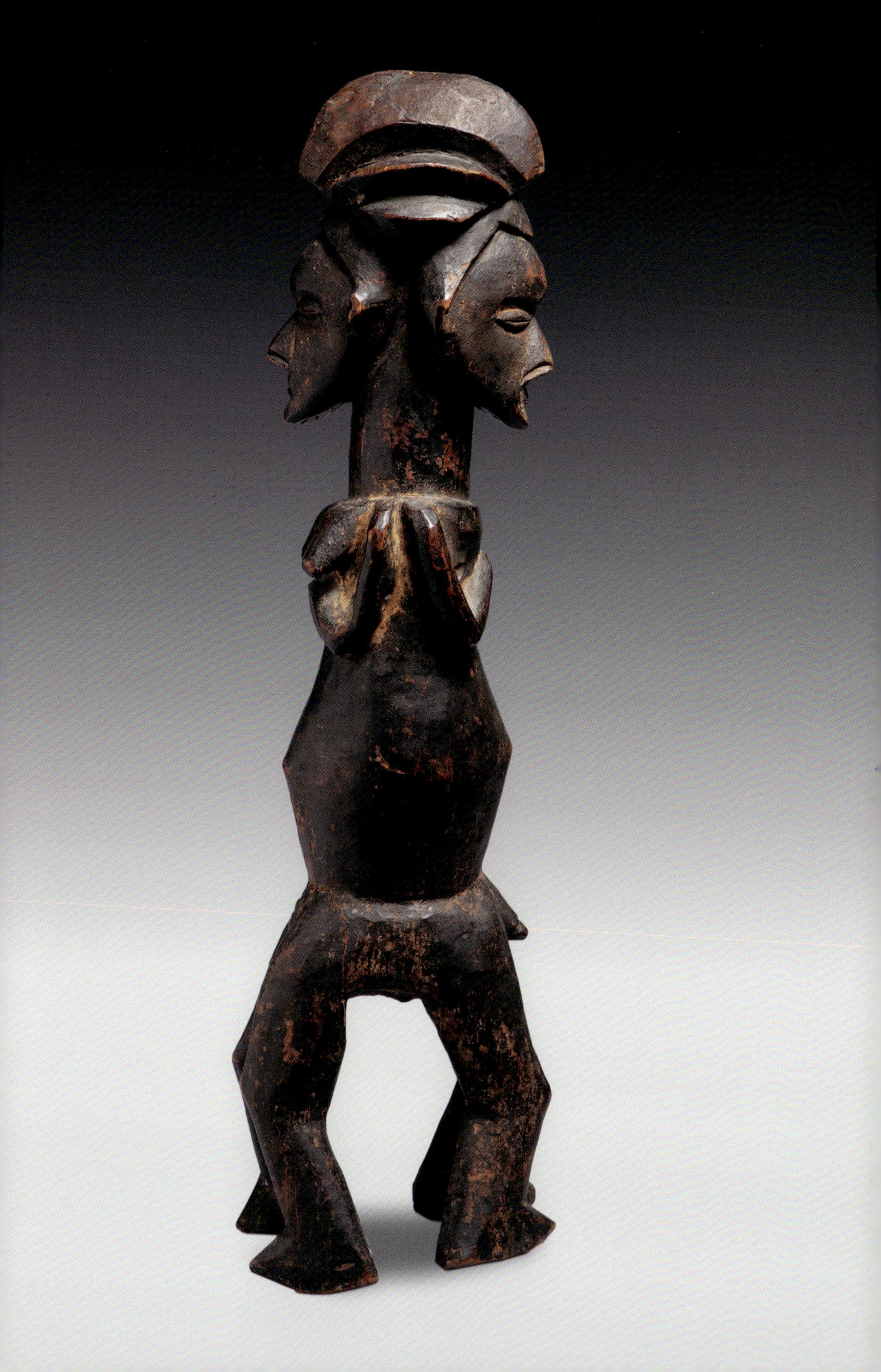

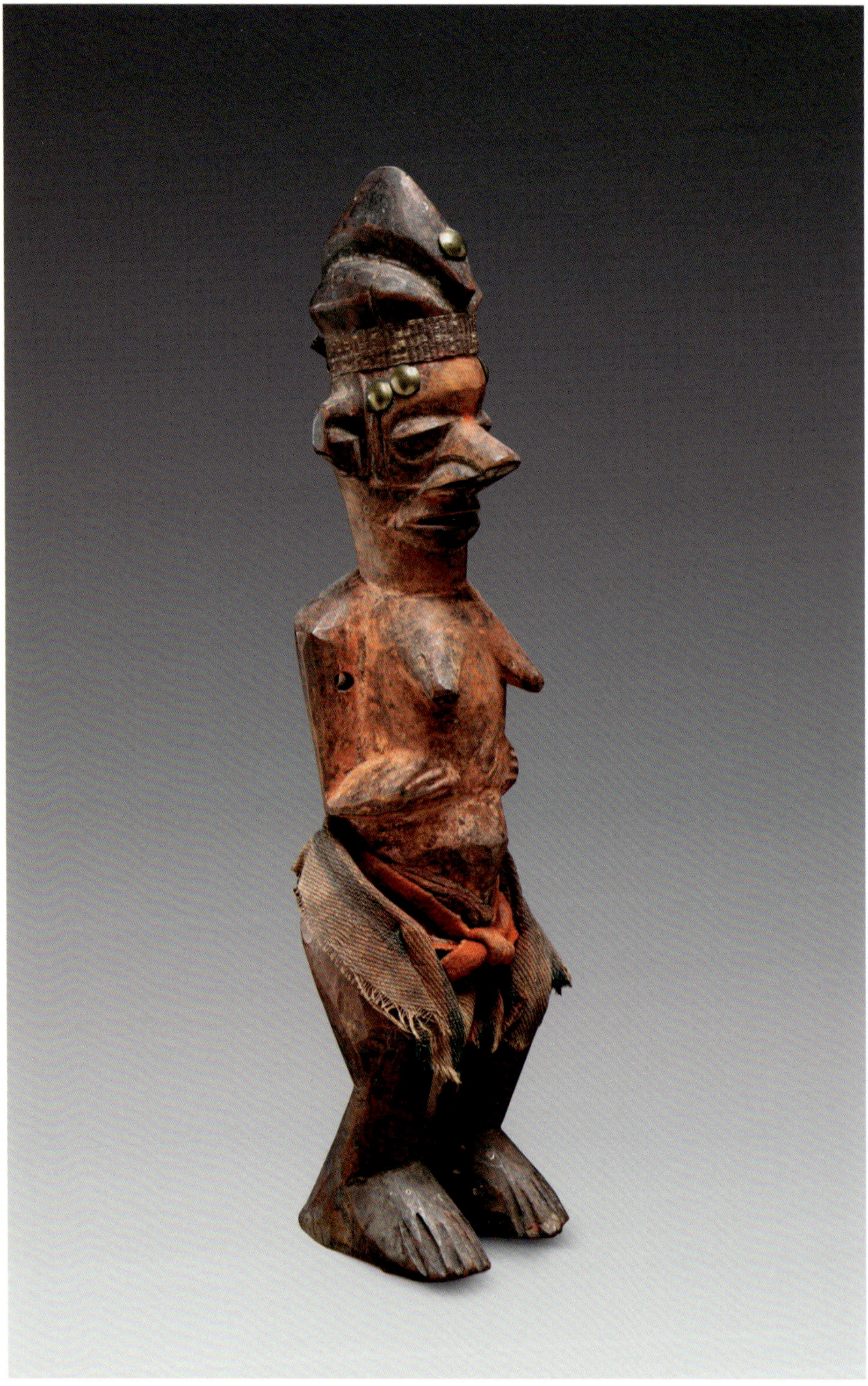

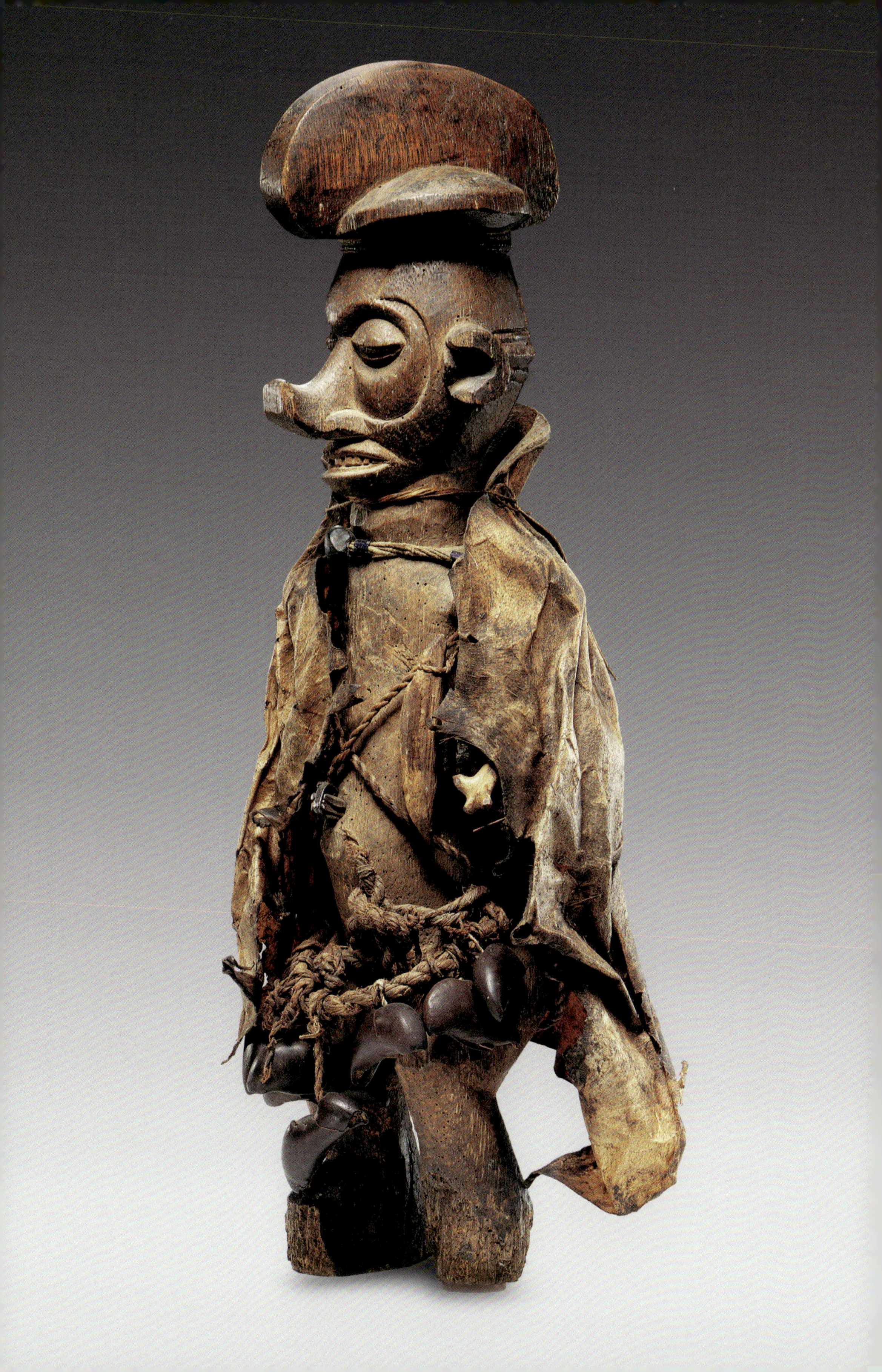

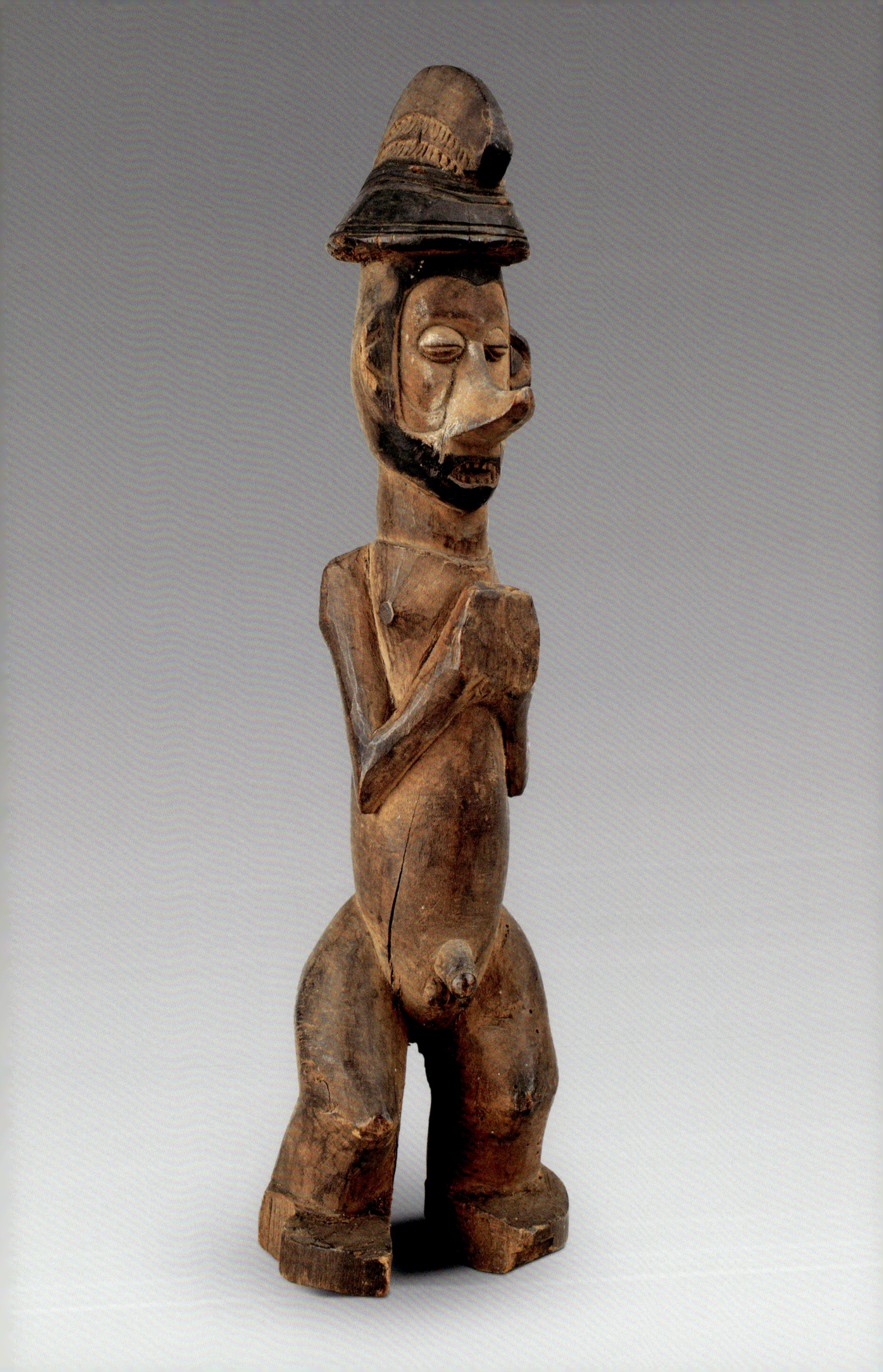

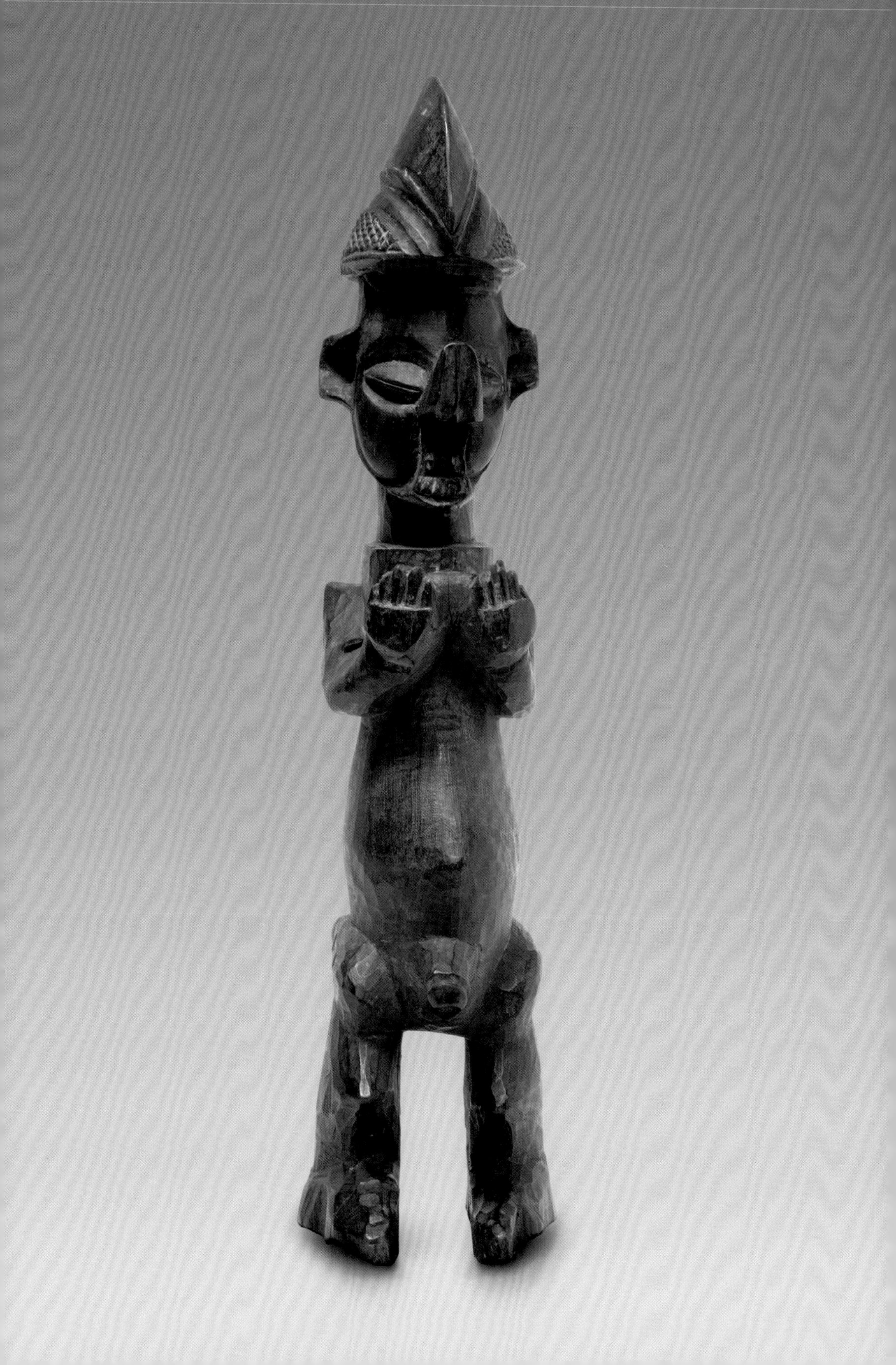

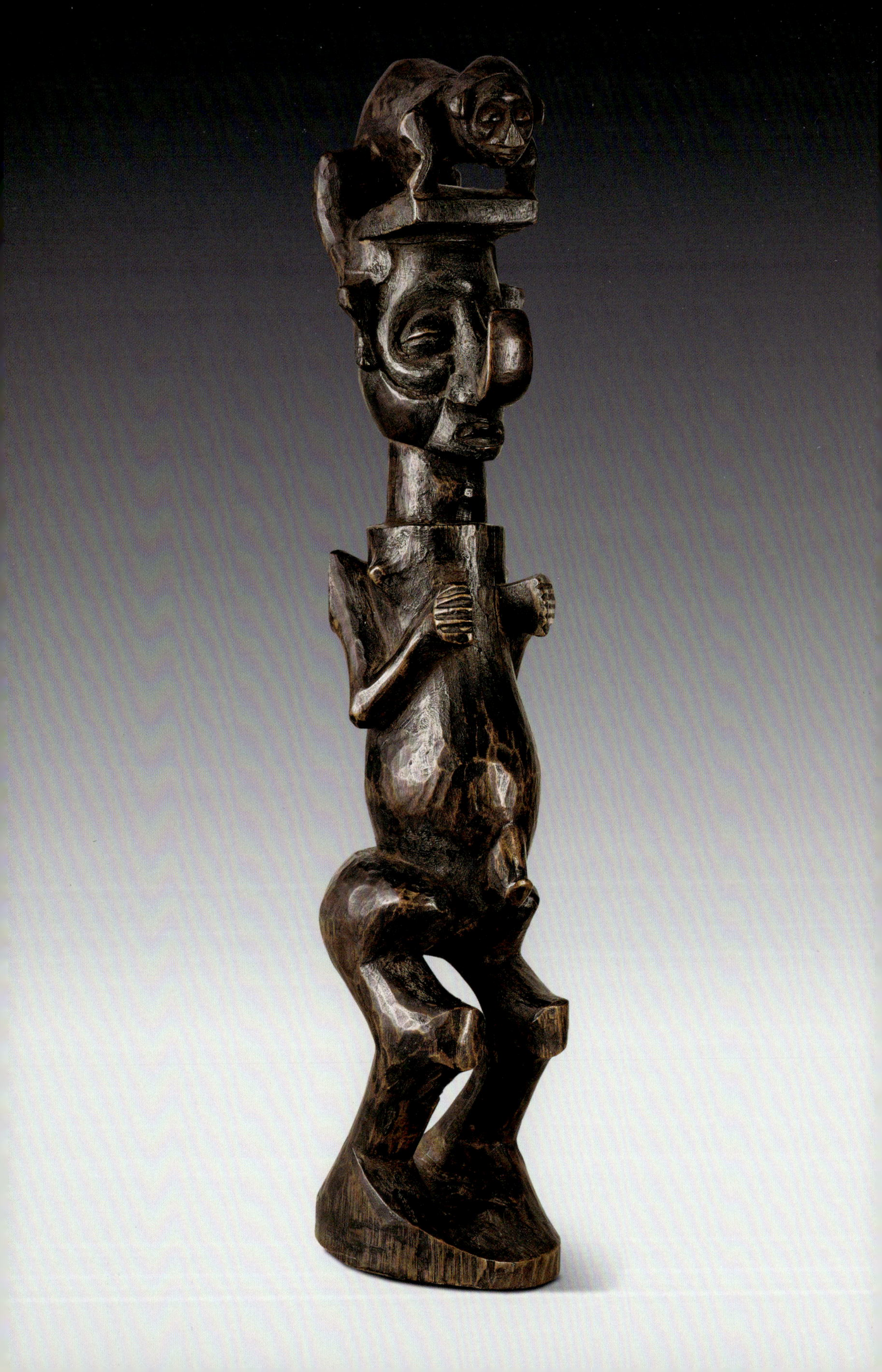

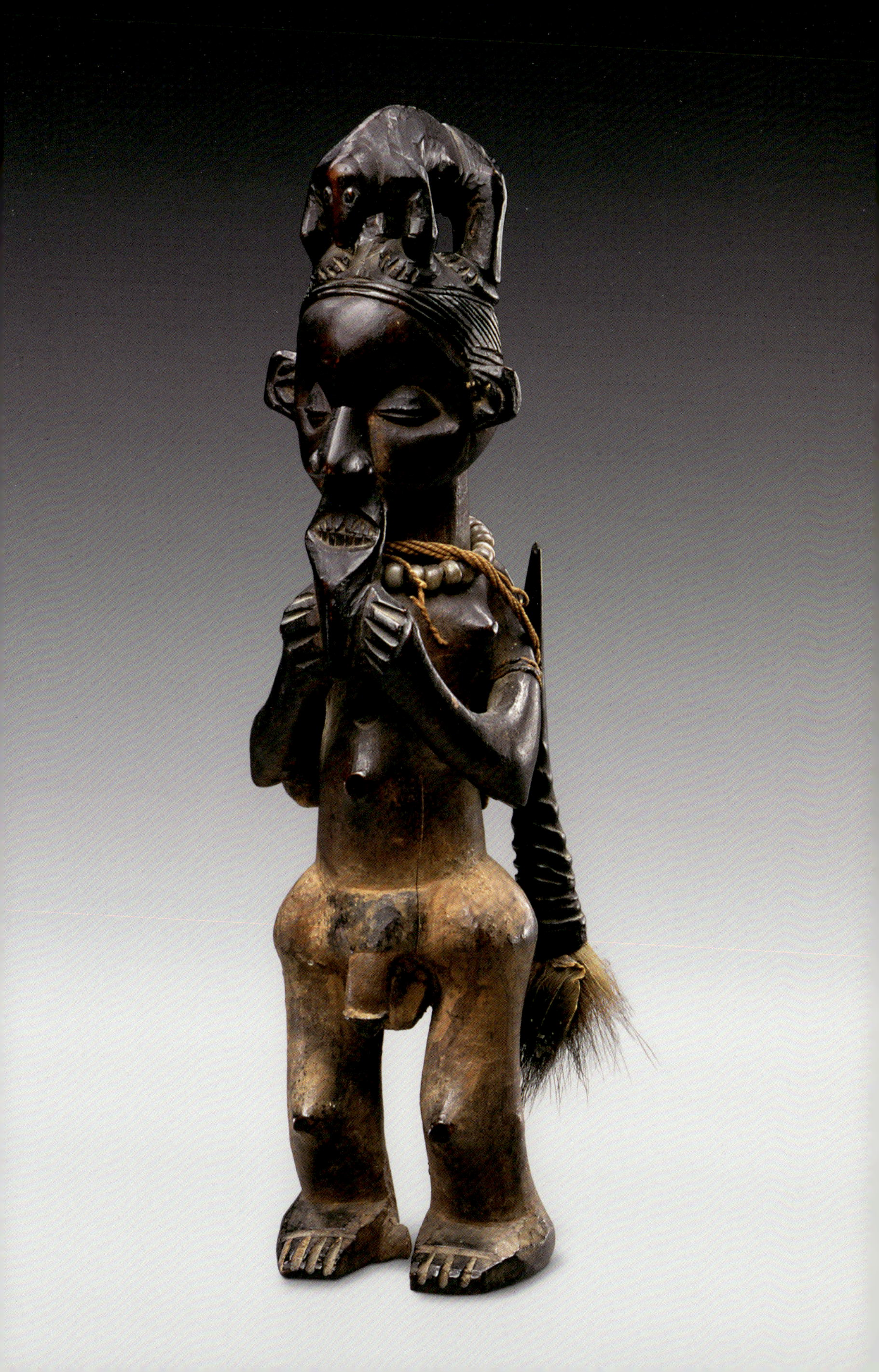

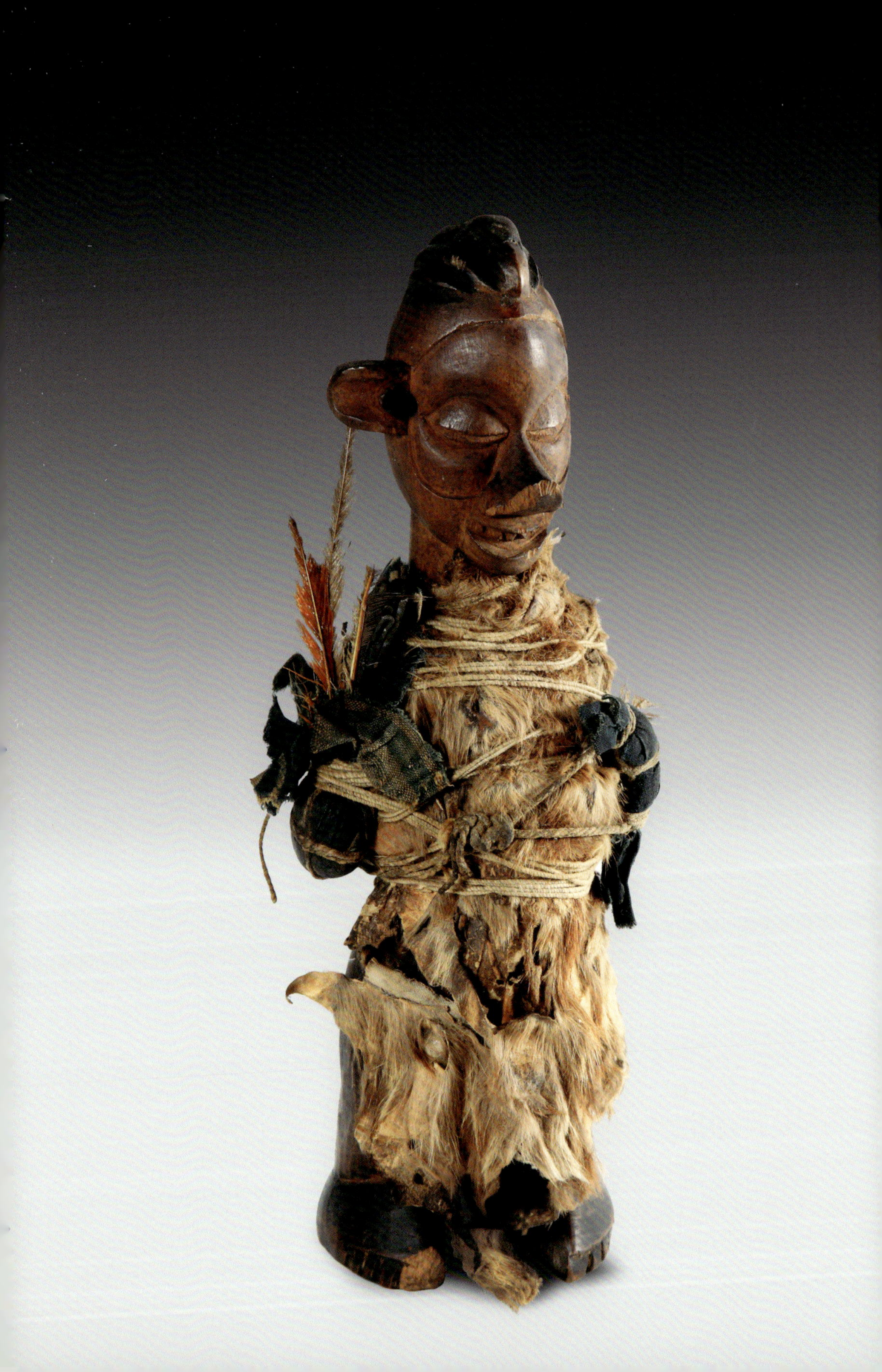

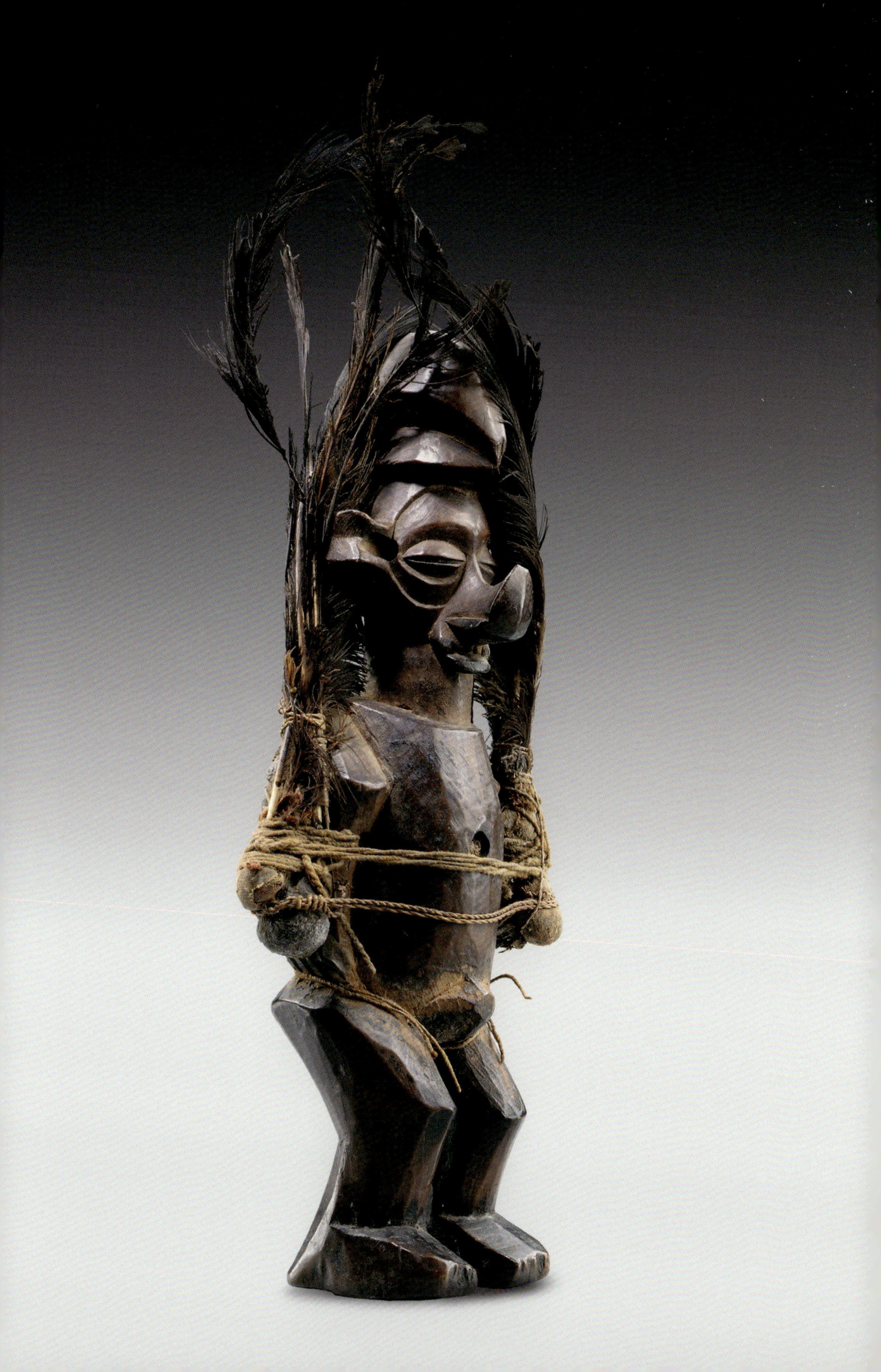

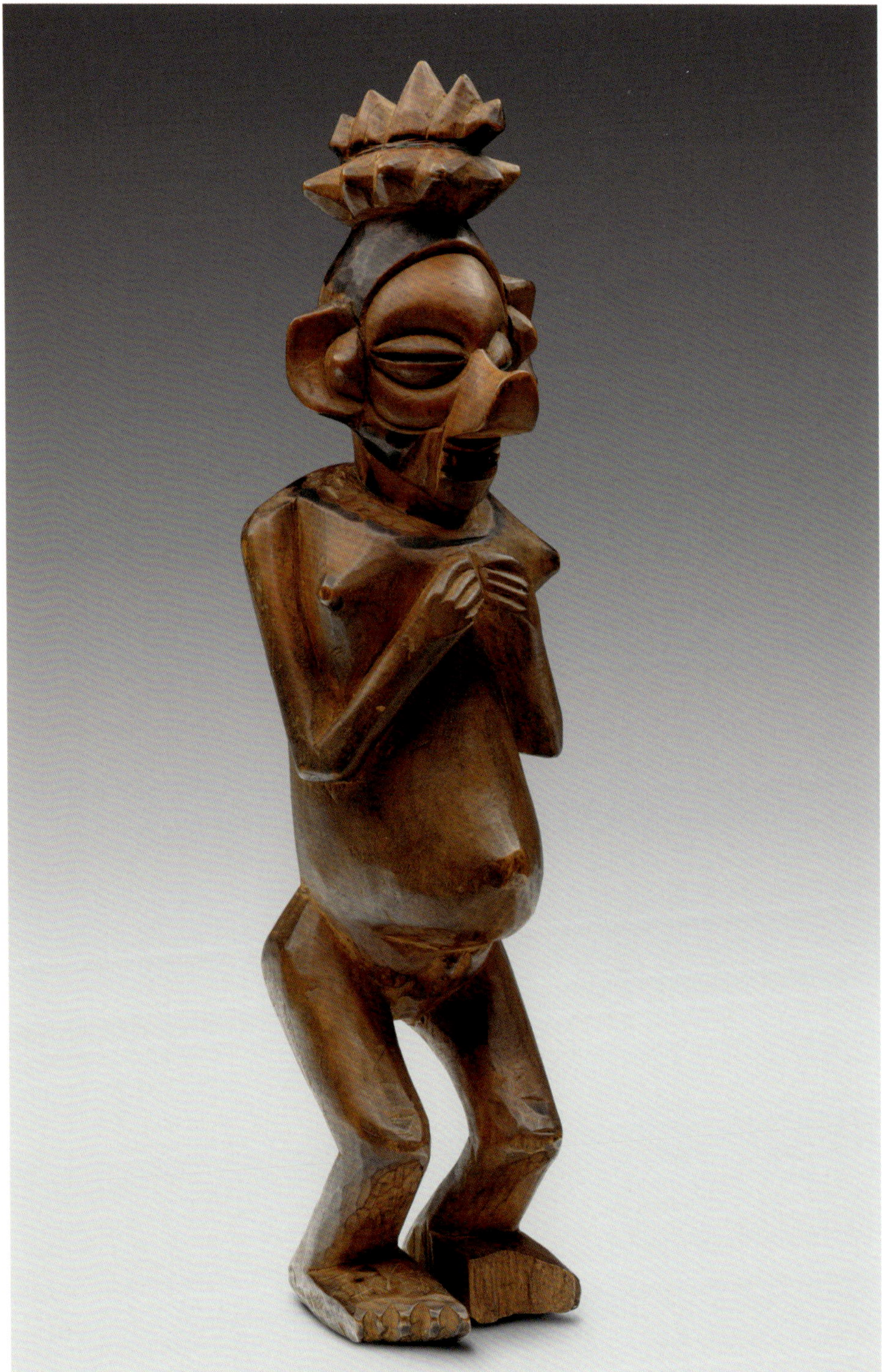

19-20 | 21

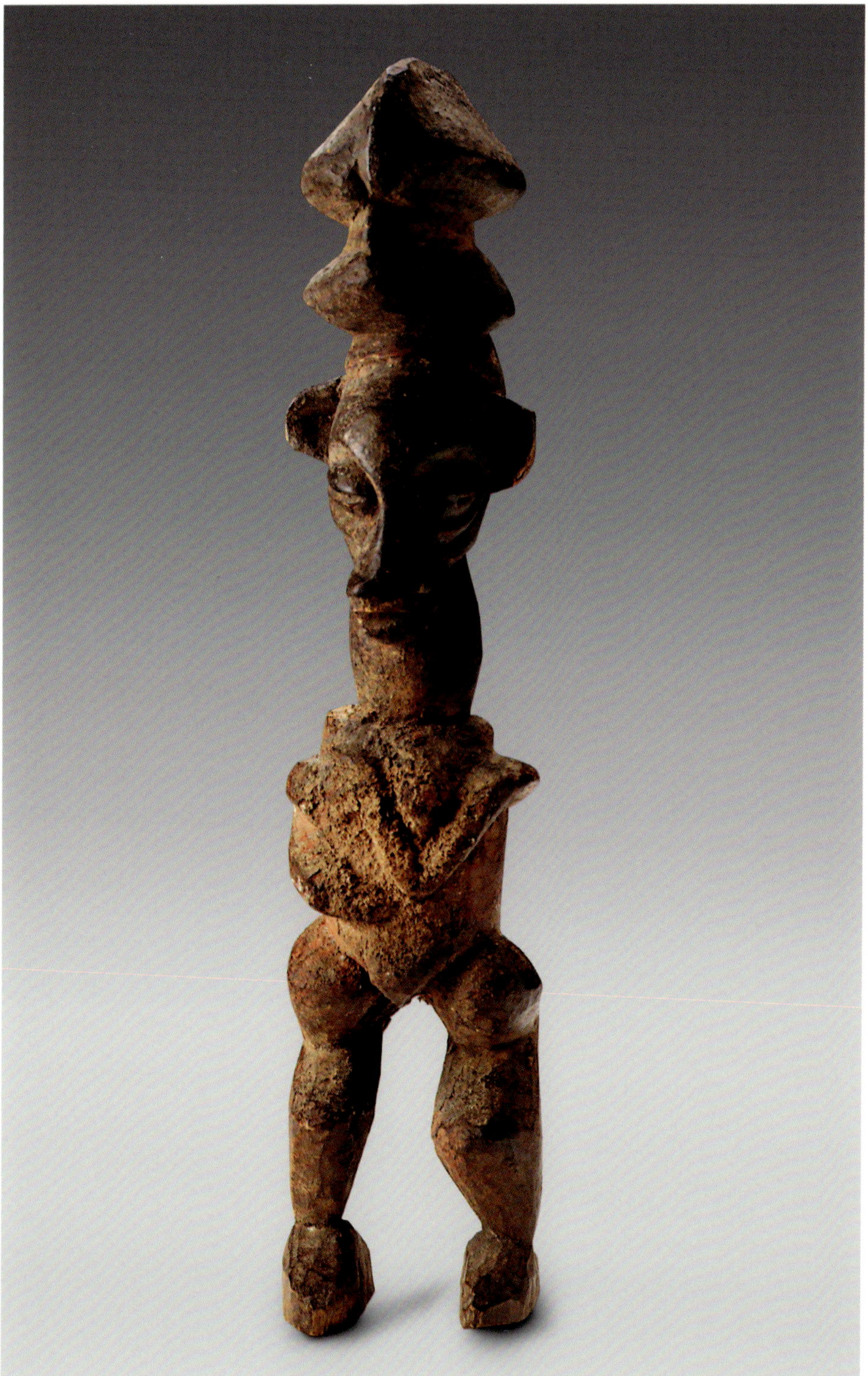

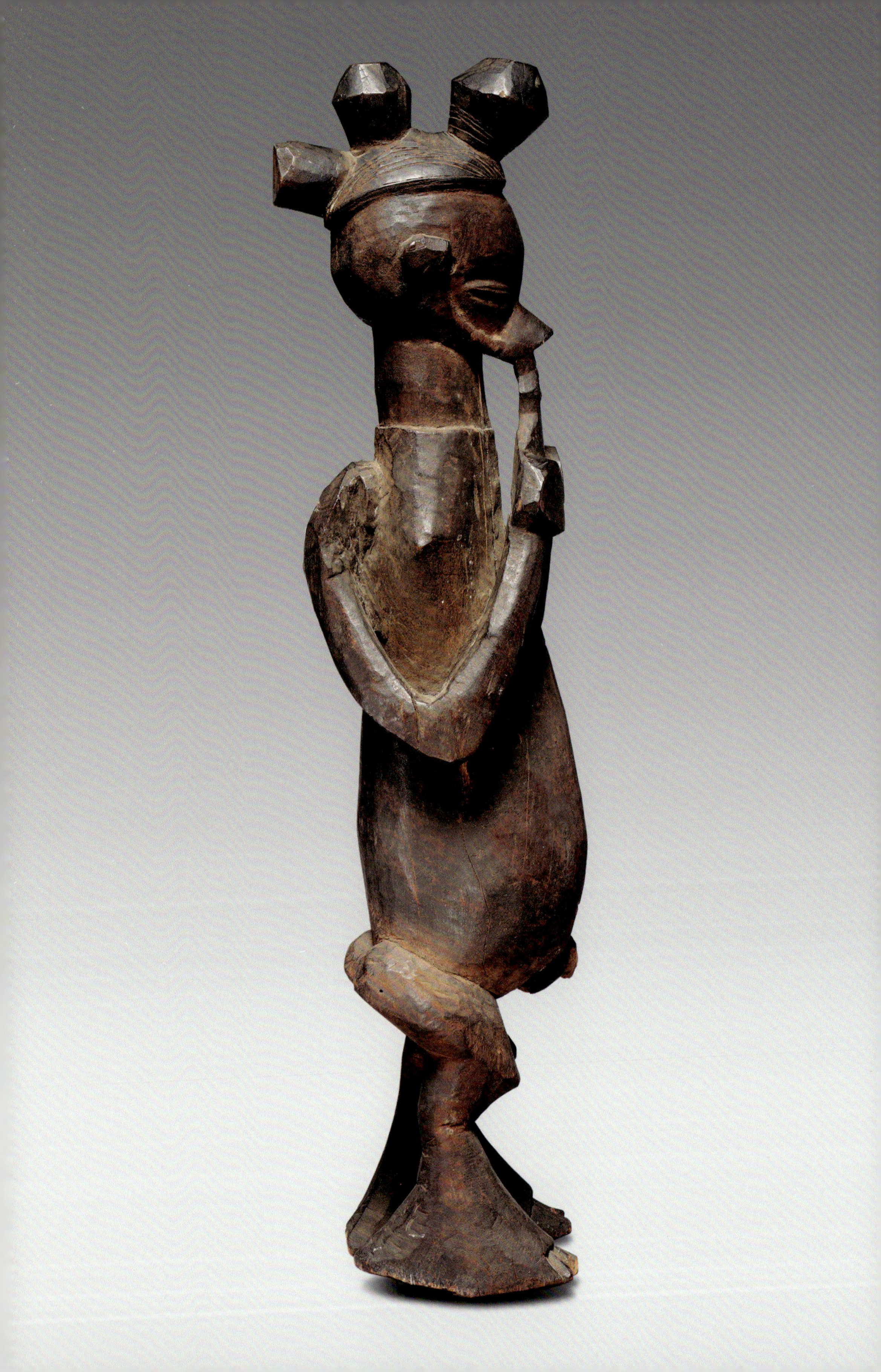

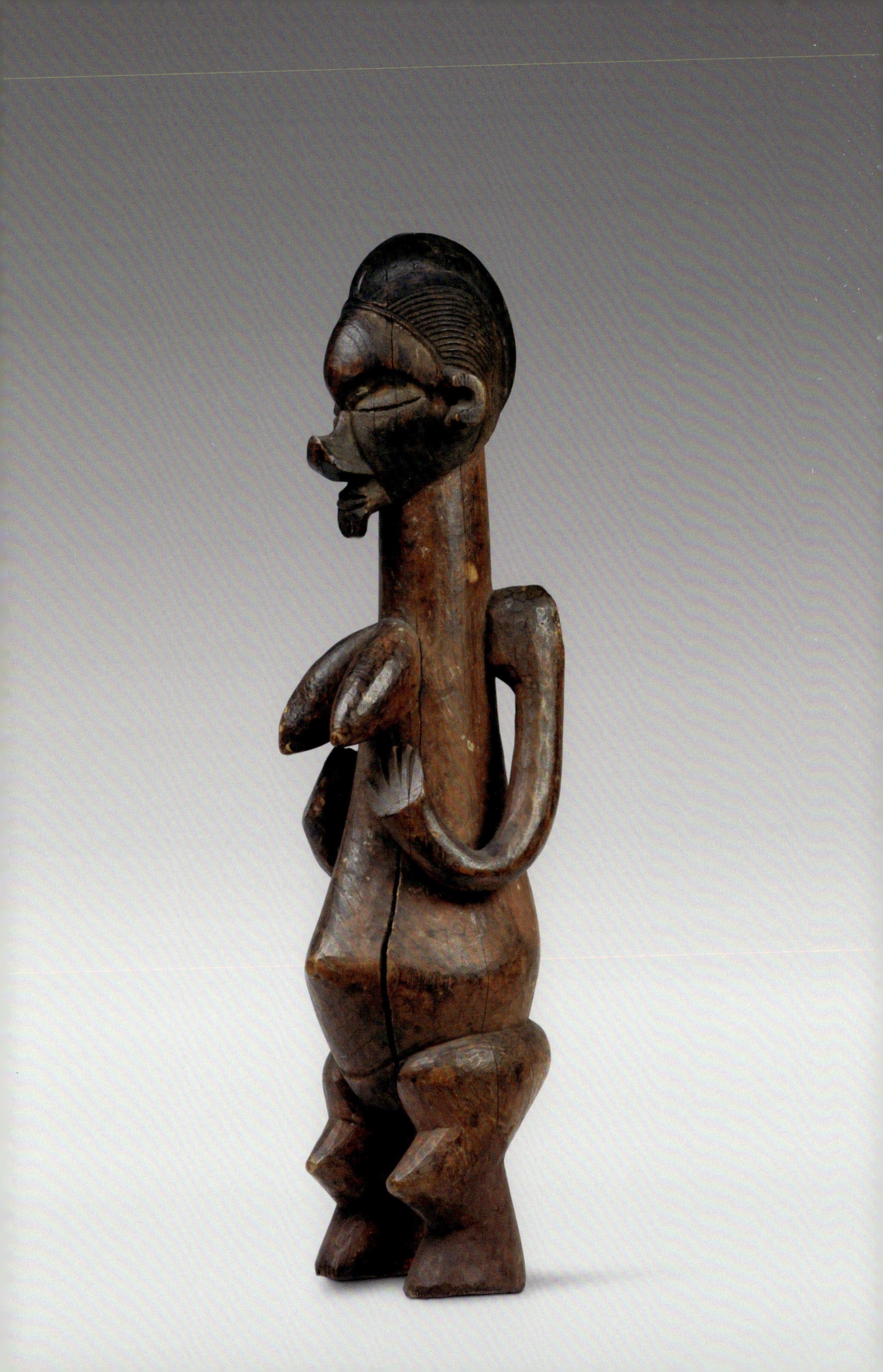

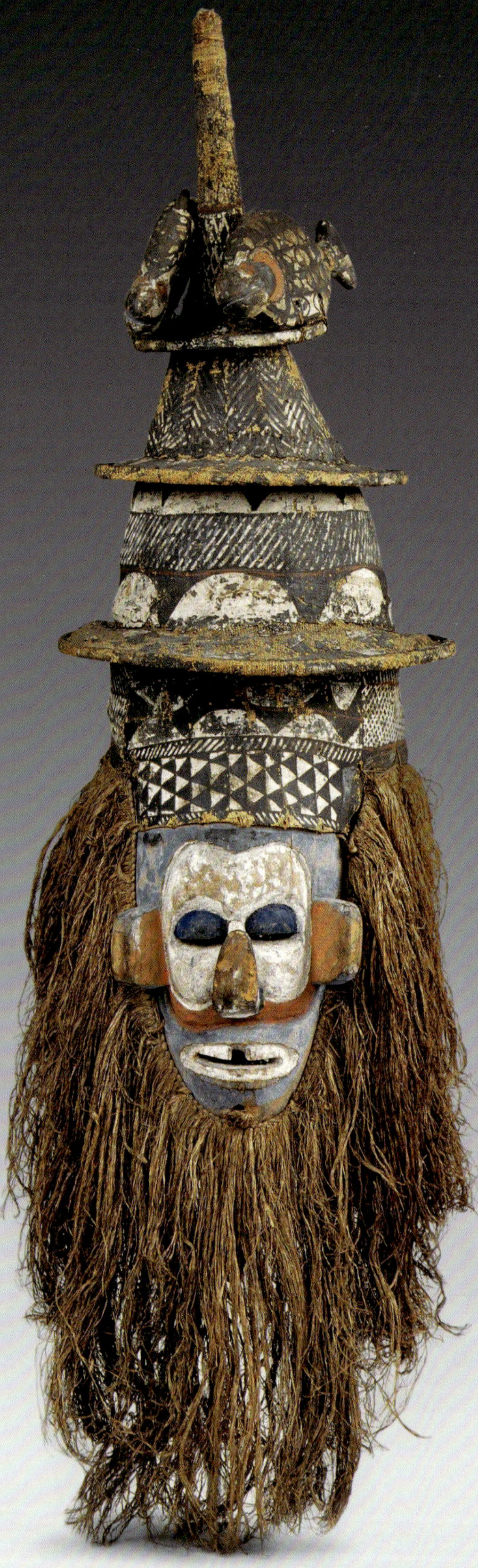

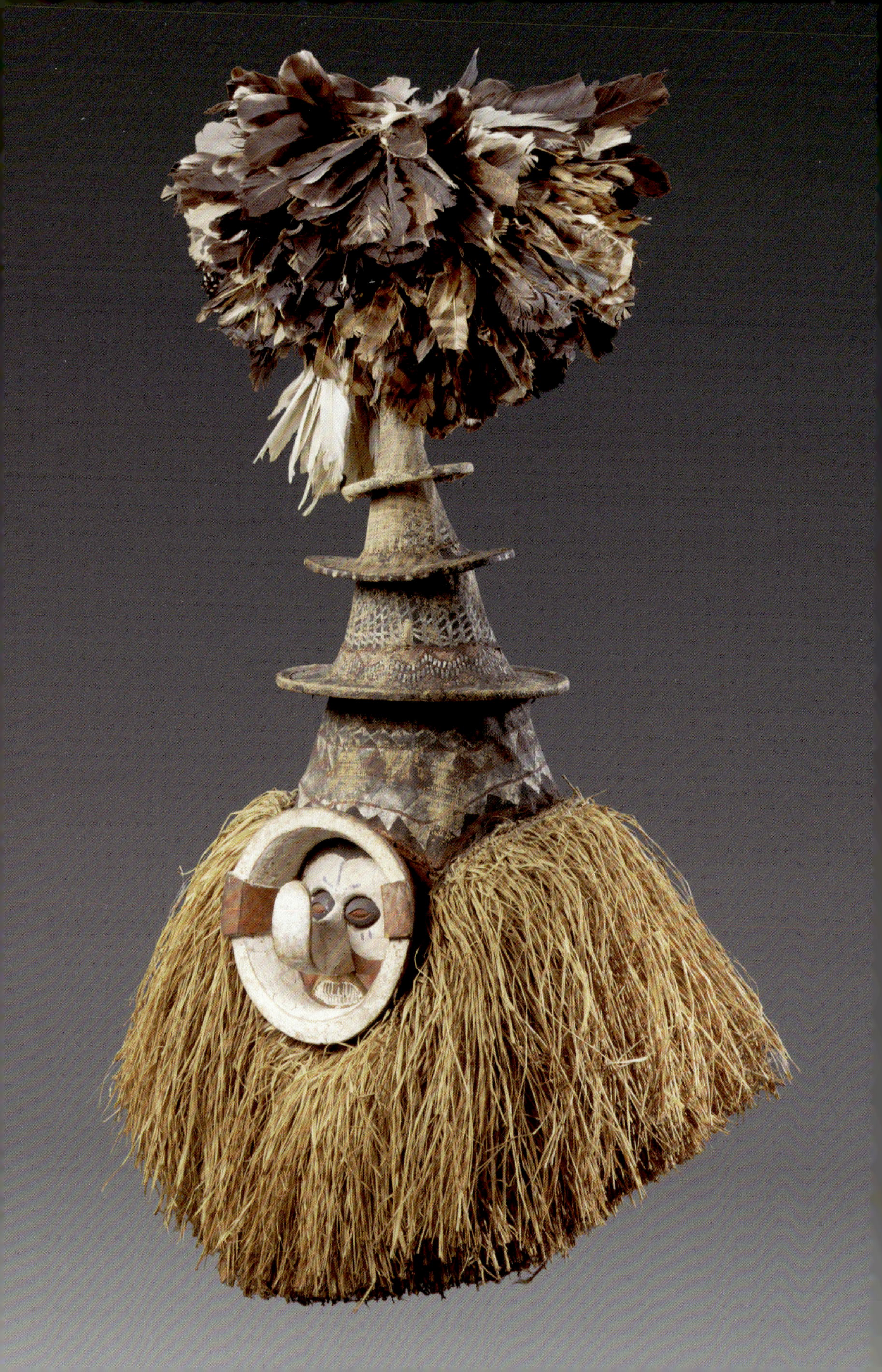

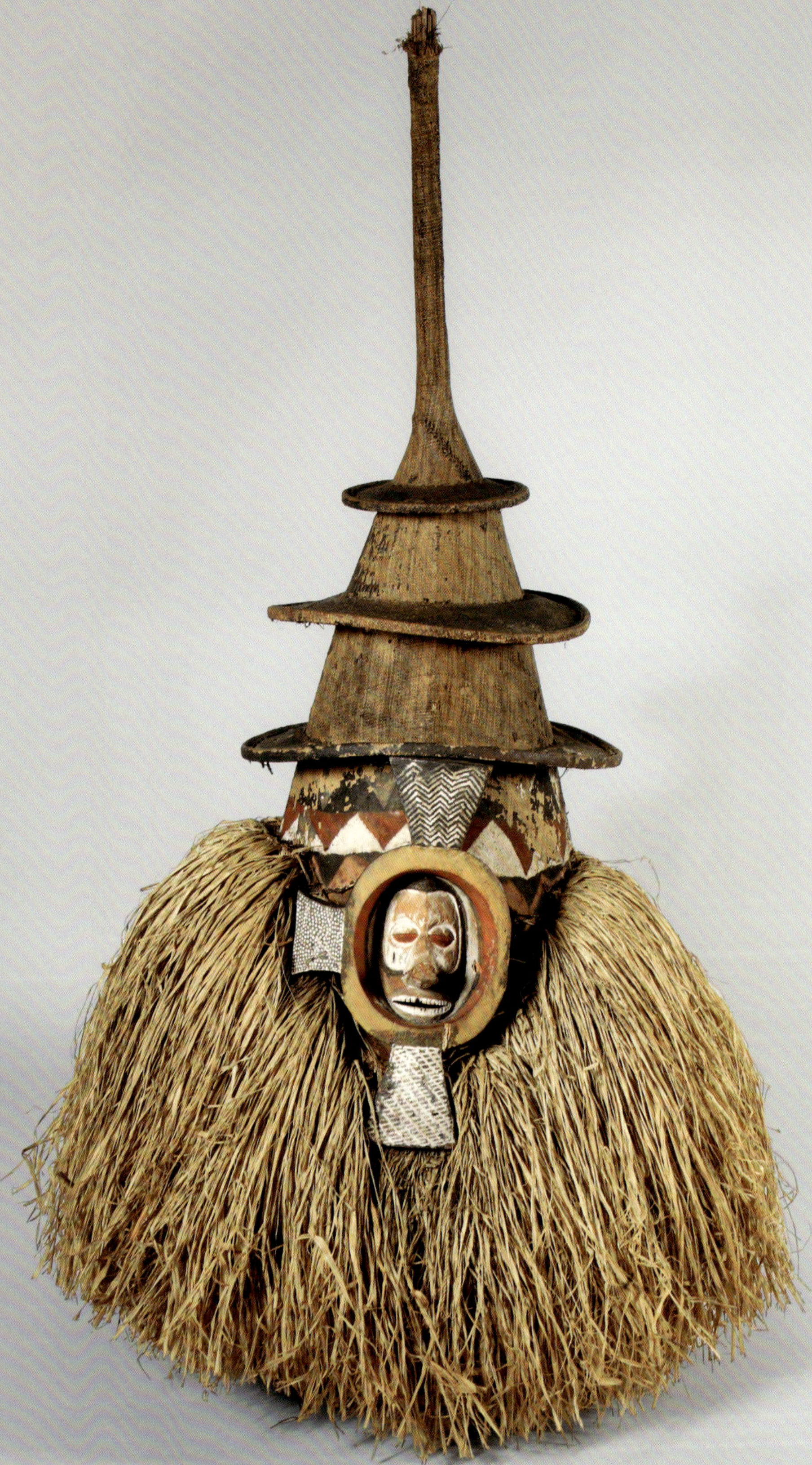

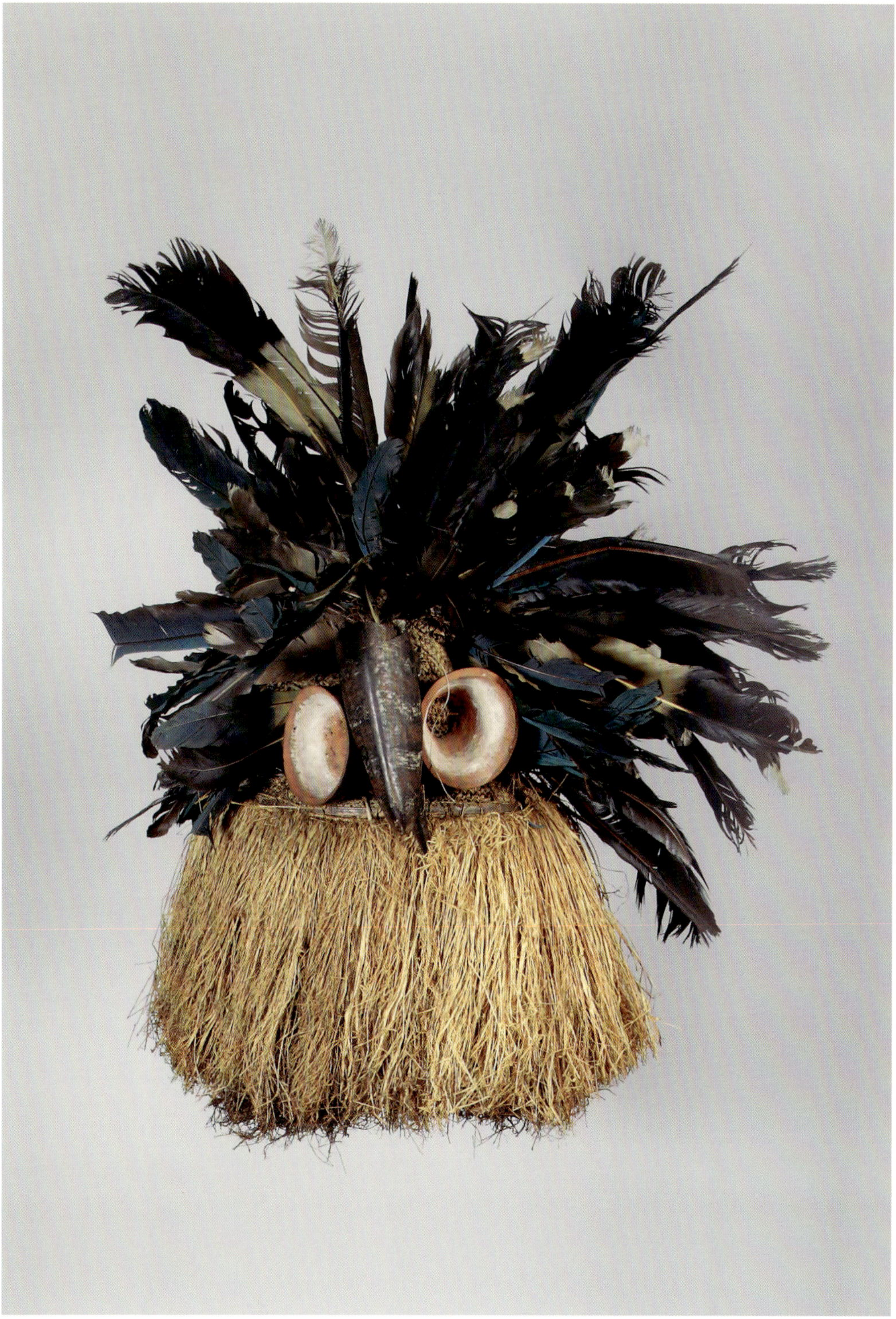

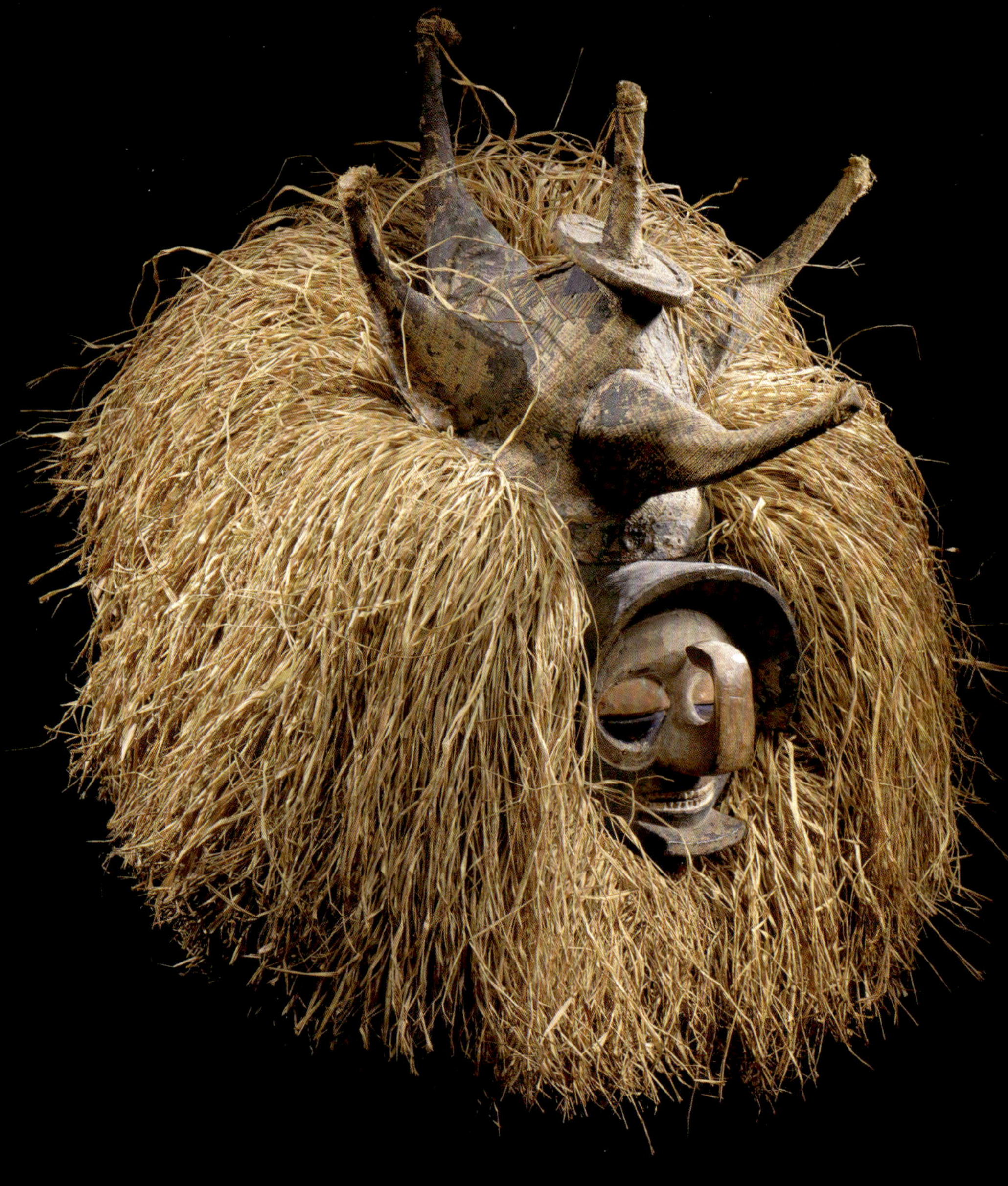

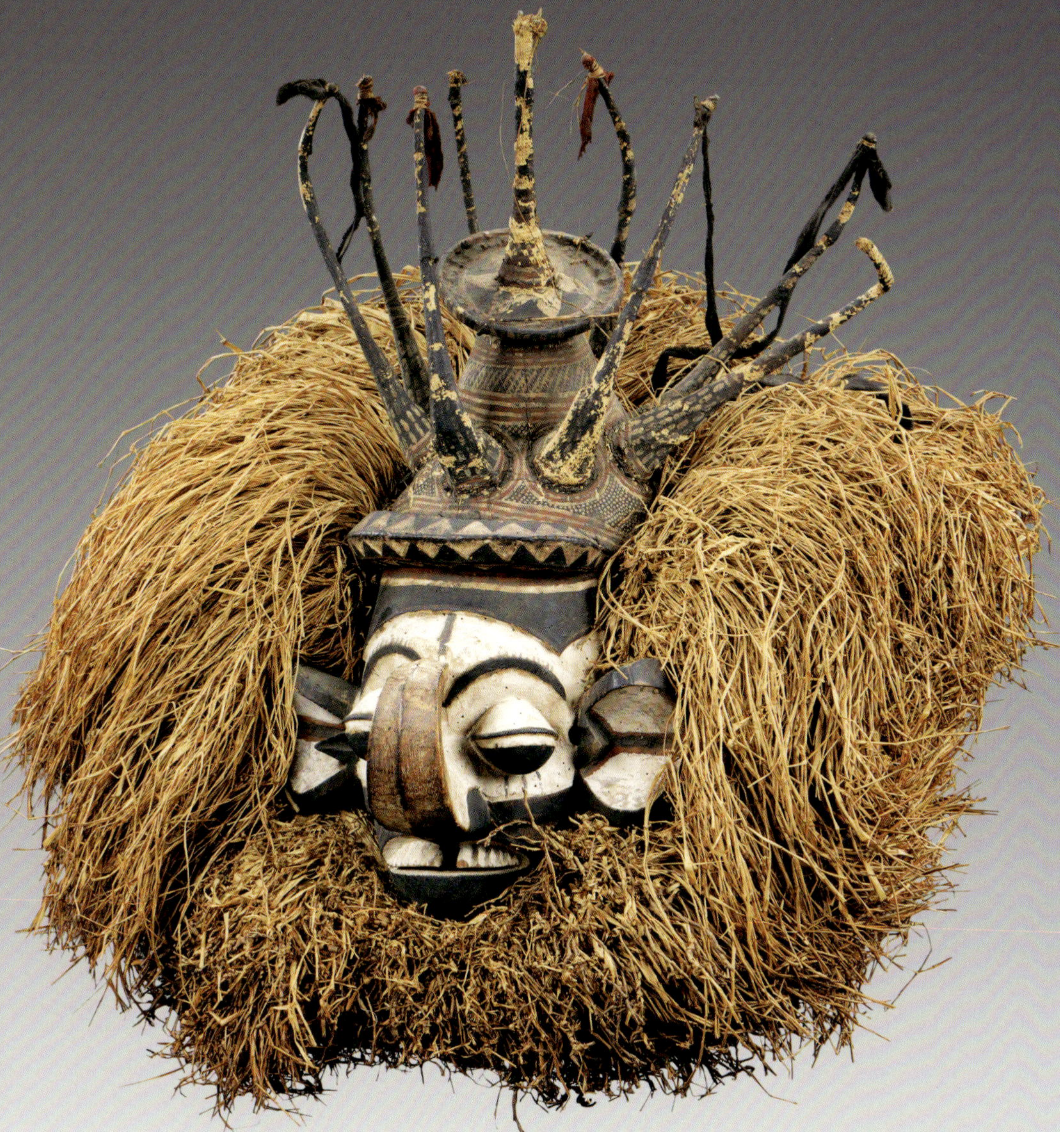

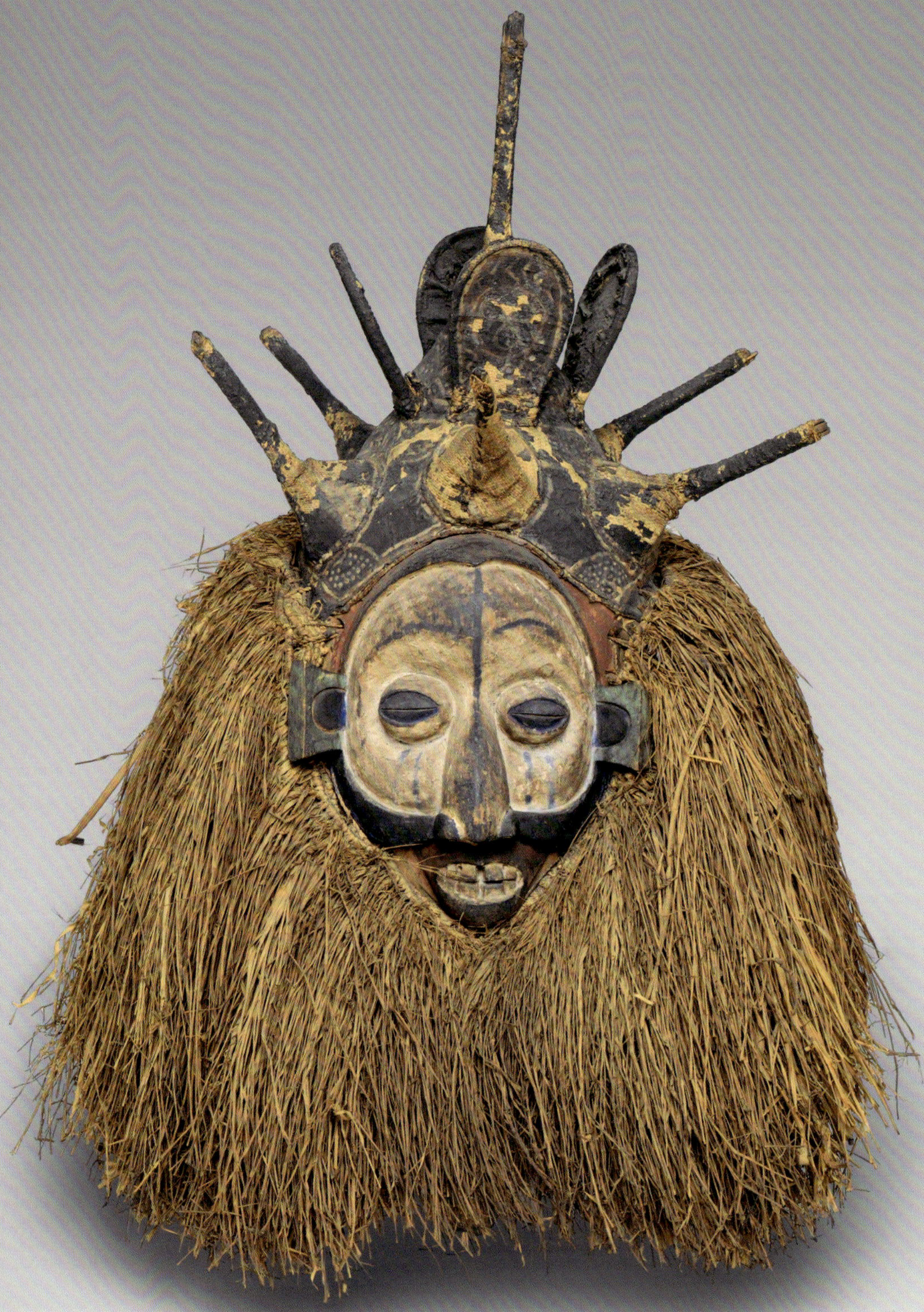

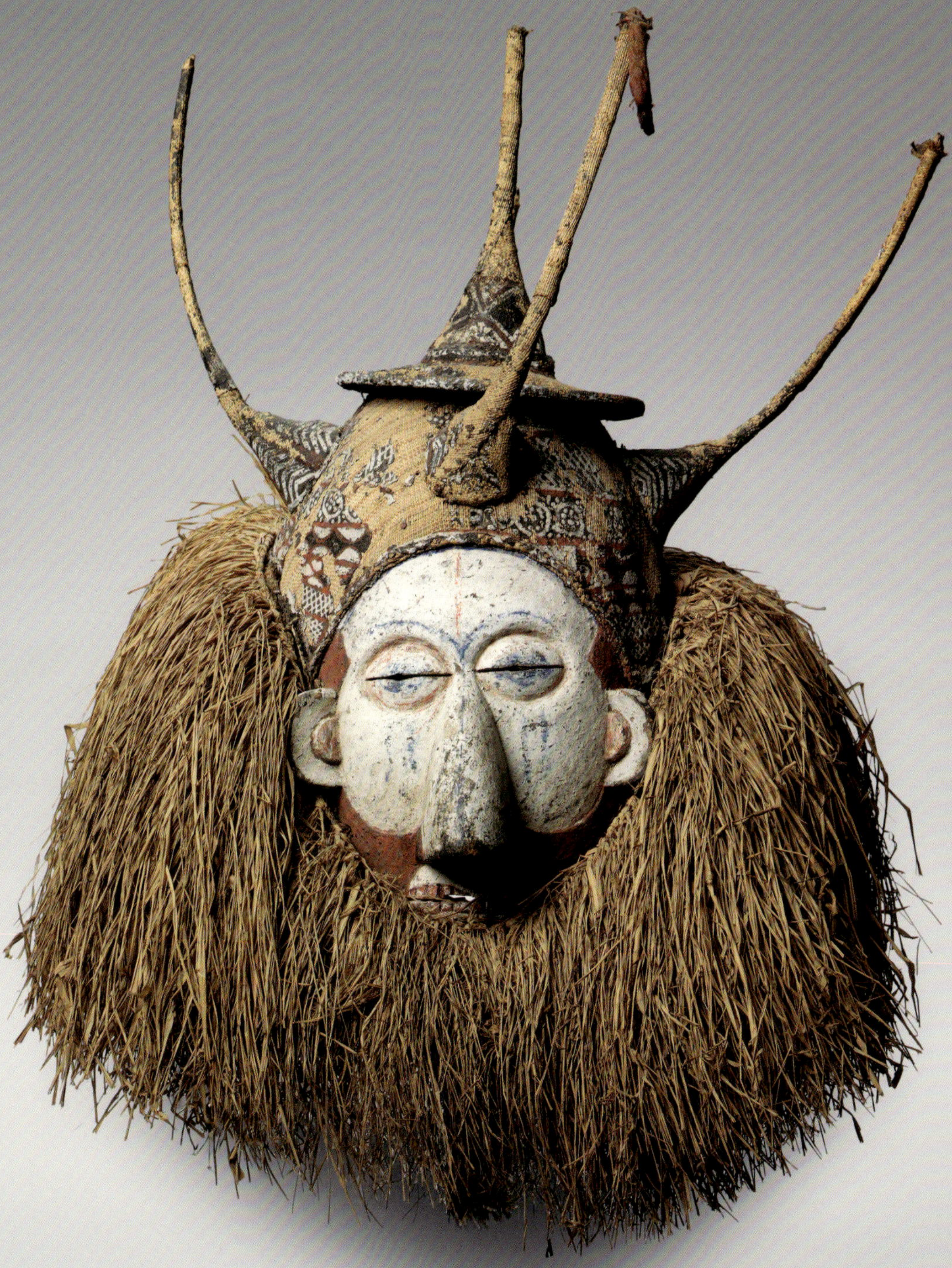

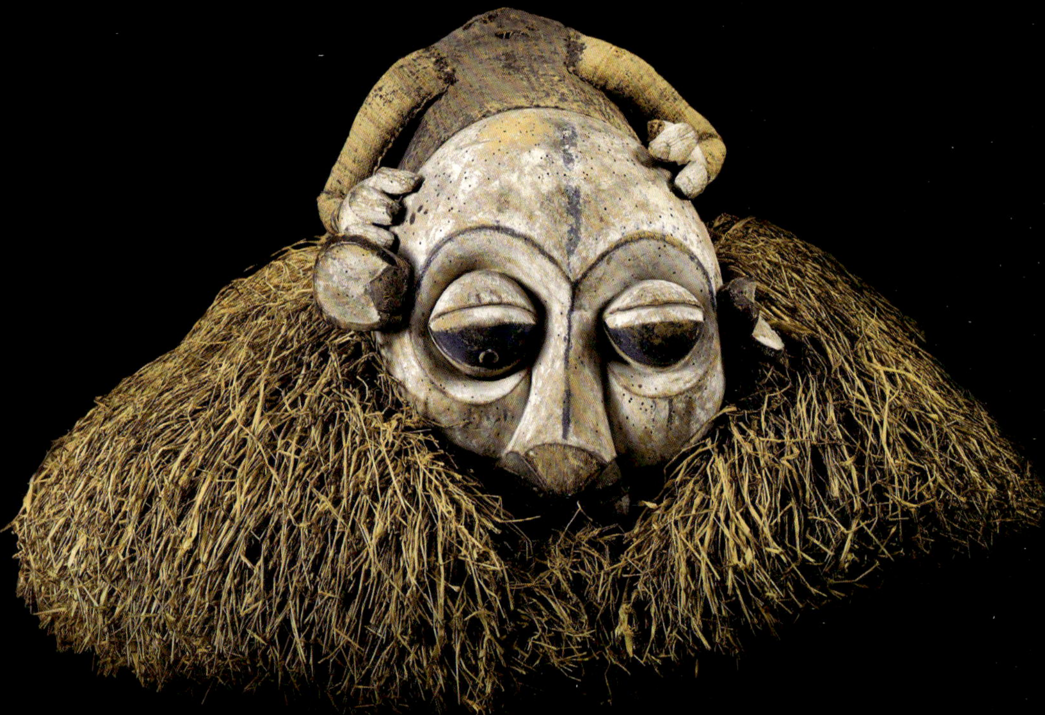

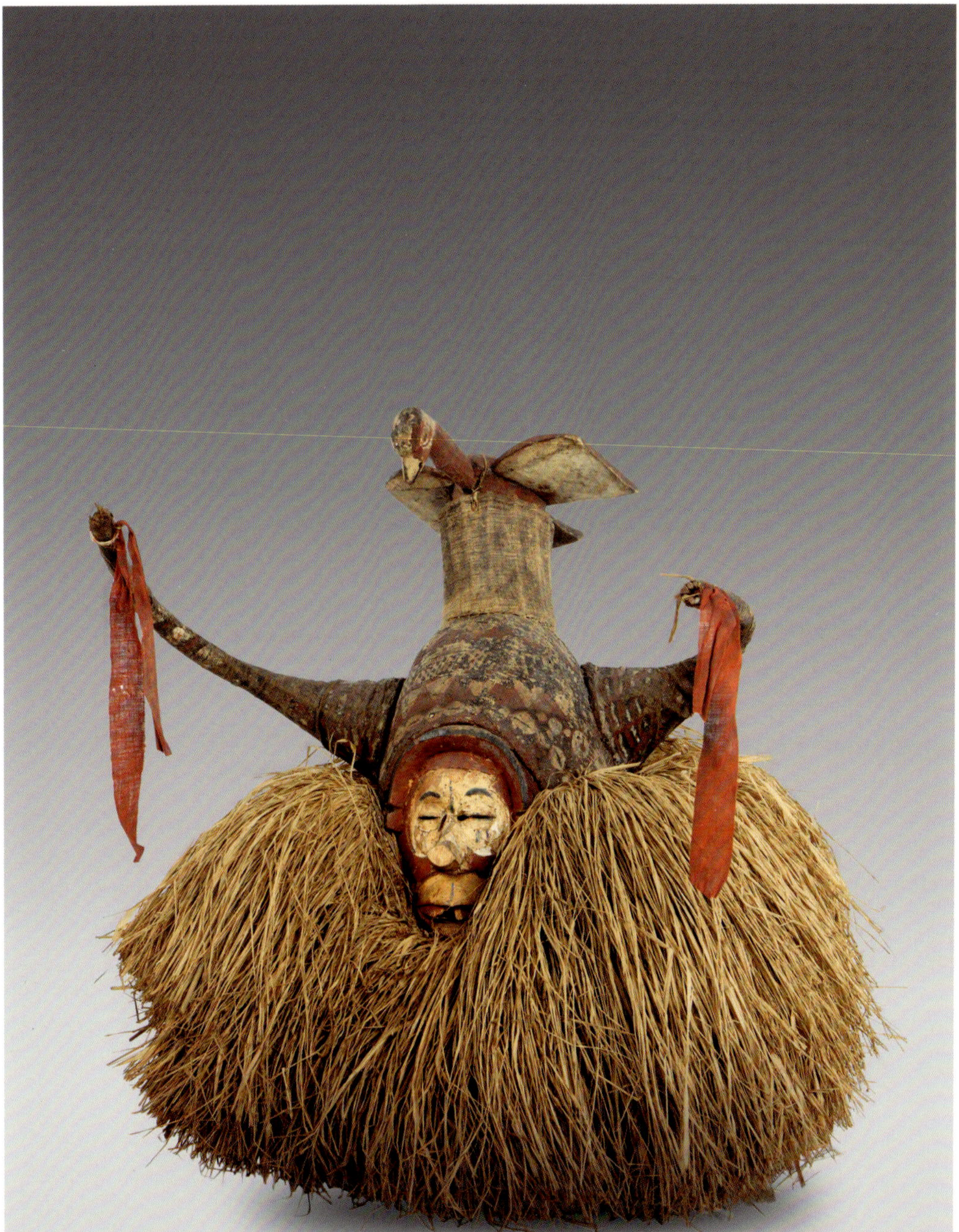

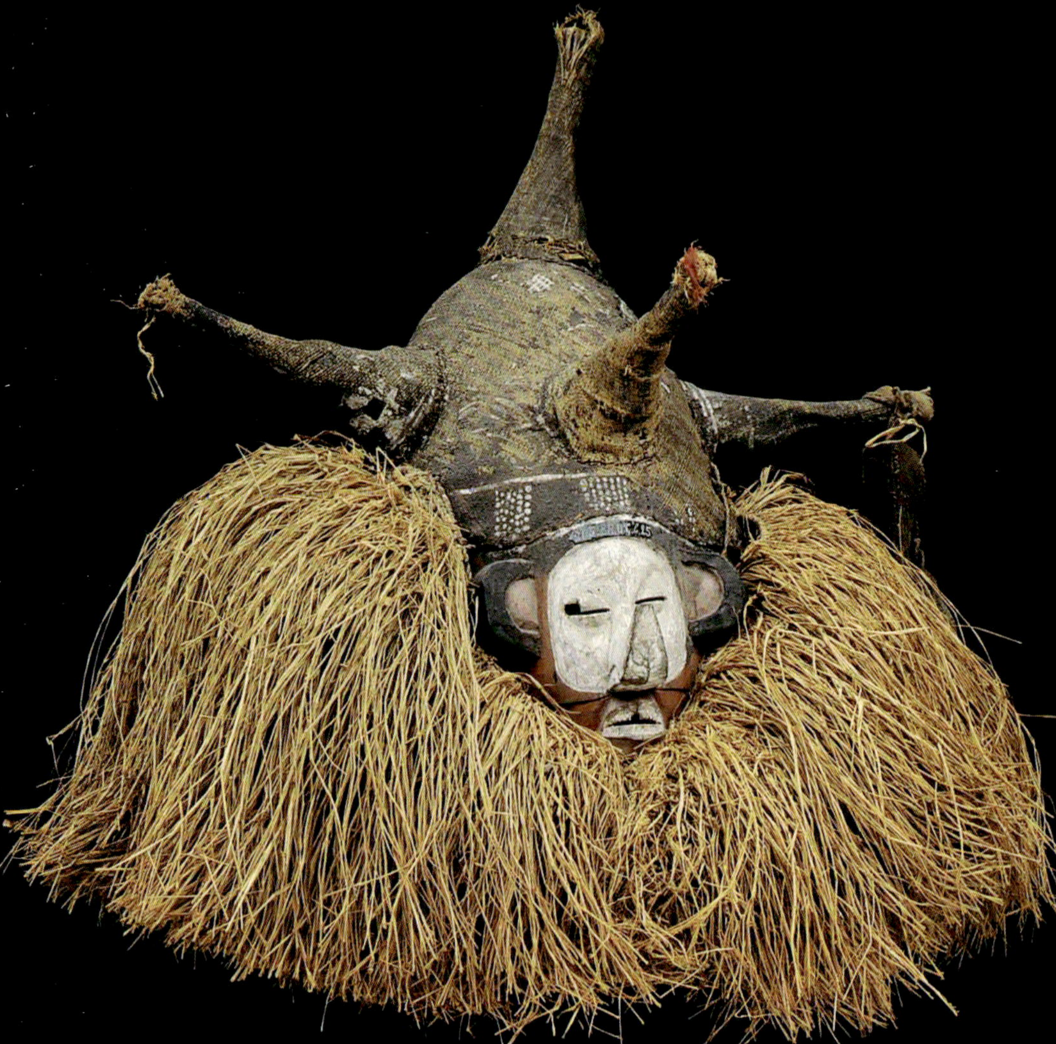

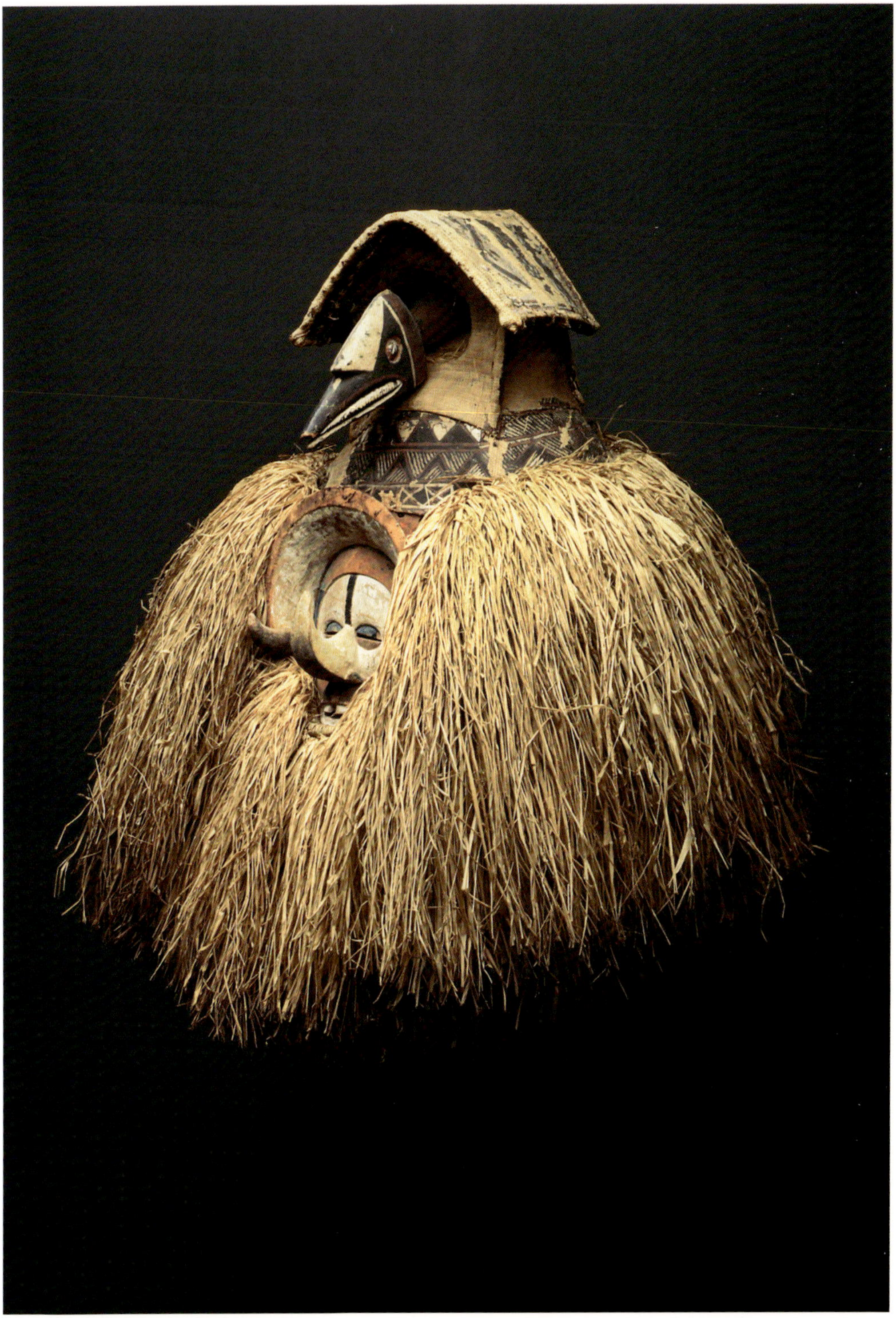

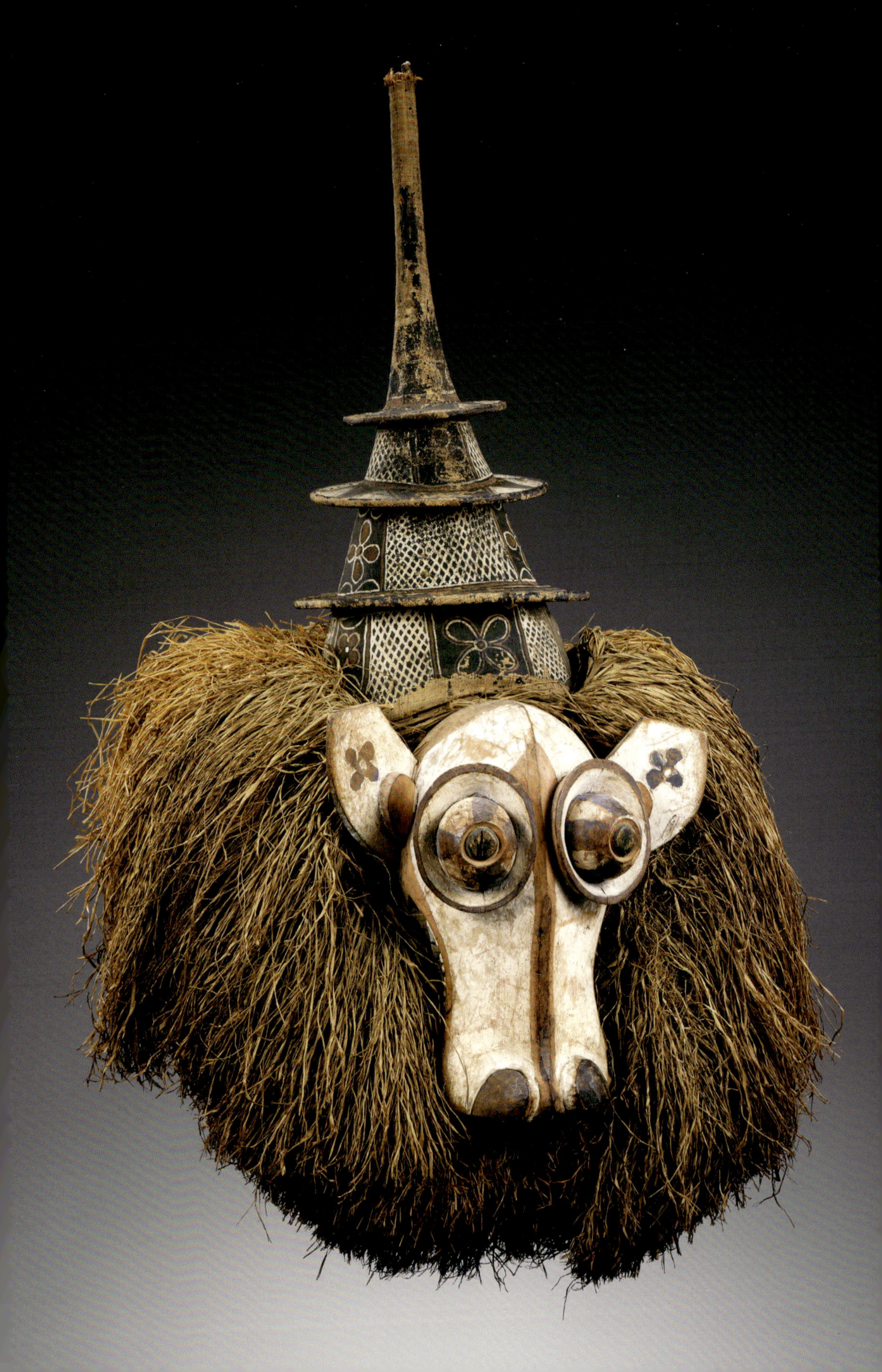

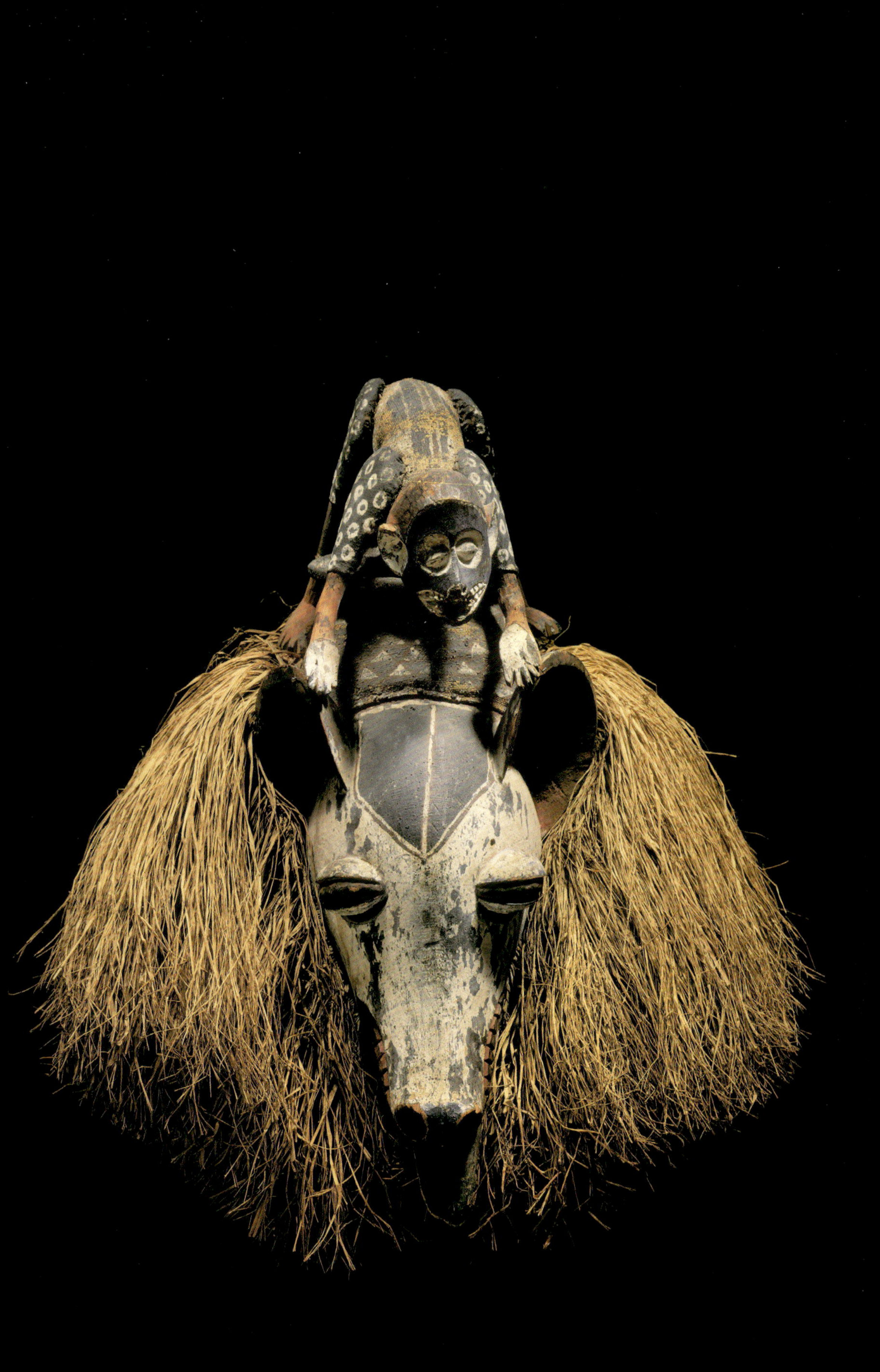

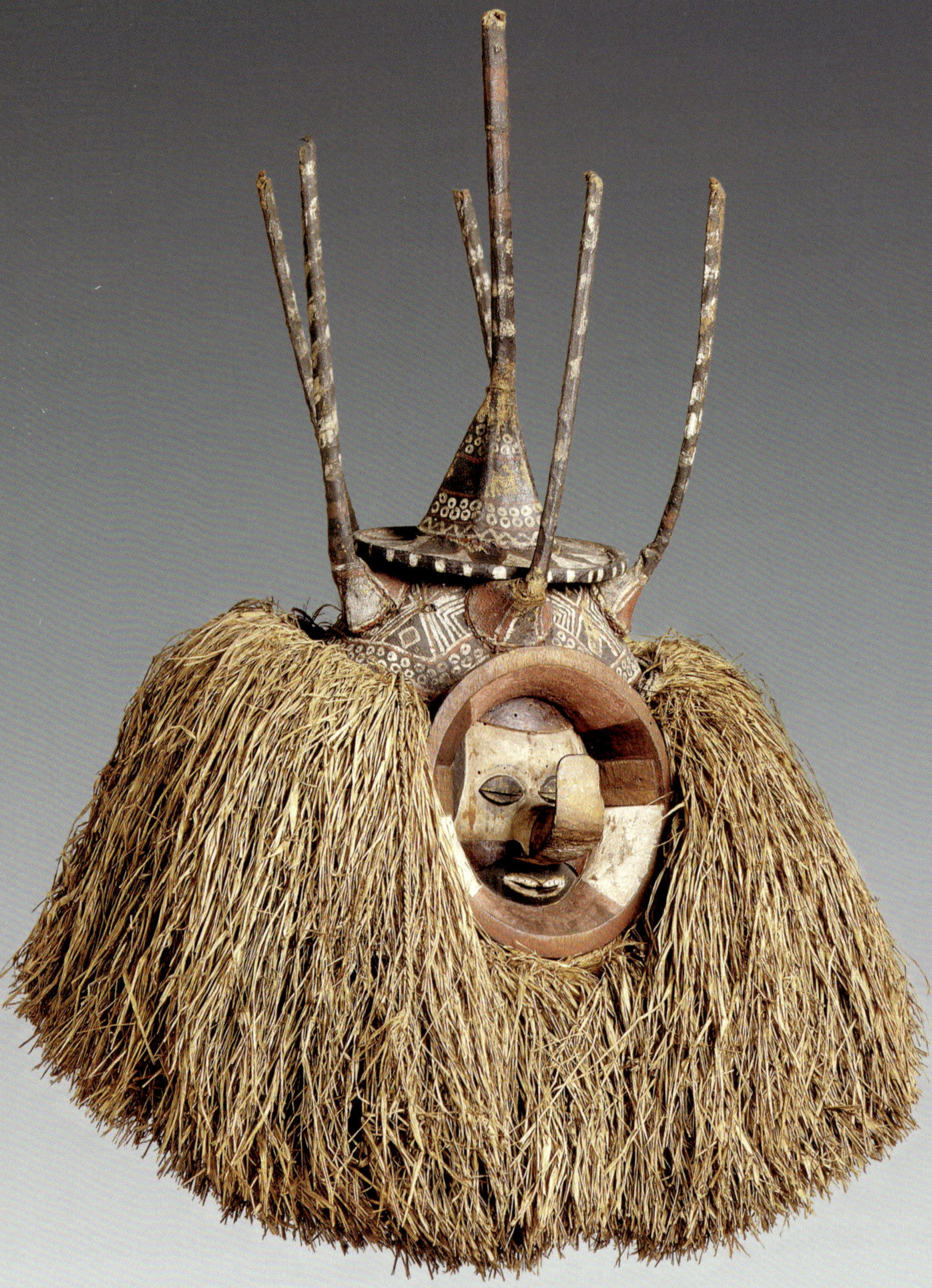

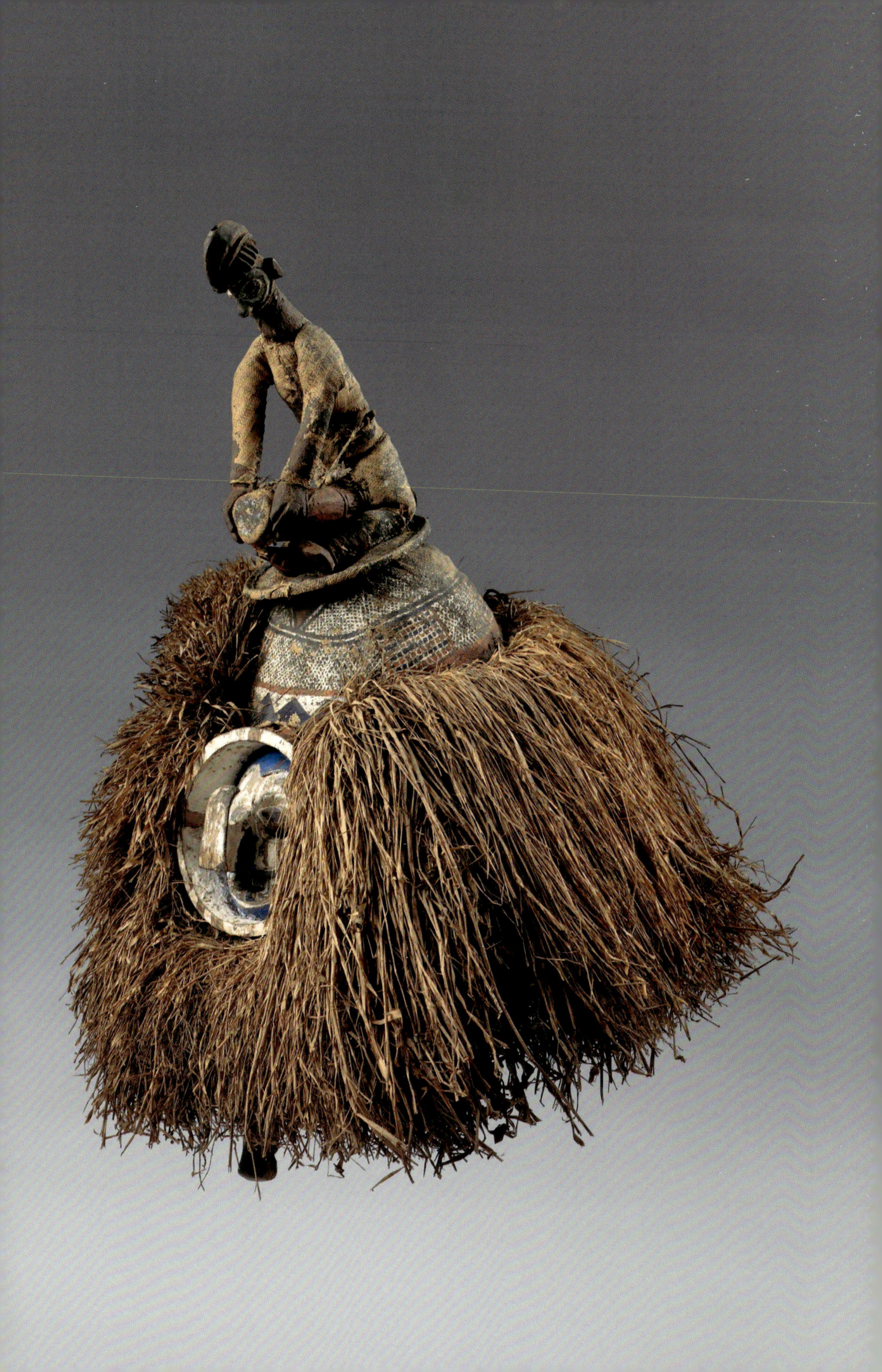

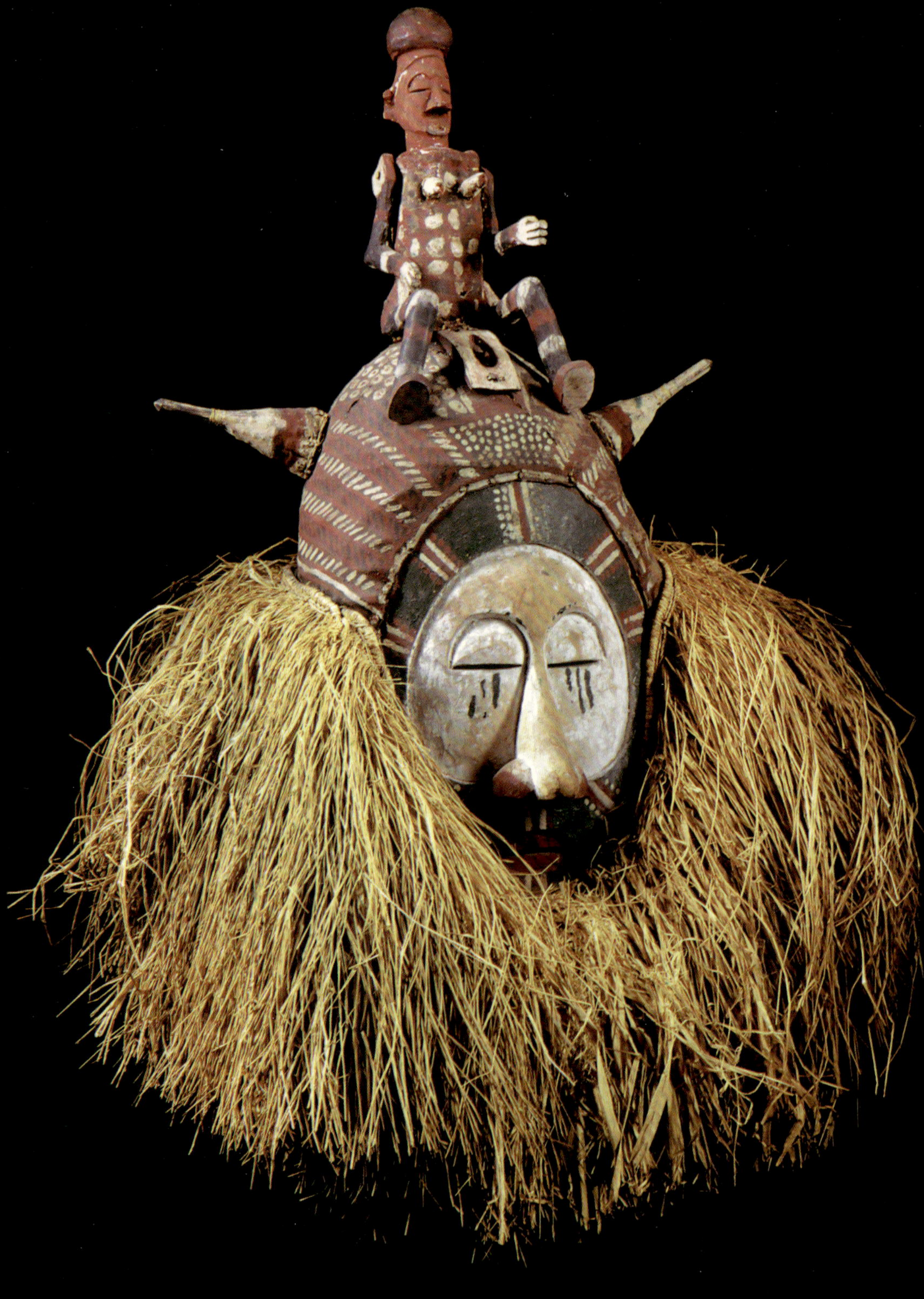

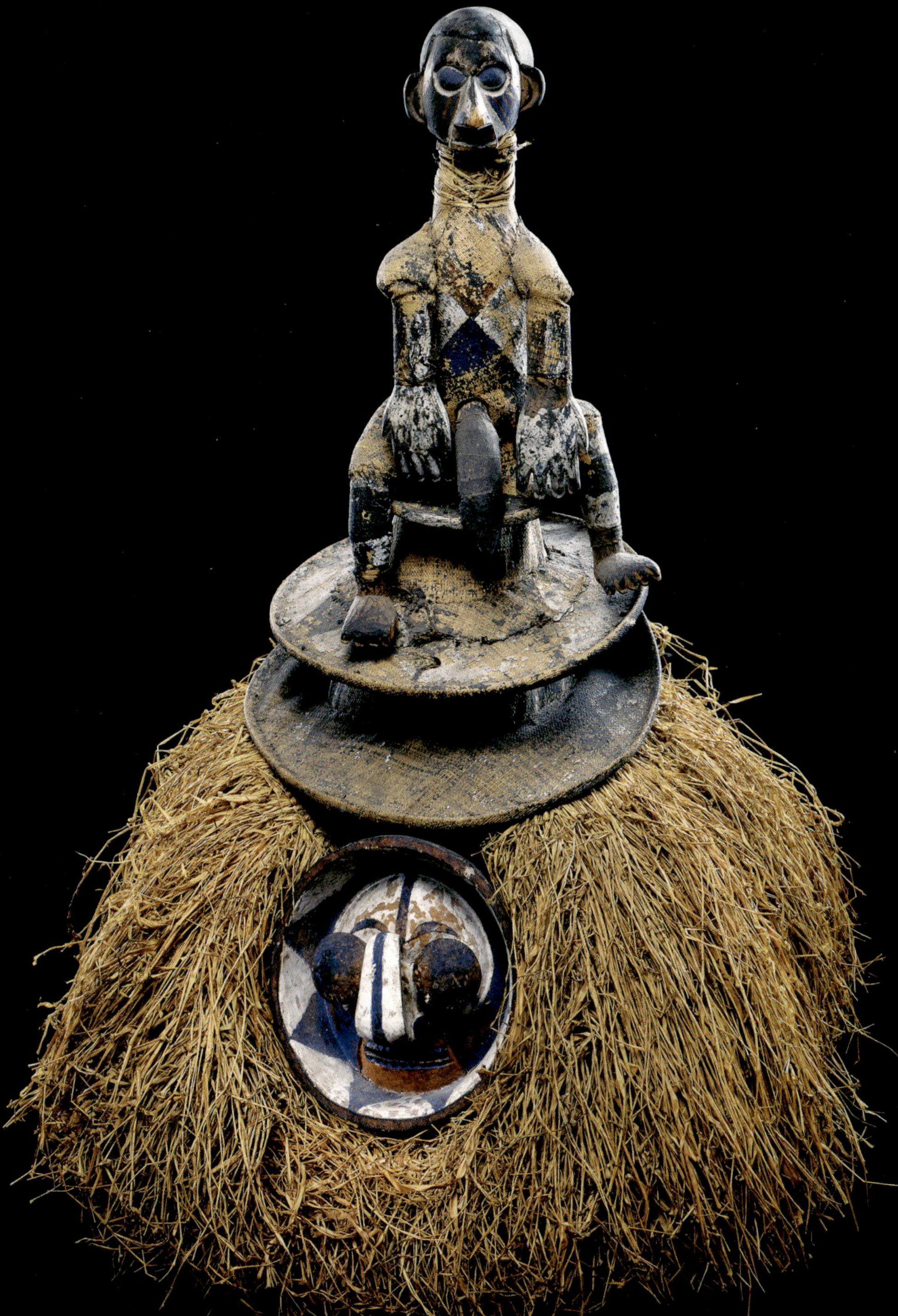

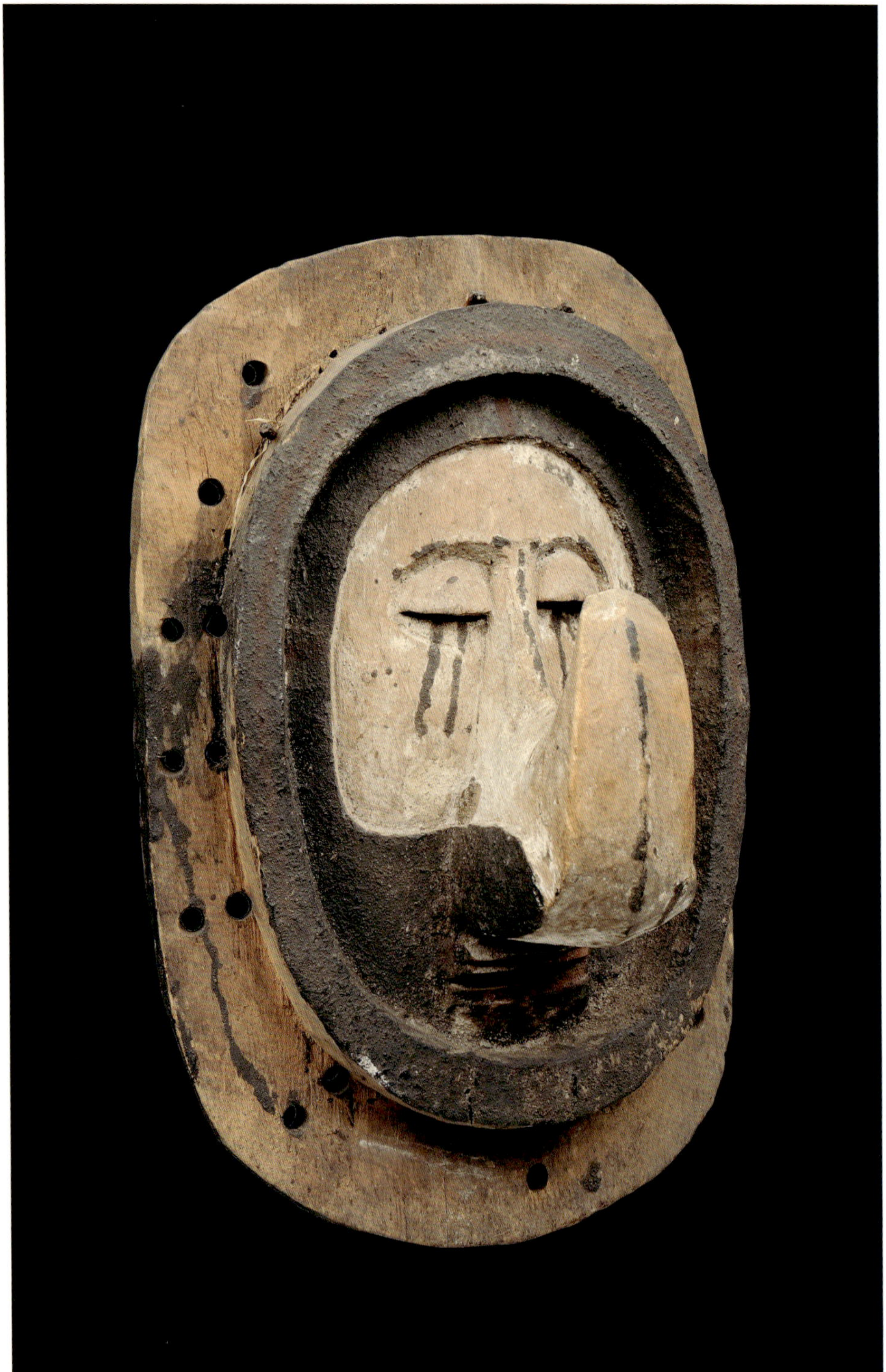

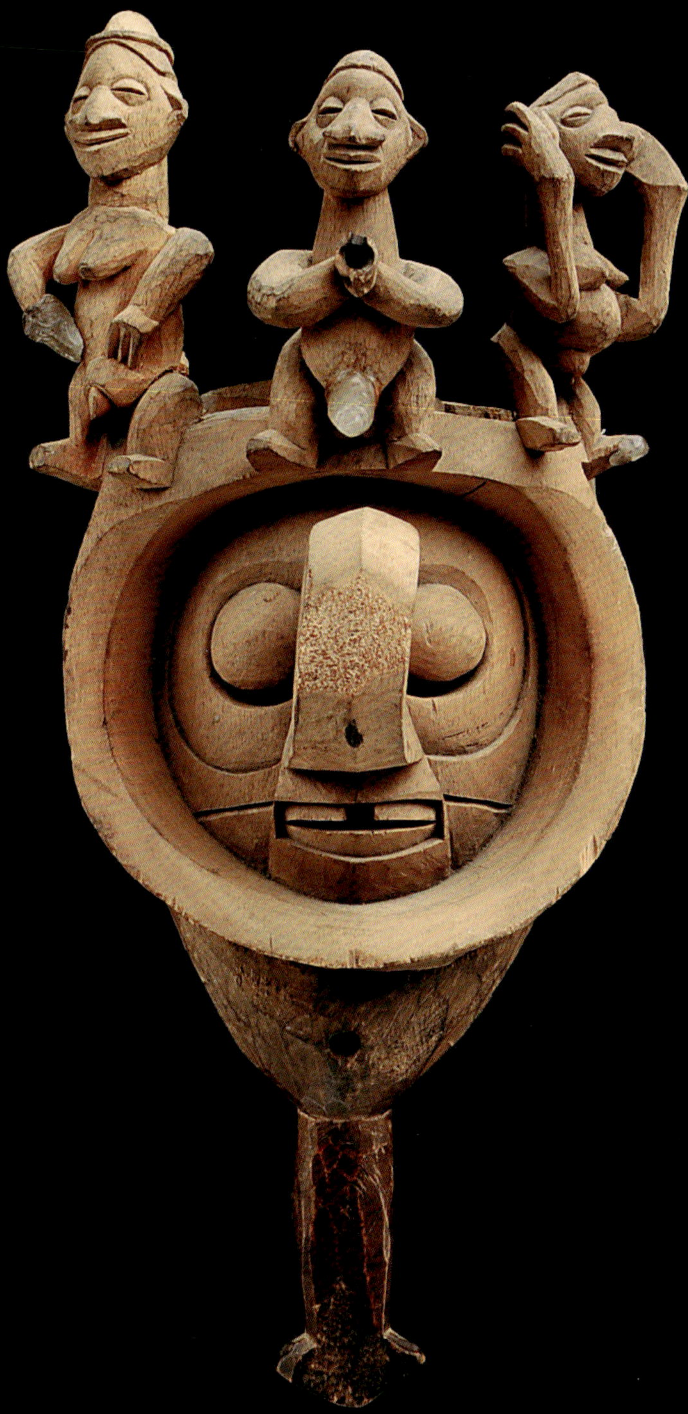

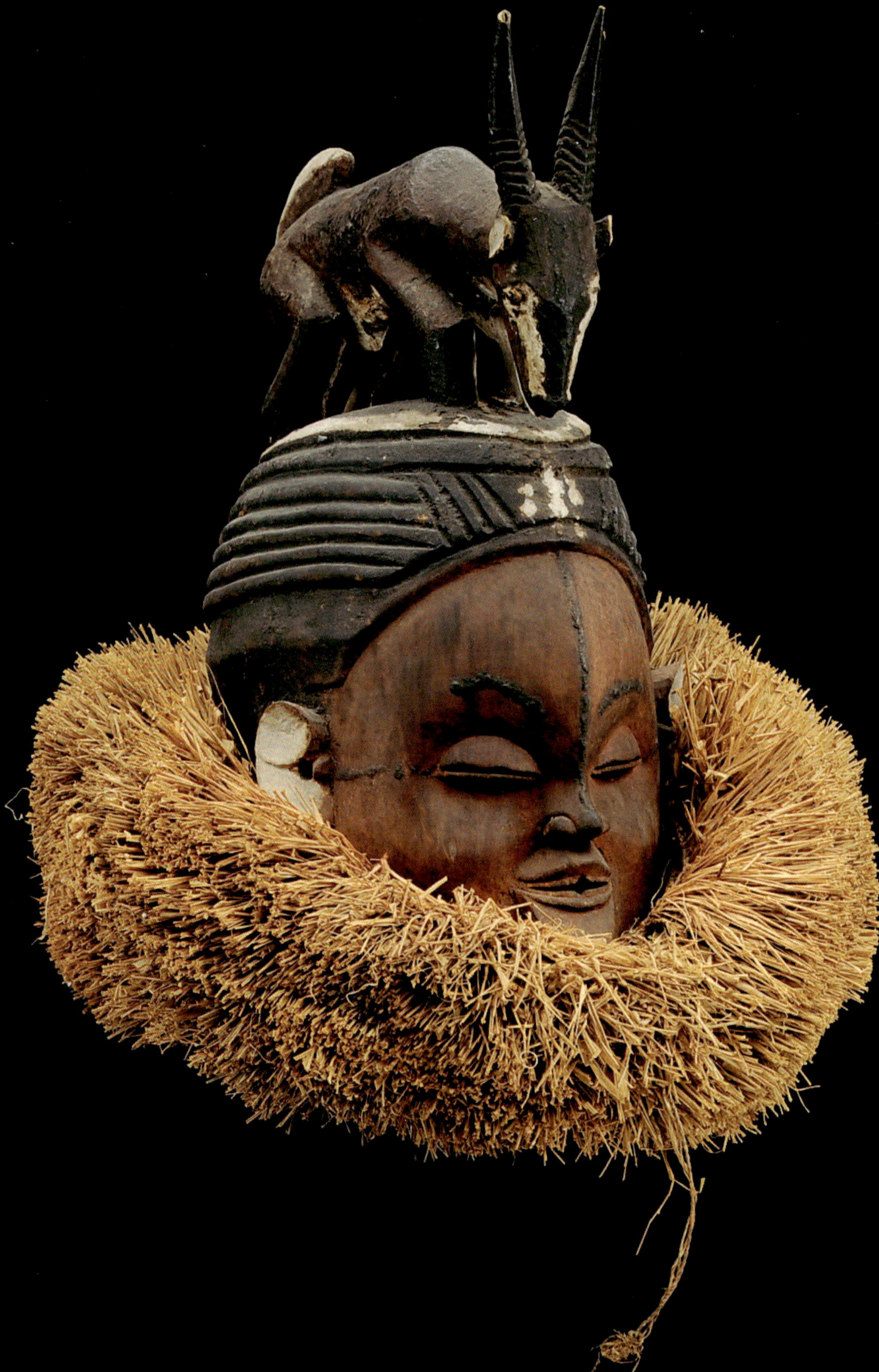

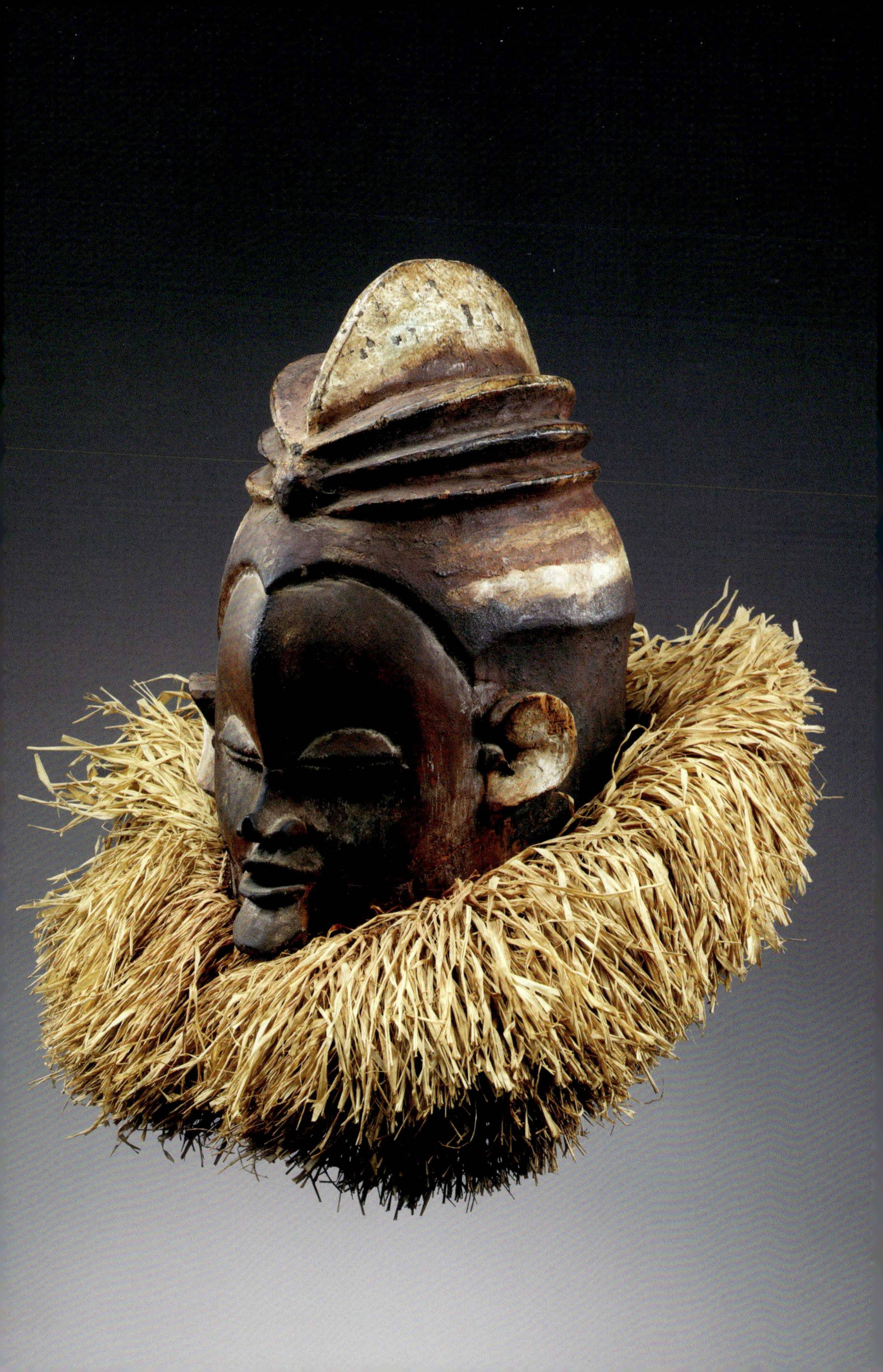

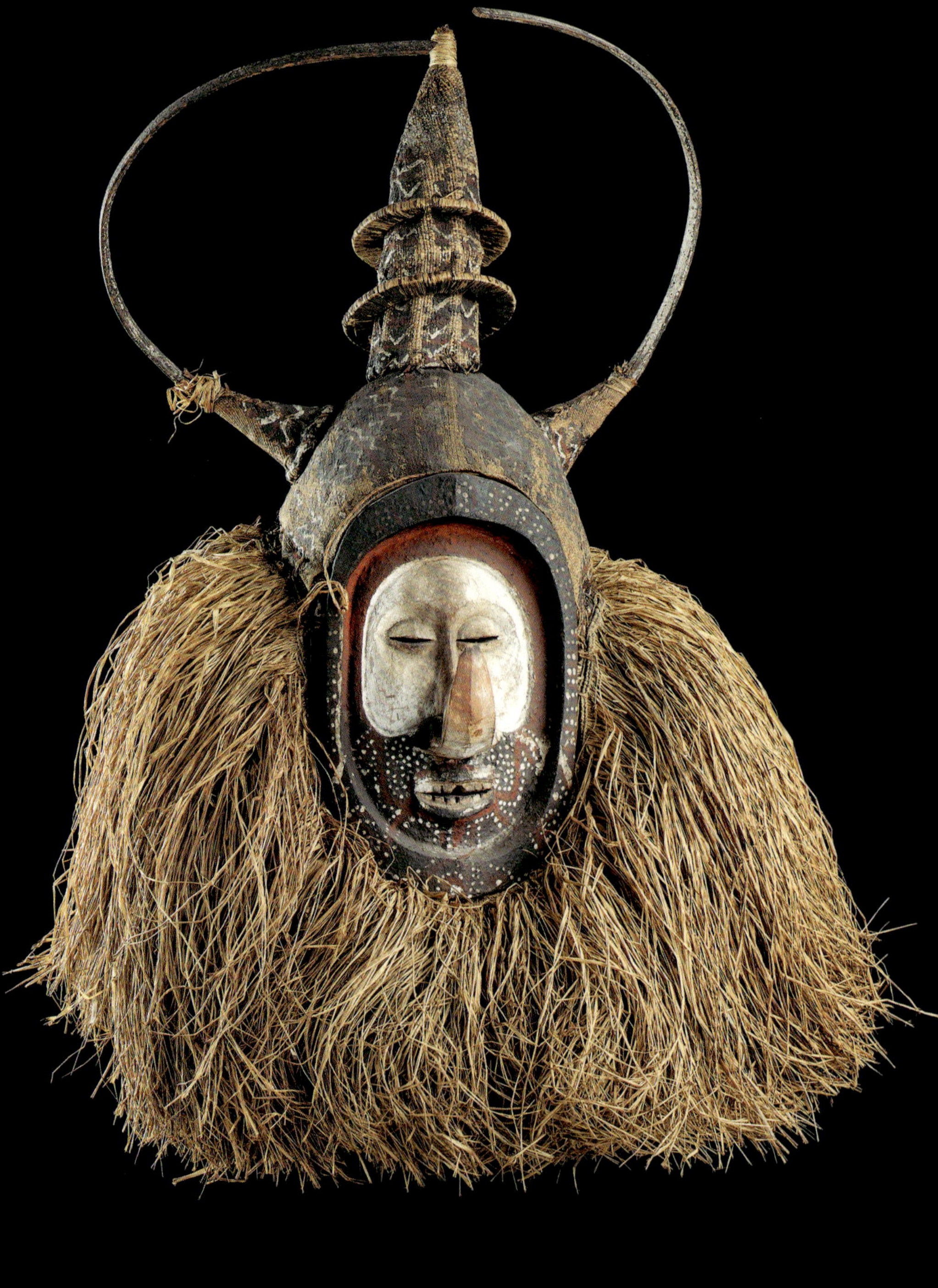

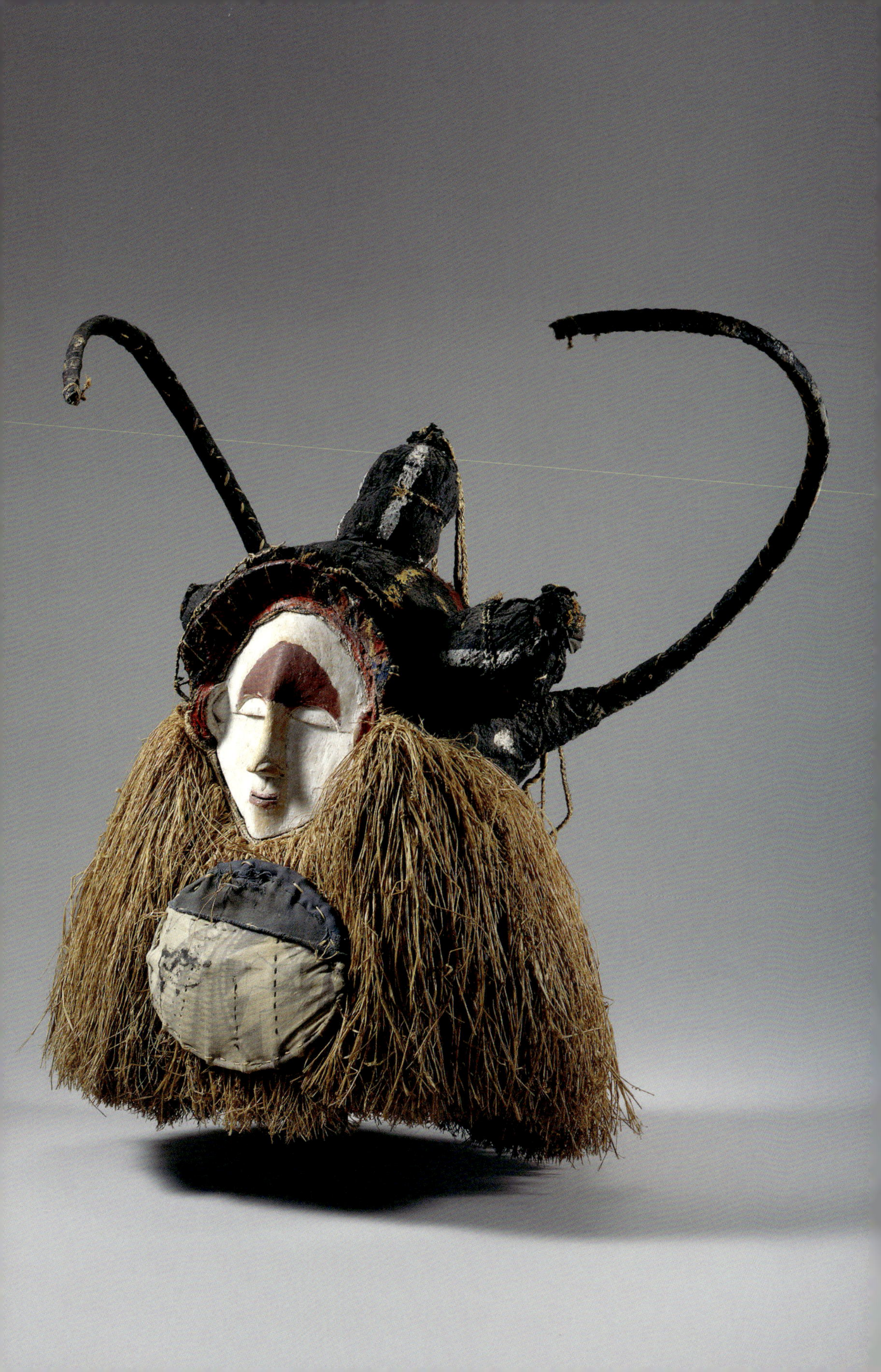

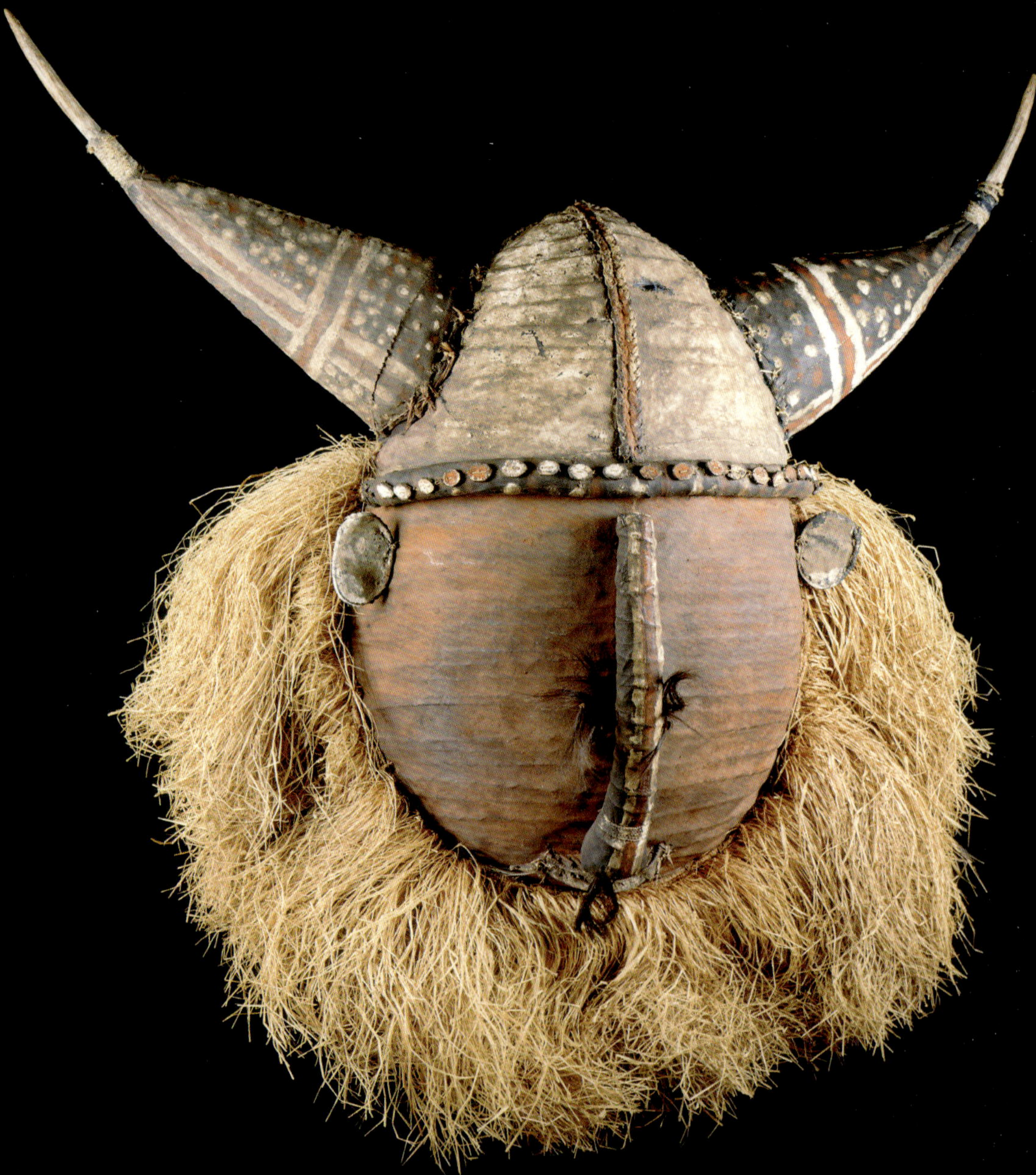

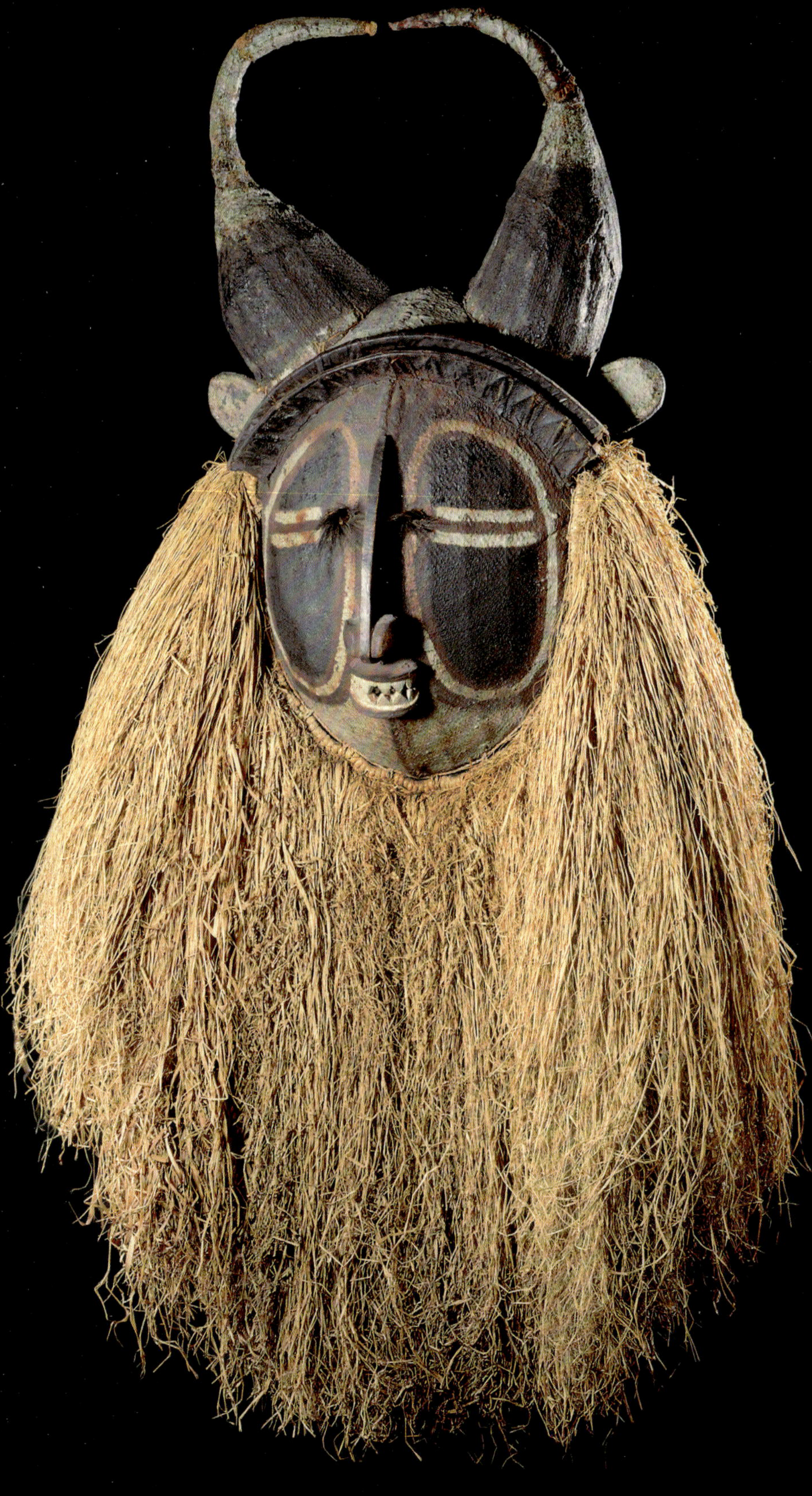

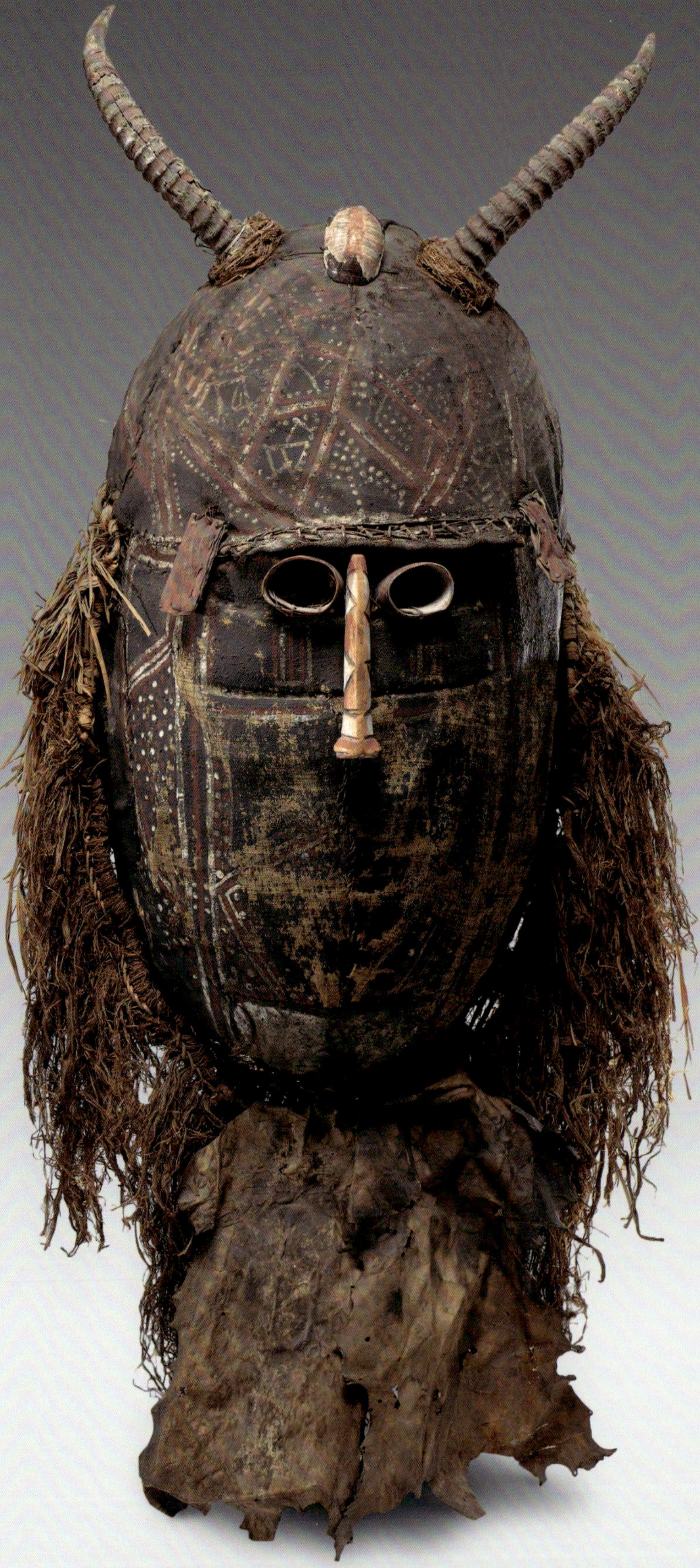

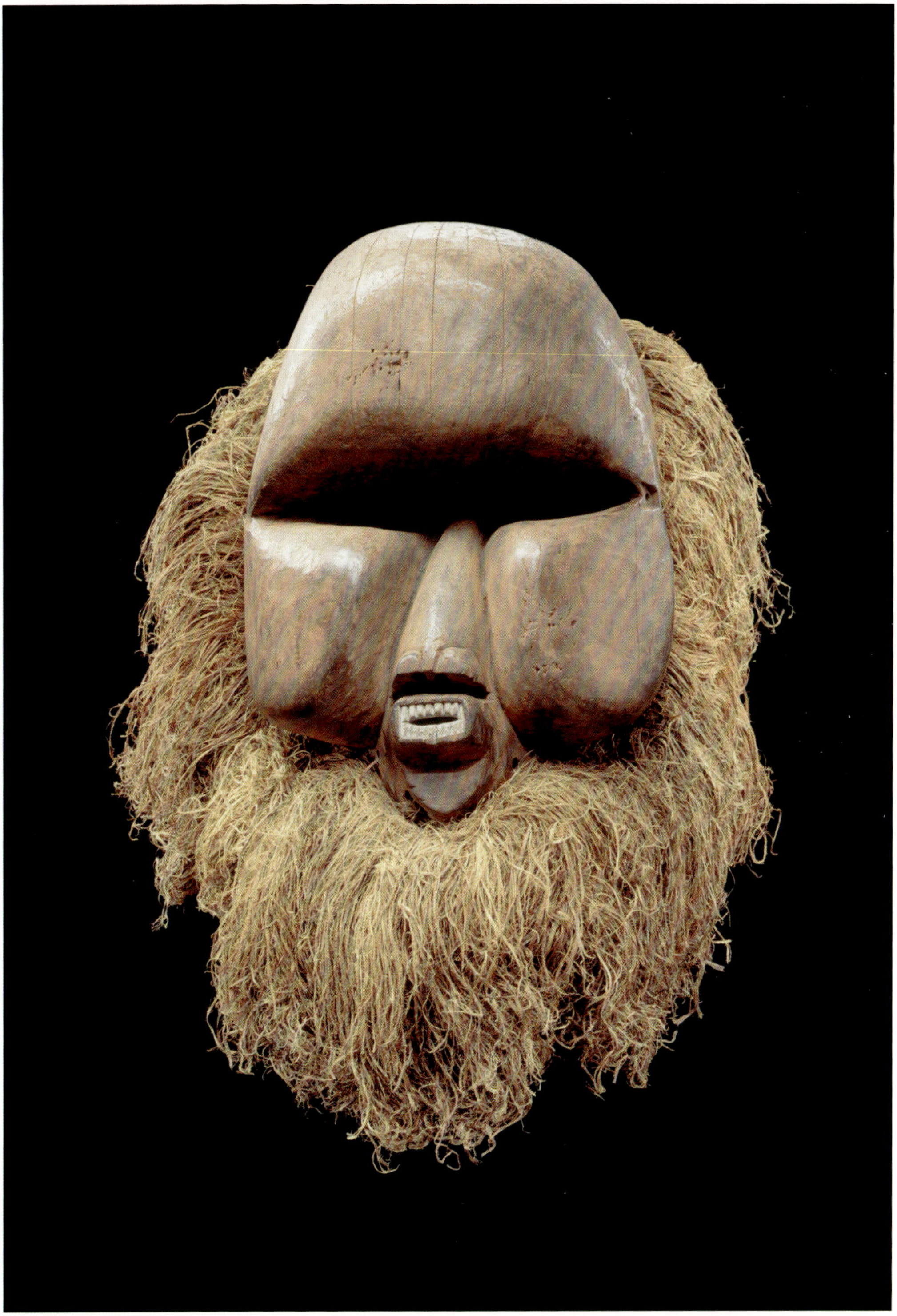

Plate Entries

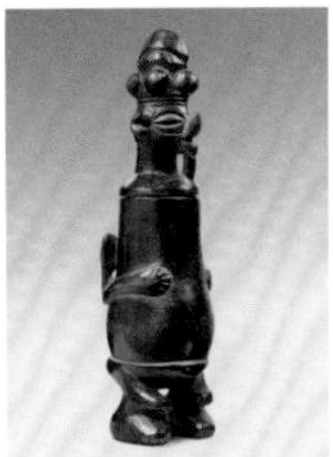

Pl. 1. Statuette container (*kumbu di mpemba*).
Wood.
H. 21.5 cm.
Max Itzikovitz Collection, Paris.

A *kumbu di mpemba* was used to contain a ball of kaolin for the installation of regional chiefs. The white clay supposedly derives from Koola, the original point of Luunda emigration and invokes the blessing of the ancestors of the chief who first occupied the land and made it productive. Moreover, at the death of a chief, the kaolin absorbs the life flow from the deceased. As regalia, it assures group unity.

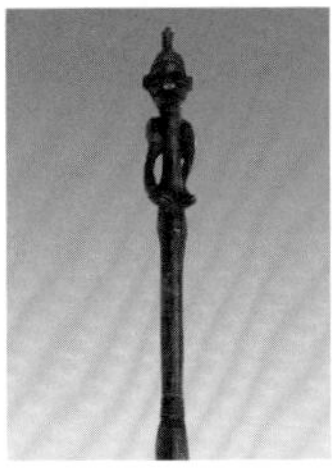

Pl. 2. Cane or staff (*yan-ti*).
Wood.
H. 128 cm.
Weltkulturen Museum, Frankfurt am Main, inv. 25389 (before 1928).

This staff presents a prognatious face, short thin arms, and a torso (shoulder-arm combination). Most likely the object collected by Frederick Van de Velde, commandant of artillery, who in 1889 led a military expedition against the Kiambvu's capital—in ref. to *Bulletin de la Société d'anthropologie* 1891–1892 v. 10, pp. 59–67, p. 64. Yaka staffs were part of chiefly regalia. Mechow collected two Yaka staffs in 1882 during his explorations (Staatliche Museen zu Berlin, Preussischer Kulturbesitz, Ethnologisches Museum, inv. IIIC1605 and IIIC1606).

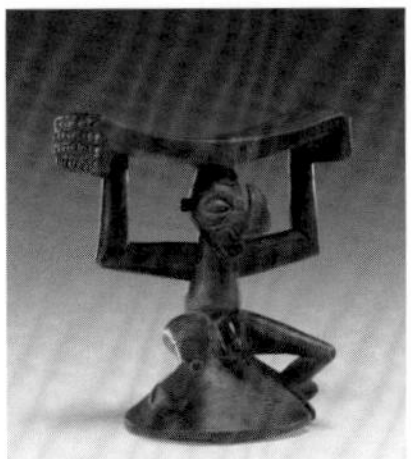

Pl. 3. Head-rest (*musaw*).
Wood, brass tacks.
H. 23 cm.
Virginia Museum of Fine Arts, Richmond. Adolph D. and Wilkins C. Williams Fund. inv. 84.81.

Collected by Hans Himmelheber in 1938, the headrest is an object of household furniture commonly used throughout Africa. The headrest was used for sleeping—placed under one ear and along the side of the chin to support one's head. Among the Yaka, headrests were used most especially by male land chiefs (*kalaamba*) and some matrilineal headmen (*lemba*) to support and protect elaborate headpieces or coiffures that worked as a charm. Generally, the headrest was kept in the bed chamber, an inner room of a pitched two-room cabin. As an item of personal property of the dignitary, they often had personal charms attached.

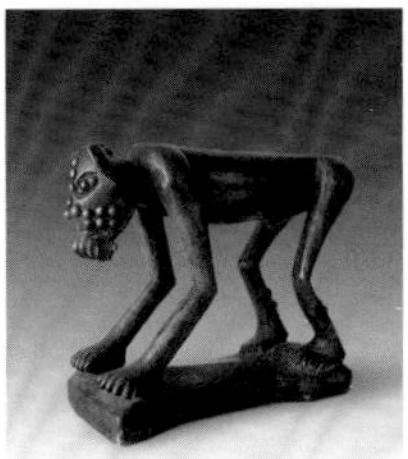

Pl. 4. Head-rest (*musaw*).
Wood, brass tacks.
H. 19.1 cm.
Private collection.

Yaka head-rest featuring a quadruped, such as a leopard, grasping an object in its mouth, the facial features accentuated with brass tacks. Yet the attenuated limbs take on almost human characteristics and suggest the capacity of a powerful individual to transform himself into the form of a predatory animal. Stylistically the head-rest would appear to derive from the central or southern Yaka.

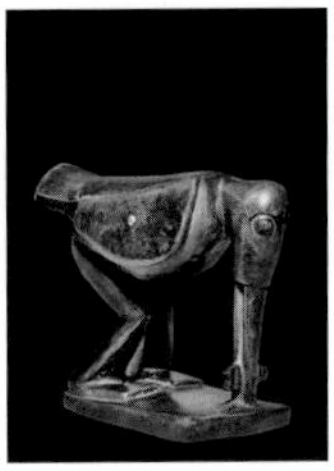

Pl. 5. Head-rest (*musaw*).
Wood.
H. 16 cm.
Felix Collection, inv. FX10 0157.

Head-rests depicting a feeding bird occasionally occur amid the more standard head-rest imagery of animals, human image, pitched roof structure, or more abstract column, or openwork "X" forms. The bird represented would appear to be a white stork of Central Africa. The black and white winged stork, known for its flight at dusk and otherwise prohibited to persons in ritual transition, refers to Venus as ruler of the night sky.

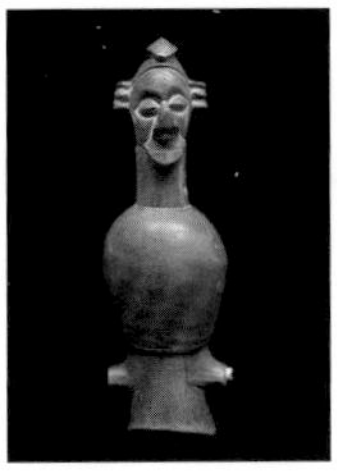

Pl. 6. Hunting whistle (*yimbila*).
Wood.
H. 13.5 cm.
Staatliche Museen zu Berlin, Preussischer Kulturbesitz, Ethnologisches Museum, inv. IIIC 19552.

Hunting whistles are used by the leader of a hunt to alert other hunters and to call his dog. A side extension is used to modulate the tone. The associated image protects the hunter from harm and brings luck to the venture. Whistles are particularly used at the height of the dry season for a grand collective hunt, driving the game into an enclosure of long nets often using a wall of fire. Collected by Leo Frobenius, this whistle presents a human head at the base although prominently displayed and worn as a pendant.

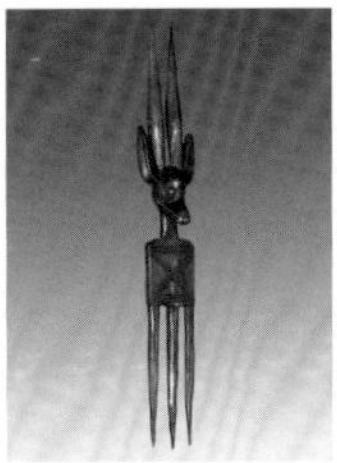

Pl. 7. Comb/hair pin (*yisanuna*).
Wood.
H. 23 cm.
MAS | Museum aan de Stroom, Antwerp, gift of Margriet Olbrechts-Maurissens, inv. AE.1975.0031.0020.

The comb presents the patron of male initiation and hero of innumerable folktales, the duiker *tsetsi*, although the animal remains a game animal whose taking heralds good fortune. In the *tsetsi* tales, the affinity between opposites (friendship and enmity, contract and violation, truthfulness and trickery) is presented and resolved with the trickster escaping and the situation returns to the way things were or ought to be.

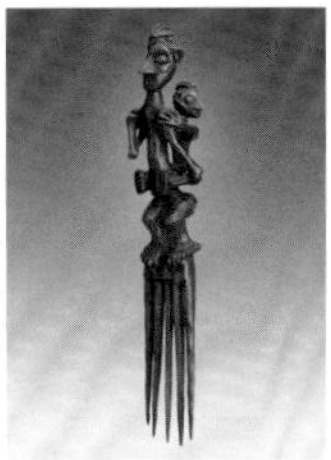

Pl. 8. Comb/hair pin (*yisanuna*).
Wood.
H. 20 cm.
Charles B. Benenson, B.A. 1933, collection. Yale University Art Gallery, New Haven, Connecticut, inv. 2006.51.78.

Yaka comb/hair pins were worn by dignitaries. The woman-carrying-child motif on this comb attests to the customary awe and preferential status of motherhood among the Yaka and serves as a metaphor for human fertility and continuity within a family or community. Given the importance of ancestors, such figures link the past and present in the hope of a propitious future.

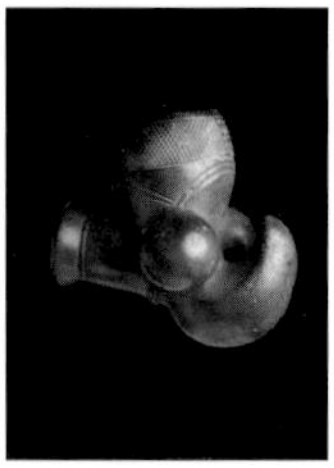

Pl. 9. Pipe bowl (*kiindzu*).
Terracotta, metal.
H. 6.6 cm.
Musée Barbier-Mueller, Geneva, inv. 1026-122 (1982).
A Yaka pipe bowl made of terracotta in the form of a highly stylized face with upturned nose and short clay stem. The ceramic bowl is carefully incised with expressive globular eyes and upturned nose rendered beneath.

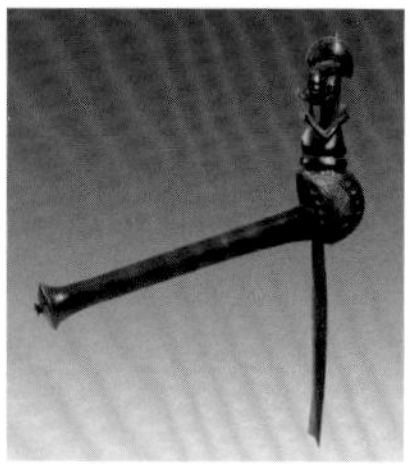

Pl. 10. Adze (*khaandu*).
Wood, metal tacks.
H. 30 cm.
Private collection.
The Yaka adze is insignia of a matrilineage headman (*leemba)* that is carried over the left shoulder when visiting lineage members. It can equally be part of the regalia of a regional chief and *ngaanga ngoombu* diviner. Less decorated examples serve as a basic tool of a sculptor. Here the mouth of the figure is shown as a line on an atrophied beard and a hole in the stomach likely held charm substances.

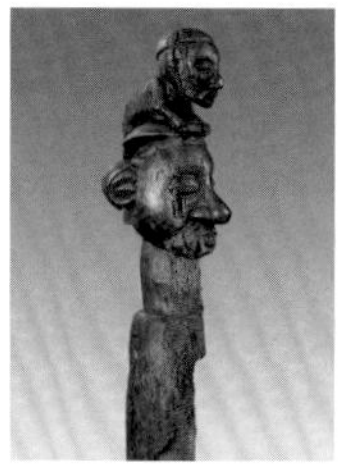

Pl. 11. Slitdrum fragment (*nkoku ngoombu*).
Wood.
H. 42.5 cm.
Royal Museum for Central Africa, Tervuren, inv. MO.0.0.32 887.
Slitdrum fragment with head on the handle surmounted by a reclining human image wearing a skullcap. The reclined position and hand gesture of the figure may allude to the digging habits of the otter shrew that are re-enacted during the diviner's initiation. The closed eyes of the main image suggest the interior or extra-vision attributed to those in authority but specifically the *ngoombu* diviner who "dreams" on the matter presented to him or her. This example was collected in the locale of Popokabaka.

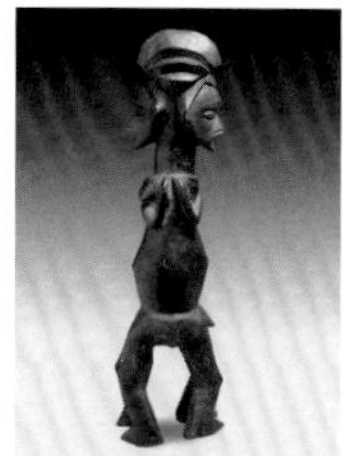

Pl. 12. Statuette (*yiteke*).
Wood.
H. 56.5 cm.
Private collection, Belgium.
Double or back-to-back figure of a variety associated with the *Khosi* charm institution, they are the largest variety of freestanding sculpture throughout the region, averaging from 30 to 76 centimeters in height. Often they are vertically divided with red on one side and white on the other while the body is decorated with red and white dots. However, as objects of power, the Yaka regard the ingredients, verbal formulae, and rituals associated with the object as activating the figure rather than any indwelling spirit.

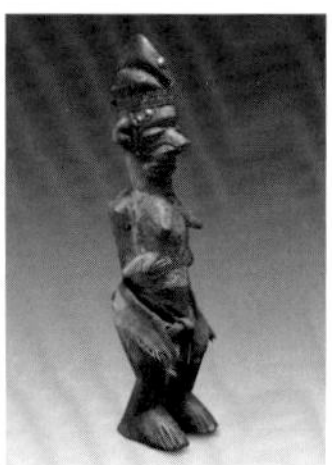

Pl. 13. Statuette (*yiteke*).
Wood, metal.
H. 26 cm.
Staatliche Museen zu Berlin, Preussischer Kulturbesit, Ethnologische Museum (SMPK), Berlin, inv. IIIC 3437.
Yaka female figure, like the male figure above, originated within a given lineage when some variety of transgression entered lineage blood as a whole, and one of the lineage members is "seized." The particular charm-curse is revealed by the diviner (*ngaanga ngoombu*) and its effect ritually contained and its rules observed. Acquired from the early Kwango explorer R. Büttner, 1886. Buttner had visited the Kiambvu at Kasongo Lunda in 1885. Object is wrongly cataloged "Mfumungu or Boma, Kongo."

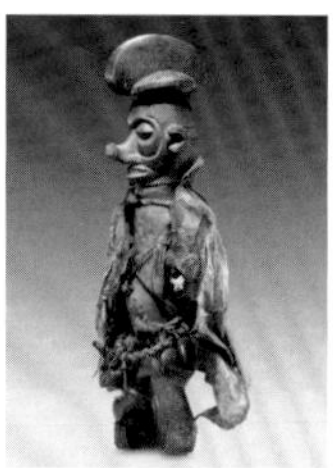

Pl. 14. Statuette (*yiteke*).
Wood, cord, beads, pods, nails, wire, and seeds.
H. 41.5 cm.
Staatliche Museen zu Berlin, Preußischer Kulturbesitz, Ethnologisches Museum, Berlin, inv. IIIC 32159.
A Yaka male figure that is used as a lineage charm to contain and control evil influences of a hereditary curse but also to protect property and inflict injury on witches. Carving of the headgear and mouth of this statuette is distinctive of early Yaka combs, masks, and statuettes collected between 1894 and 1901. The hide wrap and attached objects present an accumulative sensibility found within the Kwango region but equally served a defensive and offensive function. Collected by Pruwert in 1919.

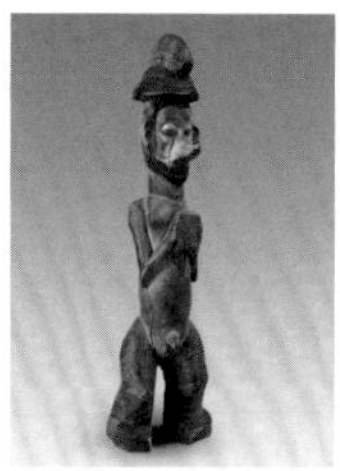

Pl. 15. Statuette (*yiteke*).
Wood.
H. 34 cm.
Rijksmuseum Volkenkunde, Leiden, inv. 1370-33 (1902).
Yaka male figure with arms and hands joined at the chest. As with the previous two examples, this gesture begins to dominate the figure. While the gesture of hands to chin or mouth commonly signifies reflection, sadness, and grief, the gesture of hands-together-at-the-upper chest pertains to a person confessing guilt or swearing secrecy but is also similar to the Yaka custom of a corpse prepared for burial.

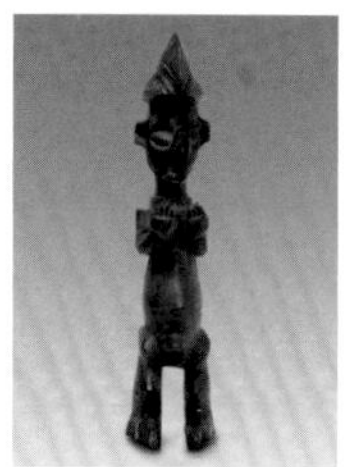

Pl. 16. Statuette (*yiteke*).
Wood.
H. 29 cm.
Agnes Etherington Art Centre, Queen's University, Kingston, Canada, gift of Justin and Elisabeth Lang, 1984, inv. M84-348.
Yaka male figure with a side aperture for insertion of charm concoctions and thighs presented in a near-seated posture. As in the previous example, the head and neck unit appear more like a cork inserted in a wine-bottle body. Curving arms arise from behind the upper torso. All sculpture used in this context appears to represent elders in their role of mediating misfortune, sickness, and death, past or present.

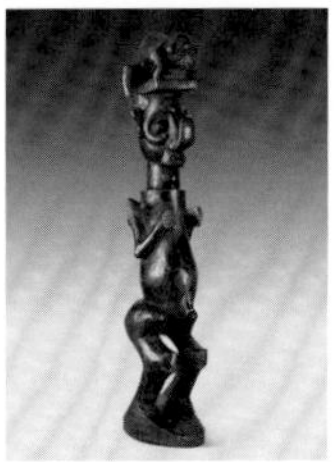

Pl. 17. Statuette (*yiteke*).
Wood.
H. 33 cm.
Private collection.
This Yaka male figure is exceptional for its clarity of expression and fine attention to detail throughout the statuette. Surmounted by a humanized animal form above the head, the upturned nose and body treatment present one of the finest carvings found among the Yaka. Like the previous examples of statuettes, it is northern Yaka in style and likely derives from the Popokabaka locale at the time of first contact with explorers in the Independent State. It was probably commissioned by an important regional chief, in conjunction with a *ngaanga* ritual specialist, who employed only the best of sculptors.

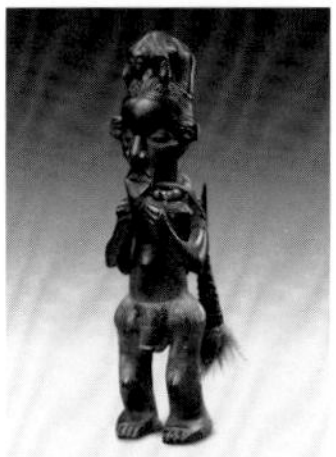

Pl. 18. Statuette (*yiteke*).
Wood, horn, cloth, beads.
H. 30.7 cm.
Private collection.
This finely carved Yaka male figure presents a quadruped animal surmounting the head while both hands touch the chin. Pod beads decorate the neck together with a suspended animal horn container bearing special medicines. The differing coloration of the lower torso indicates that the figure once wore a wrap and therefore clothed. This is generally the case with larger-sized images.

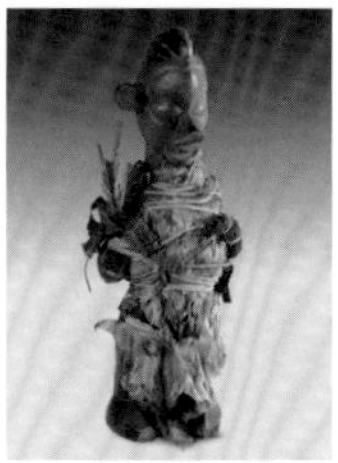

Pl. 19. Statuette (*yiteke*).
Wood, feathers.
H. 28.5 cm.
Ethnographic Museum, Zagreb, inv. 1/337. D. Lerman Collection (before 1894).
Among the earliest Yaka statuettes collected, this lineage charm comes from the collection of Dragutin Lerman, who served the Congo Independent State as a District-Commissioner and Capitaine-Commandant between 1882–1896. He was in charge of Popokabaka during his tenure in office. The abraded nose appears to have been intentional in it use. The fur covering and lateral medicine packets affirm its potency.

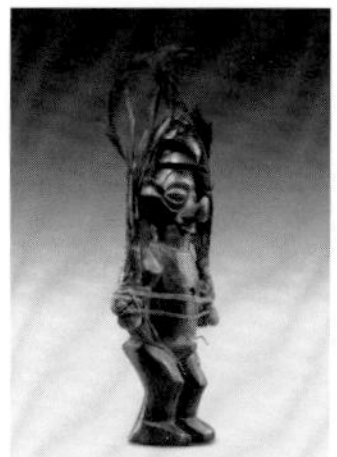

Pl. 20. Statuette (*yiteke*).
Wood, feathers, cloth.
H. 32.5 cm.
Private collection.
Yaka male figure displaying packets and feathers attached to each arm with the face and coiffure detailed while the remainder of the figure is summarily carved. This variety, owned by a patrilineal kin group and referred to as *phuungu*, unlike lineage charms, does not involve a special initiation or communal participation although blood offerings are made at its inception and food restrictions are imposed.

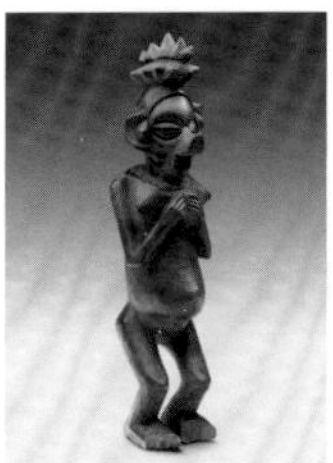

Pl. 21. Statuette (*yiteke*).
Wood.
H. 28 cm.
Peabody Museum of Archaeology and Ethnology at Harvard University, Cambridge, Massachusetts, gift of Mrs. George P. Howe. inv. PM#17-41-50/B1554.
Yaka figure with characterization of the human figure based on repetition of pointed projecting elements such as headgear, nose, breasts, pointed belly, knees, and feet demonstrate sculptural imagination. The headpiece featuring lateral projections is that of an earth chief. The fiber cord around the neck indicates that the figure was suspended from something.

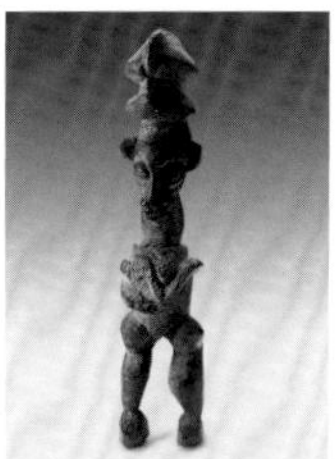

Pl. 22. Figure (*yiteke*).
Wood with encrustations.
H. 28 cm.
Iris & B. Gerald Cantor Center for Visual Arts at Stanford University, California, anonymous gift, inv. 1997.122.
Unique presentation of arms that hug the torso together with undulation of the legs and the double hat give this female figure unusual appeal. The double hat shown on the head is curious although an example of this is documented in a photograph taken of the Yaka chief at Panzi [see page 2].

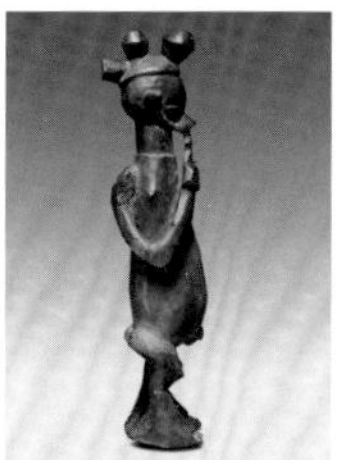

Pl. 23. Figure (*yiteke*).
Wood.
H. 61 cm.
The Cleveland Museum of Art, James Albert and Mary Gardiner Ford Memorial Fund, inv. 1970.34.
This unusual lineage charm features a male figure with three basket-like elements on the coiffure. Breast-like extended nipples are positioned to the side of the chest. From behind the figure, arms and hands curve upward to a summary chin and mouth; male genitals are placed high on the abdomen and undulating legs with expanded feet support the figure. As a lineage charm it was credited with personal attributes although no mystical "force" is involved.

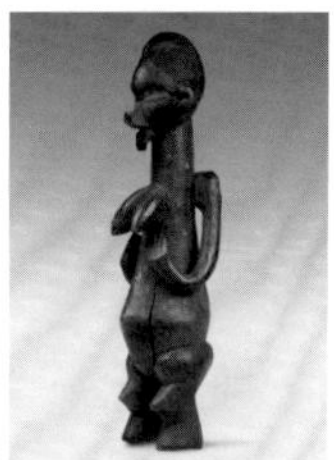

Pl. 24. Figure (*yiteke*).
Wood.
H. 49 cm.
University of Iowa Museum of Art, Iowa City, inv. X1986.425.
Although the neck-torso, shoulder-arms, and leg treatment can be found in either Yaka or Suku carving, the nose-mouth-chin combination featured here is distinctly Yaka and foreign to the known repertoire of Suku statuette variations. Attachments were undoubtedly suspended from the arms and/or a bag enclosing charm-medicines originally accompanied this figure.

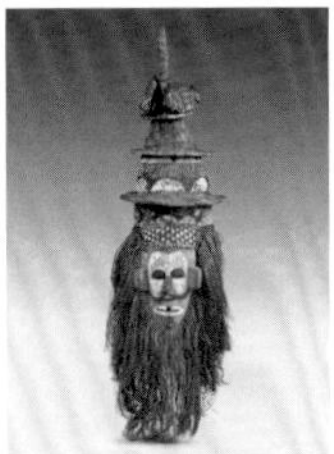

Pl. 25. Mask (*n-kisyan-khanda*).
Wood, cane, raffia fiber, pigment.
H. 70.5 cm.
MAS | Museum aan de Stroom, Antwerp, inv. AE.0516.

This northern Yaka mask features three disks on a tall cone coiffure topped by a pair of fish. Fish for the Yaka are not a prized food but are commonly collected by women and children with baskets or by damming a stream. Juxtaposition of a bright orange with a deep blue or dull red and blue presents color complements, or opposites on the color spectrum, resulting in a jarring visual effect that is further highlighted by the central white area.

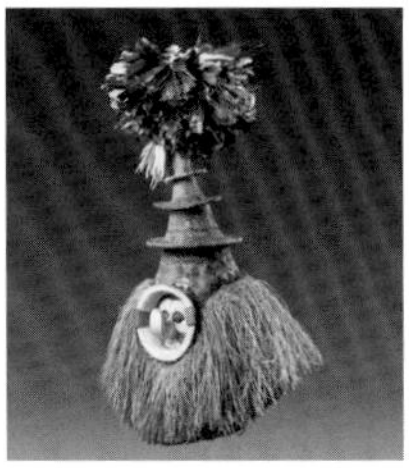

Pl. 26. Mask (*n-kisyan-khanda*).
Wood, cane, raffia fiber, pigment.
H. 80 cm.
Royal Museum for Central Africa, Tervuren, inv. EO.O.O. 1929-2 (1910).

A circular frame highlights a face with upturned nose, double-lidded eyes, and incorporates the ear extensions. The painted conical headpiece features three disks with a burst of feathers at the top while the base is surrounded by a palm leaf ruff. Such northern Yaka masks appear in pairs and are worn with a raffia-knit costume with bells or sounding nuts on their ankles. Fly whisks with goat hair tassels (*misesa*) are carried in the hands to express dance gestures.

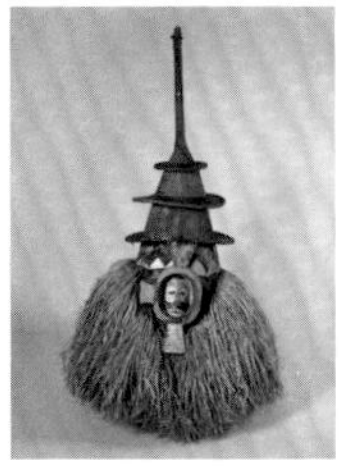

Pl. 27. Mask (*n-kisyan-khanda, kholuka*).
Wood, cane, raffia fiber, pigment.
H. 77.5 cm.
Ethnographic Museum, Zagreb, inv. 1/406, D. Lerman Collection (before 1894).

A conical northern Yaka mask with three disks, the circular frame about the face and once had four radiating projections. The facial portion of such masks, together with supporting handle, are one piece of wood carved in the shape of a paddle or scoop as viewed from within and held before the wearer's face. Perimeters of the face are often given a frame that minimally appears as a visor, more fully as a bonnet-like oval or enclose in a circle or square frame as demonstrated in this and the previous examples—in this example, the nose being ritually broken at the conclusion of *n-khanda* initiation.

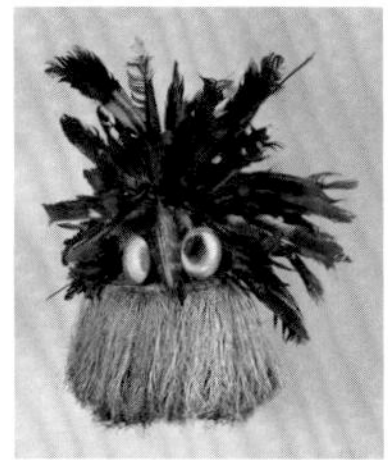

Pl. 28. Mask (*n-kisyan nkanda, mweelu*).
Fiber, calabash, and feathers.
H. 24.5 cm (without feathers or fiber).
Ethnographic Museum, Zagreb, inv. 1/405, D. Lerman Collection (before 1894).

The most widespread variety of *n-khanda* mask, *mweelu* is used to procure food supplies, and as an instrument of safe-conduct leads the initiated back to village life. In some regions it has a terrorizing aspect and is considered the "chief mask" of *n-khanda* initiation. Facial features are made of attached painted calabash or bamboo sections together with the beak of a hornbill bird added as a nose.

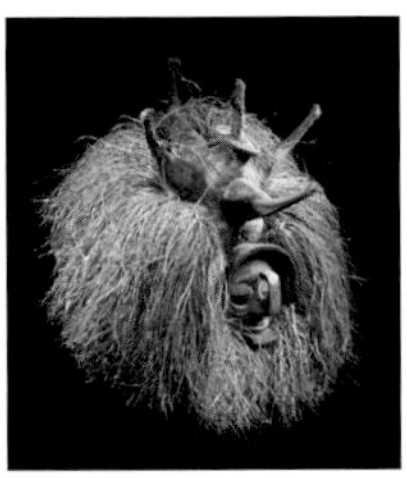

Pl. 29. Mask (*n-kisyan-khanda*).
Wood, cane, raffia fiber, pigment.
H. 52 cm.
Private collection.

Northern Yaka *N-khanda* mask featuring a bonnet-like visor about the face that is continued with a projecting beard/chin. With its single disk in the coiffure, it is likely a mask of lesser rank that appears in pairs worn by initiates representing the two distinct groups of boys within *n-khanda* initiation, those under the leadership of the guardians *mbala* and *kapita*.

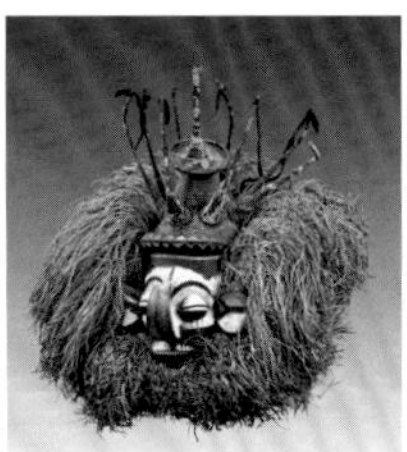

Pl. 30. Mask (*n-kisyan-khanda*).
Wood, cane, raffia fiber, pigment.
H. 47 cm (without raffia).
Private collection.

A single-disk northern Yaka mask but with multiple antennae-like extensions and exceptionally expressive eyes, ears, nose, and mouth, and painted with restrained coloration of black and white. Decoration follows the basic carved divisions treated as single color areas or follows carved ridges of eyebrows and descending nose line. Tear streaks beneath the eyes are said to symbolize the sufferings of initiation.

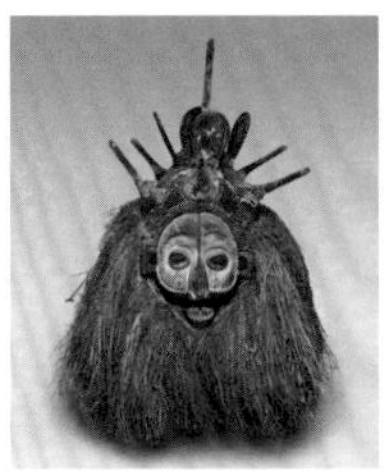

Pl. 31. Mask (*n-kisyan-khanda, ndeemba*).
Wood, cane, raffia fiber, pigment.
H. 50.8 cm.
Brooklyn Museum, New York, inv. 73.179.3

This northern Yaka mask presents a clearly demarcated extension of the hairline relief that encircles the upper portion of the face and touches the nares, giving the lower portion a darkened aspect. On top of the coiffure, made of raffia cloth painted with designs and *tsala*-like extensions, rise brim-like forms in a container-like structure that loosely enclose the central spire.

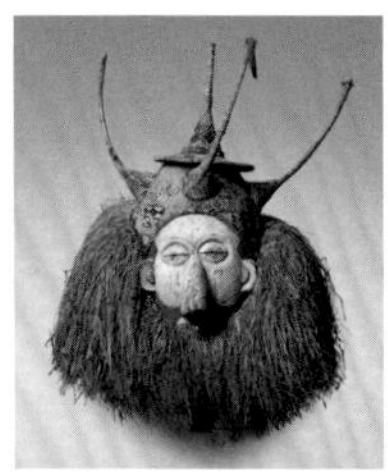

Pl. 32. Mask (*n-kisyan-khanda*).
Wood, cane, raffia fiber, pigment.
H. 47 cm.
The Cleveland Museum of Art, Ohio, gift of Katherine C. White, inv. 1969.8.

Single disk northern Yaka mask with four *tsala*-like extensions, the raffia cloth coiffure bears traces of painted cellular designs in encircling panels placed below, between, and above the coiffure projections. The surface of disks is painted with large triangular forms resulting in a star-like configuration. The differing designs are collectively referred to as *bibemba bia n-khanda*, meaning *n-khanda* designs, but they do not have individualized names. The massive facial proportions here seem to outrank the single-disk feature normally given to lesser paired masks.

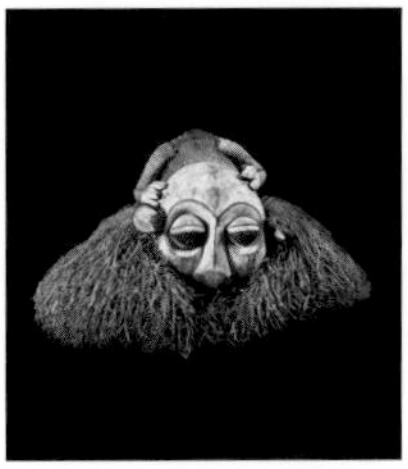

Pl. 33. Mask (*n-kisyan-khanda*).
Wood, cane, raffia fiber, pigment.
H. 45.1 cm.
The Metropolitan Museum of Art, New York, inv. 1979.206.235.
Here the surmounting image takes over the entire mask form, that of an animal with human head. Near spherical eyes dominate the face. The allusion here may be to the powers of those in authority to possibly transform themselves at night into an animal, such as a leopard, in order to stalk and kill one's enemies.

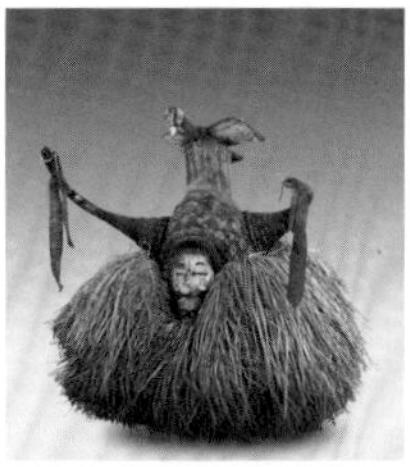

Pl. 34. Mask (*n-kisyan-khanda*).
Wood, cane, raffia fiber, pigment.
H. 37.5 cm.
Rijksmuseum Volkenkunde, Leiden, inv. 1290-2 (1901).
This northern Yaka mask presents two broad *tsala* or horns in the coiffure surmounted by a bird on a cylindrical form. If it is a nest, this alludes to raising a family but if it is a beaker the reference is to either palmwine drinking or a measuring container used in the latex trade.

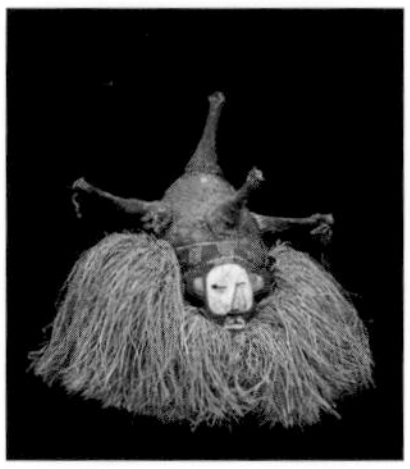

Pl. 35. Mask (*n-kisyan-khanda*).
Wood, cane, raffia fiber, pigment.
H. 56 cm.
Royal Museum for Central Africa, Tervuren, inv. 205 11/1 (1903).
Northern Yaka mask with distinctly fine facial features collected by Commandant Alphonse Cabra, of the Congo Independent State between 1889 and 1897, and presented to MRAC Tervuren in 1903. In 1901–1902 Cabra set the boarder between the Independent State and Angola. The inner portion of the face in *n-khanda* masks is consistently painted white to "make the mask more visible" while the surrounding areas are painted red or blue or gray-black.

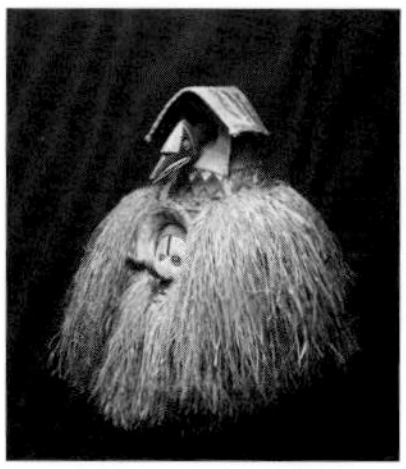

Pl. 36. Mask (*n-kisyan-khanda*).
Wood, cane, raffia fiber, pigment.
H. 45.7 cm.
The Art Institute of Chicago, gift of Neal Ball, inv. 2009.118.
Northern Yaka mask presenting a domestic dwelling with a bird's head and neck bobbing from a doorway. Dwellings placed on *n-khanda kholuka* masks generally refer to marital conjugation. A single and long awaited *kholuka* mask completes the dance exhibition both in the sponsoring home village and at dance tour performances and is associated with an unusually extroverted performer. The surmounting image partakes of major motifs introduced by dance leaders and sung in chorus by bystanders or dancing crowd.

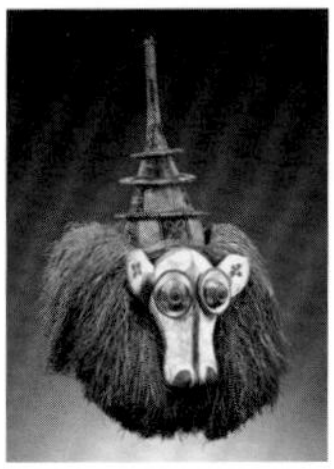

Pl. 37. Mask (*n-kisyan-khanda*).
Wood, cane, raffia fiber, pigment.
H. 68 cm.
Private collection.
This ranking northern Yaka initiation mask with three disks on a conical coiffure presents an expressively rendered face of a young buffalo with spectacular eyes. Generally, such imagery signifies animal attributes that parallel the behavior of humans and may refer to the perplexity of newly initiated youth.

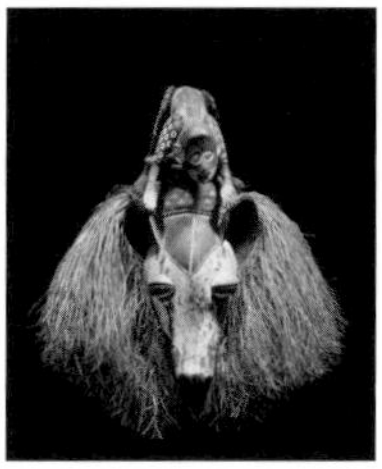

Pl. 38. Mask (*n-kisyan-khanda*).
Wood, cane, raffia fiber, pigment.
H. 55 cm.
Museum Rietberg, Zürich, gift of Baron Eduard von der Heydt, inv. RAF 503.
This northern Yaka mask displays a creature, possibly a duiker or monkey, on the back and holding on to the ears of an antelope. The subject suggests a folktale narrative. The particular representation remains ambiguous as individual animal markings are suppressed to emphasize overall decorative effects. The original context of sung verses and refrains or interviewing the sculptor is often the only clue.

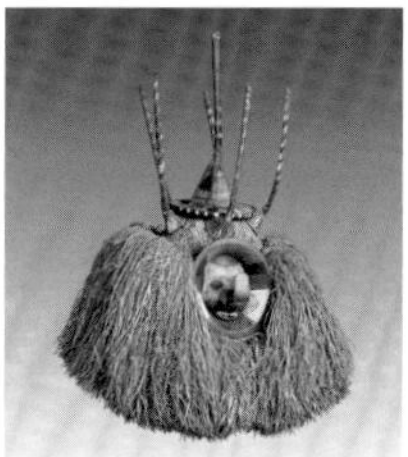

Pl. 39. Mask (*n-kisyan-khanda, kholuka*).
Wood, cane, raffia fiber, pigment.
H. 60.5 cm.
MAS | Museum aan de Stroom, Antwerp, inv. AE 0515.
Northern Yaka *n-khanda* mask featuring a single disk and four antennae-like extensions to the painted coiffure that once had strips of cloth connecting them and a bust of feathers on the central spire. The antennae-like projections (*mizanga*) as well as cone-like coiffures derive from traditional constructions worn by Yaka notables called *tsala*. *Tsala* are made of thin wooden strips rising from a circular frame in the shape of a cone whose summit is adorned with feathers. The *n-khanda* headmaster (*khyudi*) often wears a *tsala* at the crown of the head for the closing festivities.

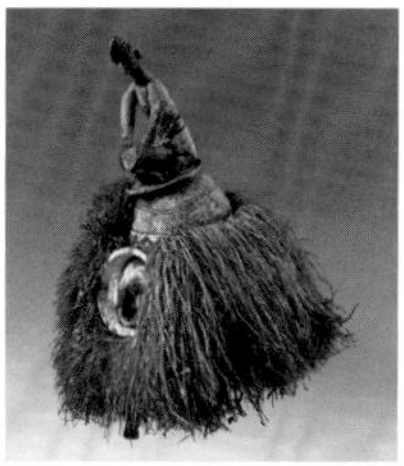

Pl. 40. Mask (*n-kisyan-khanda*).
Wood, cane, raffia fiber, pigment.
H. 50 cm.
Peggy Guggenheim Collection, Venice, inv. 76.2553 PG 254.
Kholuka mask of the northern Yaka with a single disk surmounting the head together with a puppet-like image of a *ngoma* drummer. Positioned with the drum held between his legs, the drummer plays a leading role in initiation contests performing in proximity to the circumcision operation and as principal musician in coming-out festivities.
In a broader context, the *ngoma* drummer also represents the auxiliaries of a leader and musicians of the chiefly court. Animated, he serves as a signifier of vital force and life in its sexual aspect, as demonstrated in such figures with a full erection.

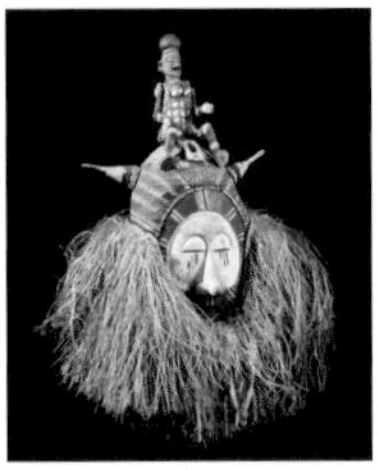

Pl. 41. Mask (*n-kisyan-khanda*).
Wood, cane, cotton cloth, raffia fiber, pigment.
H. 74 cm.
Private collection.
This double-horned mask is from the central Yaka, Kasongo Lunda Sector, as evidenced by its camber-shaped eyelids yet bearing the influence of northern Yaka manikin additions to a mask coiffure. The surmounting image features a seated female with genitals separately depicted beneath her. This imagery partakes of sung refrains that humorously disparage women. The use of green color surrounding the head betrays its more recent manufacture.

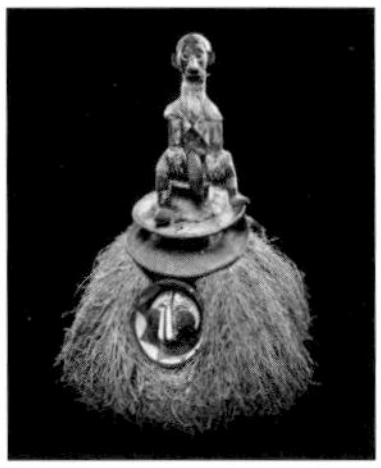

Pl. 42. Mask (*n-kisyan-khanda, kholuka*).
Wood, cane, raffia fiber, pigment.
H. 70 cm.
Musée Barbier-Muller, Geneva, inv. BMG 1026-99 (acquired before 1939).
Kholuka mask of the northern Yaka surmounted by a manikin with carved head, hands, feet, and prominent phallus. The explicit eroticism of the figure together with that of the mask's upturned nose evokes the religious link with the fertility of the young initiates together with their solidarity with adult men in erotic humor.

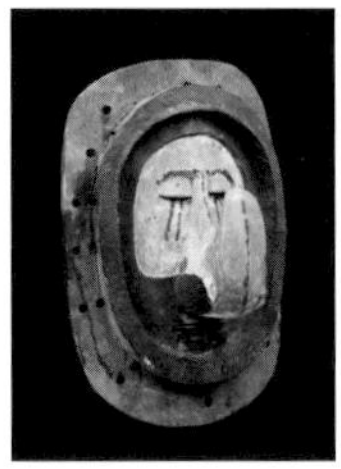

Pl. 43. Mask fragment (*n-kisyan-khanda*).
Wood, pigment.
H. 24 cm.
Jesuit Heverlee Collection, Royal Museum for Central Africa, Tervuren, inv. 2334.
Facial portion of a mask from the central Yaka collected by Jesuit missionary A. Pauwels in 1934 at Munigunda, Kasongo Lunda Sector. The camber-shaped eyes and boot-like nose are typical and the mask lacks a supporting handle.

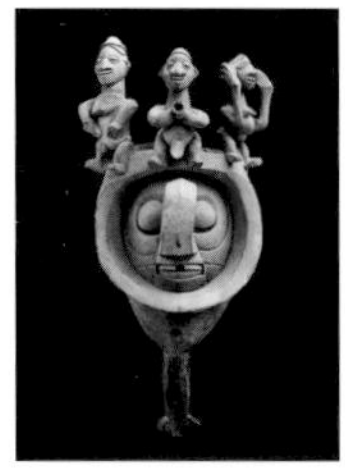

Pl. 44. Mask fragment (*n-kisyan-khanda*).
Wood.
H. 35 cm.
Royal Museum for Central Africa, Tervuren, inv. 55.134.50 (collected by G. Passau before 1905).
This unfinished northern Yaka mask displays three finely carved personages above the mask face, a phallic male figure between two females, one with hands touching groin and the other covering her ears. This illustrates the facial portion of the mask together with supporting handle carved in the general shape of a paddle or scoop. To this wooden strips are looped into the side or dowelled into the top. Woven raffia or more recently cotton cloth is stretched and sewn over this armature; then a resin is painted and when dry, colors are added.

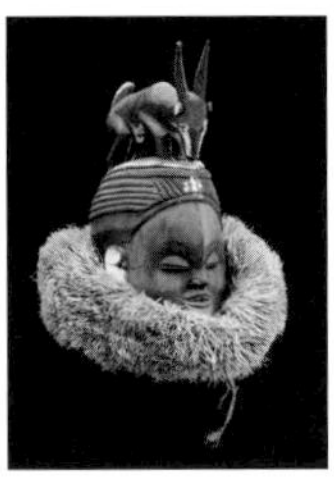

Pl. 45. Mask (*n-kisyan-khanda*).
Wood, cane, raffia fiber, pigment.
H. 45 cm.
Royal Museum for Central Africa, Tervuren, inv. RG. 42.19.12.
Mask from the southeastern Yaka of Panzi locale distinguished by its helmet form, naturalism of both face and surmounting image, projecting mouth-chin, red and white painted surface and short cropping of raffia fringe. The surmounting image carved of one piece with the mask is that of the duiker *tsetse*, sly trickster of Yaka folktales and patron of young initiates. Such masks are retained in the owner's house and occasionally used in circumstances other than *n-khanda* initiation.

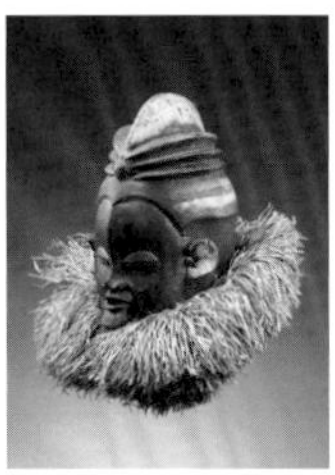

Pl. 46. Mask (*n-kisyan-khanda*).
Wood, raffia fiber, paint.
H. 45 cm.
Private collection.
N-khanda mask from the southeastern Yaka Panzi locale displaying a multi-crested hairpiece, double lidded eyes, red and white painted areas, and projecting mouth-chin. Entitled *ludemba*, the mask is regarded as female and dances in quest of food. Within this spectrum of southern masking there is a marked individualization of particular performances in behavior, accompanying songs, and audience response—reminiscent of masked performances among the Katundu Pende more than that of the northern Yaka.

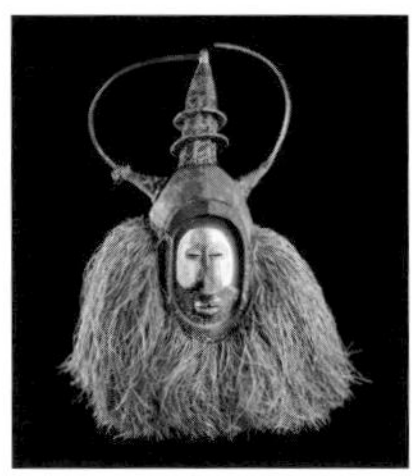

Pl. 47. Mask (*n-kisyan-khanda*).
Wood, cane, raffia cloth, pigment.
H. 68 cm.
Jesuit Heverlee Collection, Royal Museum for Central Africa, Tervuren, inv. SJ.1421.
Mask from the region of Kasongo Lunda with two disks on the central spire and wood slats encircling the coiffure of the mask. The face presents camber-shaped eyes and a massive nose and lacks a supporting handle beneath.

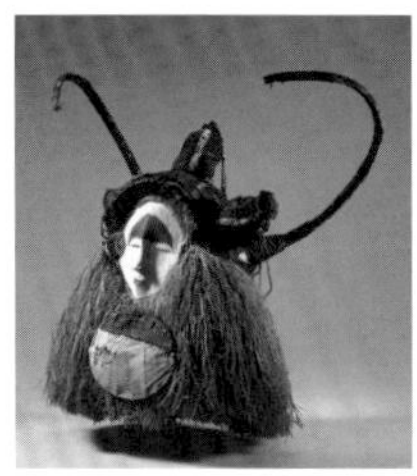

Pl. 48. Mask (*n-kisyan-khanda*).
Wood, cloth, fiber, pigment and resin.
H. 61 cm.
Iris and B. Gerald Cantor Center for Visual Arts at Stanford University, California, given in honor of Ralph J. Spiegl, M.D., by Marilyn J. Spiegl, inv. 2003.29.
N-khanda mask from the southern Yaka displaying lateral horns, constructed visor, and face painted red surrounded by white. A miniature shield is attached. The mask is likely of a variety called *kawesi*, the first to perform in coming-out festivities. The masker approaches the wife of the chief and bows profoundly and then briefly dances. Later he will return to insert the small *lukaw* baton into the ground before festivities can begin.

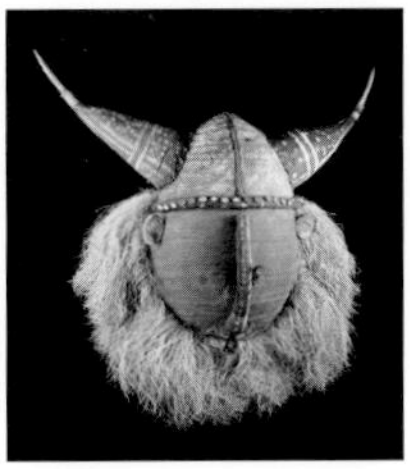

Pl. 49. Mask (*n-kisyan-khanda, mbawa-pakasa*).
Cane, raffia fiber, pigment.
H. 130 cm.
Royal Museum for Central Africa, Tervuren, inv. EO.0.0.2289 (1910).
Mbawa masks, like that of *kakuungu*, intervened at various moments during *n-khanda* initiation in order to protect initiates and frighten them into obedience and respect for their elders. *Mbawa* appears the day of circumcision, day of departure from the *n-khanda* camp, and occasionally for breaking food restrictions. *Pakasa* was also regarded as the most effective mask for averting or summoning rain. This particular southern Yaka mask is also documented as being used in warfare. Collected by Alphonse Joseph Marie Verhavert in 1910.

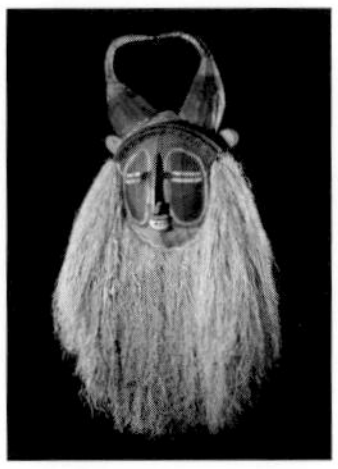

Pl. 50. Mask (*n-kisyan-khanda, mbawa*).
Wood, raffia fiber, pigment.
H. 165 cm.
Royal Museum for Central Africa, Tervuren, inv. 34 147.
Mbawa mask from the eastern Yaka, like all *mbawa* masks, alludes to the power of the African buffalo, *Syncerus caffer*, yet this example bears a human face. In the mask, animal power and virile sexuality together with avenging aspects are appropriated, concentrated, and materialized in a result more dreadful than the animal itself and then held in reserve against any proven malefactor or communal weakness. Collected by the missionary, O. Butaye before 1932, at Kimbao.

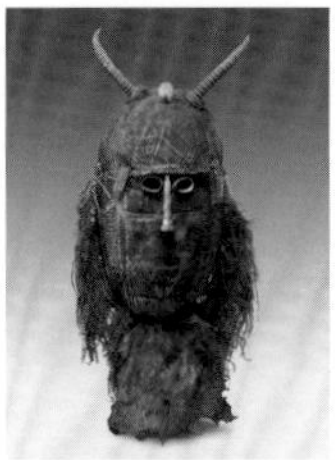

Pl. 51. Mbawa Mask.
Cane, raffia cloth, fibre, resin, polychrome, wood, bark, antelope horns, turtle shell, hide, palm leaf.
H. 160 cm.
Virginia Museum of Fine Arts, Richmond. Adolph D. and Wilkins C. Williams Fund, inv. 89.81.
Collected by Hans Himmelheber in 1939 in the Yaka village of Kisubu, on the Bakali River, the mask features actual antelope horns appended to the spherical mask. This mask, held by an individual in front of the shelter in which it is kept, is shown together with a *kakuungu* and *mwelu* mask, in a Himmelheber photo. Mbawa masks are said to be the work of a *ngaanga* specialist not that of a sculptor.

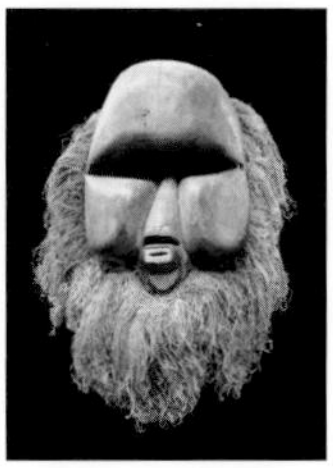

Pl. 52. Mask (*n-kisyan-khanda, kakuungu*).
Wood, raffia fiber, paint.
H. 60 cm.
Royal Museum for Central Africa, Tervuren, inv. RG 34145 (collected by the Jesuit missionary O. Butaye, in 1932).
This massive mask, deriving from the eastern Yaka of Kimbao region, presents deep-set eyes that assert the mask's haunting reputation of limitless power. The Kakuungu mask is worn and owned by the initiation charm specialist, *isidika*; essentially, it is a terrorizing mask intended to prevent witches, the *baloki*, from entering the camp and causing harm to the initiates. For this purpose the mask was often kept in a special shelter near the initiation site.

Annotated Bibliography

Baumann 1932
Baumann, Hermann. "Die Mannbarkeitsfeiern bei den Tsokwe (N.O. Angola: West Afrika) und ihren nachbarn." 1932. *Baessler-Archiv* 15, 1-53.
Baumann presents an early ethnological study of northern Angola and the Congo that treats Mukanda masks of the Chokwe and related groups as part of cultural exchange in a broader historical context.

Bourgeois 1978
Bourgeois, Arthur P. "Suku Drinking Cups." *African Arts* XII, 1, 76-77, 108.

Bourgeois 1979a
Bourgeois, Arthur P. "Nkanda-Related Sculpture of the Yaka and Suku of Southwestern Zaire." Unpublished Ph. D. dissertation, Indiana University, Bloomington.

Bourgeois 1979b
Bourgeois, Arthur P. "Mbwoolo Sculpture of the Yaka." *African Arts* XII, 3, 58-61, 96.

Bourgeois 1980
Bourgeois, Arthur P. "Kakungu among the Yaka and the Suku." *African Arts* XIV, 1, 42–46, 88.

Bourgeois 1982a
Bourgeois, Arthur P. "Yaka Masks and Sexual Imagery." *African Arts* XV, 2, 47–50, 87.

Bourgeois 1982b
Bourgeois, Arthur P. "Leadership Headgear of the Yaka and Suku." *African Arts* XV, 3, 30–35, 92.

Bourgeois 1983
Bourgeois, Arthur P. "Mukoko Ngoombu: Divination Paraphernalia of the Yaka." *African Arts* XVI, 3, 56–59, 80.

Bourgeois 1984
Bourgeois, Arthur P. *Art of the Yaka and Suku.* Meudon: Éditions Alain et Françoise Chaffin.

Bourgeois 1985
Bourgeois, Arthur P. *The Yaka and Suku.* Leiden: Brill.

Bourgeois 1990a
Bourgeois, Arthur P. "Initiation und Inthronisation bei den Yaka in Zaire." In *Männerbande Männerbunde. Zur Rolle des Mannes im Kulturvergleich.* Koln: Rautenstrauch-Joest-Museum für Völkerkunde, vol. 1, 301–308.

Bourgeois 1990b
Bourgeois, Arthur P. "Helmet-Shaped Masks from the Kwango-Kwilu Region and Beyond." *The Stanley Conferences on African Art,* vol. III, 121–136.

Bourgeois 1991
Bourgeois, Arthur P. "Mbawa-Pakasa, Image du buffle chez les Yaka et leurs voisins." *Arts d'Afrique Noire* 77, 19–32.

Bourgeois 1993
Bourgeois, Arthur P. "Masks and Masking among the Yaka, Suku, and Related Peoples." In *Face of the Spirit: Masks from the Zaire Basin,* F. Herreman and C. Petridis (eds.). Annals of the Royal Museum for Central Africa [Tervuren], Human Sciences 140. Antwerp: Etnografisch Museum; Gent: Martial & Snoeck, 49–56.

Bourgeois 1995
Bourgeois, Arthur P., "Pipes figuratives de la region du Kwango au Zaire." *Arts d'Afrique Noire* 94, 17-26.

Bourgeois 1996a
Bourgeois, Arthur P. "Central Africa." In *The Dictionary of Art,* J. Turner (ed.), 1. London: Macmillan, 400–406.

Bourgeois 1996b
Bourgeois, Arthur P. "Figures de pouvoir en Afrique centrale." In *"Magies".* Paris: Musée Dapper, 217–229.

Bourgeois 2003
Bourgeois, Arthur P. "Khosi Sculpture Among the Yaka and Their Neighbors." *Tribal* VIII, 4/33, 64–76.

Bourgeois 2007a
Bourgeois, Arthur P. "Central Africa." In *New Encyclopedia of Africa*, John Middleton (ed.). New York: Charles Scribner's Sons, vol. I, 151–156.

Bourgeois 2007b
Bourgeois, Arthur P. "Animal Imagery Among the Yaka and Suku." *Animal*. Paris: Musée Dapper, 298–322.

Bourgeois 2011
Bourgeois, Arthur P. "Of Noses and Penises: Masculine Imagery among the Yaka of Southwestern Congo." *Tribal* 60, 104-113.
Detailed analysis of various forms of Yaka and Suku art together with their place in ritual and narrative based on research undertaken in 1976 in Suku villages along the Inzia River in the Kobo, Ngombe and Kimfu Kinzadi chiefdoms and near the Kwango River in the Yaka chiefdoms of Ngowa and Ikombo but particularly in the villages of Pasanganga and Mvula-Mwanga where n-khanda *initiation was observed. This was combined with study of collections in the Royal Museum for Central Africa, Tervuren; Institut des Musées Nationaux du Zaire [Kinshasa]; Jesuit Collection [Heverlee]; The British Museum and Museum fur Volkerkunde [Basel].*

Crowley 1982
Crowley, Daniel. "Mukanda: Religion, Art, and Ethnicity in West Central Africa in African Religious Groups and Beliefs." In *Papers in Honor of William R. Bascom*, Simon Ottenberg (ed.). Meerut, India: Archana Pub., 206–221.
Crowley explores a supra-ethnic, institution-connected art style associated with mukanda *initiation.*

De Beir 1975a
De Beir, L. *Les Bayaka de M'Nene N'Tombo Lenge-Lenge.* Collectanea Instituti Anthropos, vol. 5.

De Beir 1975b
De Beir, L. *Religion et magie des Bayaka.* Collectanea Instituti Anthropos, vol. 4.
Publications of research undertaken by Jesuit missionary De Beir between 1938 and 1946 primarily in the M'Nene chiefdom: in Religion et magie des Bayaka, *beliefs in a supreme being, ancestral cult, divination, magic, and sorcery are presented together with supporting* kiYaka *text. In* Les Yaka de M'Nene N'Toombo Lenge-Lenge *[see above] levels of chieftainship and interrelations between Lunda, Kongo, Yaka, and Tsaamba political elements are treated together with stages of life, birth, education, marriage, and death.*

De Boeck and Devisch 1994
De Boeck, Filip, and René (Renaat) Devisch. "Ndembu, Luunda and Yaka Divination Compared, from Representation and Social Engineering to Embodiment and Worldmaking." *Journal of African Religions African* XXIV, 2. Leiden: Brill.
Divination is viewed as a self-generative practice establishing transitional space and transitional modes of thinking, sensing, and feeling. It involves a regenerative process that intertwines the body-self, the group and life-force in an interactional drama.

De Heusch 1982
De Heusch, Luc. *Rois nés d'un coeur de vache.* Les Essais, CCXVII; Mythes et rites bantous, II. Paris: Gallimard.

de Mahieu 1967
de Mahieu, Wauthier. *La statuaire Yaka, Essai, d'analyse ethno-morpfologique.* Licentiaats-verhandeling, Katholieke Universiteit Leuven.
Morphological analysis of a collection of statuettes from Takundi, south of Kenge; Kobangu near Popokabaka; and Muyombo and Kingunda near Kasongo Lunda where the author discovers four different patterns of proportions and details in carvings of the human figure.

Deschamps 1977
Deschamps, Roger. "L'identification anatomique des bois utilisés pour des sculptures en Afrique. La sculpture Yaka et Suku du Zaire et d'Angola." *Africa-Tervuren* XXIII, 1, 23–27.
Study based on examination of the varieties of wood used in 409 Yaka and Suku objects in the Royal Museum for Central Africa, Tervuren. While masks are carved of Alstonia or Ricinodendron trees chosen for technical reasons, the wood used in statuettes are more diverse and are likely chosen for their medicinal or supposed magical properties.

Devisch 1972
Devisch, René (Renaat). "Signification socio-culturelle des masques chez les Yaka." *Boletim do Instituto de Investigação Científica de Angola* 9, 2, 151–176.
Study of the n-khanda *initiation with a view to the ritual role and status of the sculptor, construction and variety of masks, their performance and public response.*

Devisch 1990
Devisch, René (Renaat). "From Physical Defect towards Perfection: Mbwoolu Sculptures for Healing among the Yaka." *Art and Initiation in Zaire*, C. D. Roy (ed.). Iowa City: University of Iowa (Iowa Studies in African Art, III), 63–92.

Devisch 1993
Devisch, René (Renaat). *Weaving the Threads of Life, The Khita Gyn-Eco-Logical Healing Cult Among the Yaka.* Chicago: University of Chicago Press.

Devisch 1995
Devisch, René (Renaat). "Ndemba and Tsekedye Masks." *Treasures from the Africa Museum, Tervuren*, G. Verswijver et al. (eds.). Tervuren: Royal Museum for Central Africa, 306–307.

Devisch and Brodeur 1999
Devisch, René (Renaat), and Claude Brodeur. *The Law of the Lifegivers: The Domestication of Desire.* New York: Harwood Academic Publishers.
Based on two years of anthropological research (1972–1974), among the Yaka in Taanda, M'Nene chiefdom, and subsequently in Kinshasa annually through 1991, Devisch's approach to the healing cults of the Yaka unravels ongoing ritual praxis and the structural constituents of social life. Details of the contextual and initiatory experience provide a wealth of information for analysis.

Himmelheber 1939
Himmelheber, Hans. "Les Masques Bayaka et leur sculpteurs." *Brousse* 1, 19–39.
Based on observations made in 1938/1939 between the Kwango and Bakali Rivers from Popokabaka until Kasongo-Lunda and eastward to the Lubisi River, Himmelheber treats n-khanda *initiation and associated masks, the sculptor at work, training, and attitude of the public towards the art and artist.*

Huber 1956
Huber, Hugo. "Magical Statuettes and their Accessories among the Eastern Bayaka and their Neighbors." *Anthropos* 51, 264–290.

Kopytoff 1960
Kopytoff, Igor. *Suku Religion: A Study in Internally Induced Reinterpretation.* Ph. D. dissertation, Northwestern University.

LaGamma 1996
LaGamma, Lisa. *The Art of the Punu Mukudj Masquerade: Portrait of an Equatorial Society.* Ph. D. dissertation. Columbia University.

Lamal 1963
Lamal, F. *Basuku et Bayaka des districts Kwango et Kwilu au Congo.* Annales, 56. Tervuren: Royal Museum for Central Africa.

Laman 1962
Laman, Karl. *The Kongo, III.* Studia ethnographica Upsaliensia, XVI, Upsala.

Lema Gwete 1978
Lema Gwete, Alphonse. *La statuaire dans la société Teke. Morphologie et context culturel.* Unpublished doctoral thesis, Katholieke Universiteit Leuven.

Milheiros 1956
Milheiros, Mario. *Luanda, Anatomia Social dos Maiacas (de Angola).* Luanda: Oficinas Gráficas O Apostolado.
Study of the Yaka living within Uigi Province of Angola treating both n-khanda *initiation and named varieties and use of* nkisi *charms.*

Nicolaï 1963
Nicolaï, Henri. *Le Kwilu. Étude géographique d'une région Congolaise.* Brussels: Centre scientifique et médical de l'Université libre de Bruxelles en Afrique Centrale.
Geographical study of the region between the Kwilu and Kwango Rivers, treating geology, riveraine stystems, highland morphology, plants and forests, population

density, habitation and village life with special attention to rubber and palmgrove industries.

Plancquaert 1930
Plancquaert, Michel. *Les sociétiés secrètes chez les Bayaka.* Bibliothèque Congo 31. Louvain: Kuyl-Otto.
First comprehensive study of Yaka ritual institutions: ngongi, ibwila, mkanda, *and* imboko *in 1927, principally at Kimbau with comparative data from elsewhere, by a Jesuit missionary who subsequently spent most of his active life among the Yaka.*

Plancquaert 1971
Plancquaert, Michel. *Les Yaka. Essai d'histoire.* Tervuren: Royal Museum for Central Africa.
Summary of Plancquaert's life-long interest and research on the history of the Yaka from prehistory through the colonial era based upon interviews, documents, and genealogies from the former Kasongo-Lunda Archives.

Ruttenberg 1967
Ruttenberg, Pied. *Jalons de l'évangélisation au Kwango.* Heverlee: Éditions priveés du ravitaillement intellectuel du Congo.
History of the Jesuit missions in the Kwango region.

Turner 1967
Turner, Victor. *The Forest of Symbols.* Ithaca: Cornell University Press.

Turner 1968
Turner, Victor. *The Drums of Affliction. A Study of Religious Processes among the Ndembu of Zambia.* Ithaca: Cornell University Press.
A study of ritual behavior and symbolism—including mukanda—*among the Ndembu and constitutes one of the great ethnographies of anthropological literature.*

Van Damme-Linseele 2001a
Van Damme-Linseele, Annemieke. *Spectacular Display: The Art of Nkanu Initiation Rituals.* Washington, DC: Smithsonian Institution Press, National Museum of African Art.

Van Damme-Linseele 2001b
Van Damme-Linseele, Annemieke. "The Nkanu and Other Eastern Kongo Peoples Lifted from the Shadow of the Yaka." In *Frans M. Olbrechts 1899–1958. In Search of Art in Africa*, C. Petridis (ed.). Antwerp: Ethnographic Museum Antwerp, 189–210.
A masterful study of a much neglected subject that remains within the sphere of a common cultural base with the Yaka.

Van der Beken 1978
Van der Beken, Alain. *Proverbes et vie yaka.* Collectanea Instituti Anthropos, vol. 15.

Van der Beken 1993
Van der Beken, Alain. *Proverbes yaka du Zaire.* Paris: Karthala.
Collection of 2,000 proverbs from Yaka chiefs and notables of Kasongo-Lunda Sector with translation and commentary, some proverbs are unique to each of the above.

Van Gennep 1960
Van Gennep, Arnold. *The Rites of Passage.* Chicago: University of Chicago Press.
Classic work by the first anthropologist to note the regularity and significance of rituals attached to transitional stages in human life.

Van Gool 1953
Van Gool, Désiré. "Puberteitsriten bij de Bayaka." *Anthropos* 48, 5–6, 853–888.
Based upon the unpublished notes of Jesuit missionary Henri Huveneers regarding initiation at Kabila and other villages near Popokabaka in 1941, Van Gool presents an analysis of initiation as it relates to the psychology of the adolescent MuYaka male.

Van Roy 1988
Van Roy, Hubert. *Les Byaambvu du Moyen-Kwango, Histoire du royaume luwa-yaka.* Berlin: Dietrich Reimer Verlag.

Van Roy 2006
Van Roy, Hubert. *Origines et évolution des Yaka.* CEEBA, II, 163.
Masterful research on the foundation and subsequent rulers of the yaka kingdom based upon oral traditions, some twenty succession lists and genealogies supplemented by archival material and interviews.

Van Schingen 1921
Van Schingen, R.P. "La circoncision chez les Bayaka et les Basuku." *Revue Générale de la Colonie belge*, II, 6, 51–64.
Initial description of n-khanda *initiation among the Yaka and Suku, primarily supplied by Ignace Nsoki of Ngowa, Popokabaka, edited by Jesuit missionary J. Hanquet.*

Van Wing 1920–21
Van Wing, Joseph. "Nzo Longo ou Les rites de la puberté chez les Bakongo." *Revue Générale de la Colonie belge* II, 2, 229–246, 3, 48–58, 365–389.
Study of western extensions of male initiation among the Mbata and Mpangu Kongo peoples between the Inkisi and Nsele Rivers together with translation of songs and ritual text.

Van Wing 1941-42,
Van Wing, Joseph. "MaKongo Magic." *Journal of the Royal Anthropological Institute* 71-72. London: 85-97.

Von Mechow 1882
Von Mechow, Alexander. "Bericht über die von ihm geführte Expedition zur Aufklarung des Kwango-Stromes, 1878-1881." *Verhandl. Gesellsch. Erdkunde Berlin*, 475–489.
A description of contact with the court of the kyambvu *at Kasongo Lunda.*

I would like to thank the following individuals and institutions for assistance with this project:

American Museum of Natural History, New York
The Art Institute of Chicago
Brooklyn Museum, New York
Iris & B. Gerald Cantor Center for Visual Arts at Stanford University, California
The Cleveland Museum of Art
Els De Palmenaer at MAS | Museum aan de Stroom, Antwerp
Renaat Devisch
Marc Leo Felix
Fine Arts Museums of San Francisco, de Young Museum
David Gelbard
Max Itzikovitz
The Jesuits of Heverlee, Belgium
David Joralemon
The Metropolitan Museum of Art, New York
Musée Barbier-Mueller, Genève
Musée du quai Branly, Paris
Musée Royal de l'Afrique Centrale, Tervuren
Museum Rietberg, Zürich
National Museum of African Art, Smithsonian Institution, Washington, D.C.
Rijksmuseum Volkenkunde, Leiden
Marceau Rivière
Staatliche Museen zu Berlin
University of Iowa Museum of Art, Iowa City
Virginia Museum of Fine Arts, Richmond
Ben Watkins
Yale University Art Gallery, New York
Zagreb Museum of Ethnography

and two private collectors who wish to remain anonymous.

My heartfelt thanks to Anne-Marie Bouttiaux for the translation of my text for the French edition.

Biography

Arthur P. Bourgeois is Professor Emeritus in Art History at Governors State University, University Park, Illinois. His personal fieldwork in 1976 in the Democratic Republic of the Congo (then Zaire) among the Yaka and Suku was devoted to the traditional *n-khanda*, first in the Kinshasa quarter of Masina, and then in villages along the Inzia River in the Kobo, Ngombe, and Kiamfu Kinzadi chiefdoms, and near the Kwango River in the chiefdoms of Ngowa and Ikombo. He has studied yaka collections worldwide and published four books and more than thirty professional articles.

Photo Credits

Cover, pls. 35, 43, 44, 45: © J.-M. Vandyck/ MRAC Tervuren

Pl. 1: Courtesy Max Itzikovitz

Pl. 2: © 2013 Wolfgang Günzel, Frankfurt am Main, Weltkulturen Museum Frankfurt/Main

Pl. 3: Travis Fullerton © Virginia Museum of Fine Arts

Pl. 4: © Photo Robert C. Kato

Pls. 6, 13, 14: © 2014 Photo Scala, Firenze/ BPK, Bildagentur für Kunst, Kultur und Geschichte, Berlin

Pls. 7, 25, 39: © MAS | Antwerp

Pl. 8: © Yale University Art Gallery

Pls. 9, 42: Musée Barbier-Mueller, Photo Studio Ferrazzini Bouchet

Pl. 10: © BAMW Photography

Pl. 11: © MRAC Tervuren

Pl. 12: © James Quine

Pls. 15, 34: © Rijksmuseum voor Volkenkunde, Leiden

Pl. 16: © Paul Litherland

Pl. 17: © Robert A. Kato

Pls. 19, 27, 28: Courtesy of the Ethnographic Museum, Zagreb

Pls. 20, 29, 30, 37, 46: Photo © Hughes Dubois

Pl. 21: Gift of Mrs. George P. Howe. © President and Fellows of Harvard College, Peabody Museum of Archaeology and Ethnology, PM# 17-41-50/B1554 (digital file# 99090074).

Pls. 22, 48: © Iris & B. Gerald Cantor Center for Visual Arts at Stanford University, California

Pls. 23, 32: © The Cleveland Museum of Art

Pl. 24: © University of Iowa Museum of Art, Iowa City/photo by Steve Erickson

Pls. 26, 52: photo R. Asselberghs © MRAC Tervuren

Pl. 31: © Brooklyn Museum, New York

Pl. 33: © The Metropolitan Museum of Art/ Art Resource/Scala, Firenze

Pl. 36: © The Art Institute Chicago

Pl. 38: © Wettstein und Kauf

Pl. 40: © Manusardi Art Photo Studio, Milano

Pl. 41: © Scott McCue

Pl. 47: © J. Van de Vyver, collection MRAC Tervuren

Pls. 49, 50: © D. Beaulieux, MRAC Tervuren

Pl. 51: Katherine Wetzel © Virginia Museum of Fine Arts

In the same series:

BAMANA by Jean-Paul Colleyn
BAMUM by Christraud M. Geary
BAULE by Alain-Michel Boyer
BENIN by Barbara Plankensteiner
CHOKWE by Boris Wastiau
FANG by Louis Perrois
KOTA by Louis Perrois
KUBA by David A. Binkley and Patricia Darish
IGBO by Herbert M. Cole
LOBI by Daniela Bognolo
LUBA by Mary Nooter Roberts and Allen F. Roberts
PENDE by Z. S. Strother
PUNU by Louis Perrois and Charlotte Grand-Dufay
YORUBA by Babatunde Lawal

Colour Separation
Eurofotolit, Milan

Printed in Italy in April 2014
by Grafiche Flaminia, Trevi (PG)
for 5 Continents Editions, Milan